D0931508

Autobiographical Memory: Remembering What and Remembering When

Autobiographical Memory: Remembering What and Remembering When

Charles P. Thompson
Kansas State University

John J. Skowronski
The Ohio State University at Newark

Steen F. Larsen
University of Aarhus, Denmark

Andrew Betz
GTE, Waltham, Massachusetts

LEA LAWRENCE ERLBAUM ASSOCIATES, PUBLISHERS
1996 Mahwah, New Jersey

Lawrence Erlbaum Associates, Inc., Publishers
10 Industrial Avenue
Mahwah, New Jersey 07430

Cover design by Gail Silverman

Library of Congress Cataloging-in-Publication Data

Autobiographical memory : remembering what and remembering when /
Charles P. Thompson . . . [et al.].
p.   cm.
Includes bibliographical references and indexes.
ISBN 0-8058-1514-7 (alk. paper)
1. Autobiographical memory. I. Thompson, Charles P.
BF378.A87A885 1996
153.1'3—dc20   95-37857
                                                          CIP

Books published by Lawrence Erlbaum Associates are printed on acid-free paper,
and their bindings are chosen for strength and durability.

Printed in the United States of America
10 9 8 7 6 5 4 3 2 1

Contents

Preface   vii

About the Authors   xiii

1 Theory and Overview   1

2 The Diaries   21

3 Memory for Everyday Events   39

4 Emotional Pleasantness and Intensity   67

5 Effectiveness of Self-Schema in Memory   83

6 Reconstructive Memory for Time   101

7 Reconstructing Event Dates: The Effects of Retention
       Interval, Event Characteristics, and Person Characteristics   124

8 Emotional Pleasantness and Event Dating   163

9 The Role of the Self-Schema in the Reconstruction
       of Time   182

10 Overview and Summary   204

v

Appendix   217

References   222

Author Index   231

Subject Index   235

Preface

In this book, we describe the results of our diary research, in progress for more than 15 years. Modern diary research began with an innovative study by Marigold Linton (1975) in which she recorded and tested events from her life over a 6-year period. Motivated by her efforts, our research began with a small pilot study conducted at Kansas State University by Charles (Chuck) Thompson in the fall of 1979. The pilot results were encouraging, so he began this research program with the intent of collecting event records from students for a few semesters (obviously, things got out of hand).

John Skowronski came on the scene out of desperation. He was a new PhD looking for a job, and Kansas State University was kind enough to give him a visiting position in the academic year of 1985–1986. While at Kansas State he chatted with Chuck about the diary research; the social-psychological aspect of the diaries piqued his curiosity. He thought that the diaries might ultimately provide a perspective on self and social memory that was different from the norm in social cognitive research, so he encouraged Chuck to show him how to collect diary data. The two of them collected some data that year and thus began a productive partnership in diary research.

John took a job at The Ohio State University at Newark starting in the fall of 1986. He soon forged strong ties with the faculty at the Columbus campus and managed to engage the interest of several social psychology graduate students. One of those students was Andrew (Drew) Betz. John dangled some data from the diaries (comparing self-event memory to memory for events from others' lives) in front of Drew, and with the promise of publication (perhaps exaggerated a tad, John admits), Drew rose to it like a hungry trout. Drew had a fair amount of methodological expertise, and he very rapidly became the statistics expert of our small research group. Audaciously, Drew also began suggesting studies, and several of the more recent data sets in this book have been significantly influenced by Drew's creative ideas.

Meanwhile, Steen Larsen (at the University of Aarhus, Denmark) worked on comparing the memory of self-events to memory for non-self events. In 1985, he talked to Chuck about methodology; he also spoke to Willem Wagenaar (University of Leiden, Holland). Wagenaar had just completed a 6-year diary of his own memory (Wagenaar, 1986). Being more humane, Steen decided to test himself with a several-months diary, using an adaptation of the Wagenaar method for news events. While undergoing this regime in 1986, however, he also ran a pilot study with some unsuspecting students. The results were interesting enough to prompt further studies. Conversations with the Kansas State group by e-mail and at conferences (not to mention a few meetings in a Colorado cottage on the Little Thompson River) gradually turned into collaborative research. Steen has been especially helpful in clarifying some of the theoretical ideas surrounding the role of schemata in event dating.

Indeed, our research group grew gradually based on mutual interests in research and, in no small part, pleasure in each other's company. Had we produced nothing of scientific value, we nonetheless would have enjoyed our friendly relationship.

Not only has our working relationship been collegial and productive, but the diary procedure produces very interesting data. These data are incredibly rich. We are consistently amazed at how virtually every diary seems to describe a unique personality. This richness occurs despite the fact that we specifically instruct our subjects *not* to record any events that they consider too personal to be read by strangers (we should note that we are often astonished at the events that are apparently considered not too personal for strangers!).

In addition, our subjects almost always enjoy the testing period, even though they often find that the diary-keeping stage of the experiment becomes rather tedious. Indeed, a common problem we face in testing is that subjects are delighted at the memories produced by the cues they have provided, and they would like to discuss those memories at length. Unfortunately, we have to remind them to keep their reminiscing rather brief or the test session becomes unreasonably long.

The common reaction of our subjects during testing is probably best captured by a young woman whose comments to Chuck at the end of the testing period were approximately as follows:

Woman: Are you familiar with those pictures you paint by filling in the numbered squares with the right color and a picture emerges?

Chuck: Yes, why do you ask?

> Woman: Well, this test session was like that. As you asked me about those memories, my semester got filled in—just like those pictures!

The conduct of this research has been marked by several delightful surprises. Two of these we recall rather well. One occurred during John's year at Kansas State. At that time, Chuck and John were using an old TRS-80 personal computer to tabulate data from the diaries, and its lack of memory capacity caused them to do analyses in several steps. During one session, they were sorting some preliminary tabulations with the idea of looking at some of the psychological and cognitive characteristics of good and poor daters. During one manual data sort, they happened to notice that females were going into a good dater pile and the males were placed into a poor dater pile. Thanks to the manual labor imposed by that old TRS-80, the researchers were clued into the possibility of gender differences in dating accuracy, an outcome later verified in several of the other data sets.

A second incident occurred as John and Drew were puzzling over analyses. They had some cockamamie idea about how the overall error distribution might be affected by various factors, so they took a peek at the overall distribution of absolute dating errors. Their first printout was a rough graph from SAS, and it showed a smooth, regular error distribution with a few puzzling outliers. Given the smoothness of the distribution, they had difficulty understanding those outliers until they finally noticed that the outliers were occurring about every 7 days; because of the imprecision of the printout, this regularity was not easily observed. After they got up off the floor, they knew that they had an interesting phenomenon, the day-of-week (DOW) effect. Chuck soon developed a mathematical procedure (using modulo arithmetic) for measuring the effect. Steen deserves credit for the day-of-week name: John and Drew's initial "multiple of seven" label was not nearly as elegant.

Much of our early research has been reported in separate articles in learned journals, but all those articles have focused on semester-long studies. The recent collection of several long-term diaries, extending up to 2½ years in length, replicated and significantly extended our knowledge of autobiographical memory. Given the additional information from our long-term diaries, we felt that a more complete account of all our studies under one cover would best capture the richness of the data produced by our studies. In addition, we realized that additional information could be extracted from the semester-long diaries that we had collected. Many of our early publications were quite focused, and our discussion of the diary data in those publications was somewhat limited. This book has given us the opportunity to examine commonalities and differences across our diary studies and has caused us to rethink and reanalyze much of the data from the diaries.

As in all presentations of this sort, the arrangement of the chapters in this book does not reflect the chronological order of events; instead, we have attempted to organize our presentation into the major themes suggested by our theoretical view of autobiographical memory. This organization should make it easier for the reader to keep our results in mind. We close the book with a brief summary of what our research has taught us, together with a theoretical description of those data.

ACKNOWLEDGMENTS

This project could not have been completed without the assistance of a number of people. Our special thanks goes to Rod Vogl, who was present to oversee the data collection for a large portion of this research project. Without Rod, we might not have retrieved some of the data we collected when the time came to write this book. Rod also helped review the early drafts of our manuscript.

We received assistance from a number of other people over the course of this project. We want to acknowledge the work of Jana Ortiz, Brian Perez, and David Welch, who helped us during the data collection phase and served as testers in the test phase of our long-term diary project. Among the many undergraduates who helped us with testing and data entry in the semester-long studies at Kansas State were Beverly Biggs, Sheila Clark, Todd Dautel, Allison Fox, Aleda Oettinger, Joyce Rohloff, and Carrick Williams.

Dan Aeschliman, Minida Dowdy, Will Eckels, Cosima Hadidi, Tricia Hoard, and Grant Nurnberg served as our long-term diary subjects. We are grateful that they stayed with us for as long as personal circumstances permitted. For three of them, this spanned the entire 3 years of the project.

Rich Walker and Jeff Gibbons also helped us research some of the background information, and they reviewed drafts of this book. Rich Walker, along with Laura Shannon, Julie Hott, Michelle Monroe, Robin Butler, and Laura Davis, conducted many of the studies at Ohio State, faithfully and accurately keyboarded and checked the mountains of data that were produced, and helped to develop a content coding scheme. Michael Pederson and Tia Hansen provided similar services at Aarhus. Moreover, Tia designed and conducted some innovative experimental procedures that were part of the final phase of one of these studies.

We wish to thank Academic Press HBJ for granting us their permission to reproduce materials. We also wish to thank Purdue University, which kindly provided an office and computing facilities to John during the final push to finish this book.

The long-term diary research reported here was supported by National Institute of Mental Health Grant MI I44090. The reviewers of our grant proposal, the primary focus of which was the memorist Rajan Mahadevan, recognized that we not only had a unique opportunity to systematically study a unique person over an extended period of time but also had the relatively rare opportunity to collect long-term diaries from our control subjects. We thank them and the officials at NIMH for their support and encouragement. We are also grateful to the Danish Research Council for the Humanities and to the Aarhus University Research Foundation for supporting the contributions of Steen Larsen to this research.

Charles P. Thompson
John J. Skowronski
Steen F. Larsen
Andrew Betz

About the Authors

Andrew L. Betz received his BA magna cum laude from Bowling Green State University and his MA and PhD from Ohio State University. He is now with GTE in Waltham, Massachusetts. His research interests include autobiographical memory, the effects of mental representations on social inference, and social influences on memory.

Steen F. Larsen received his BA from the University of Copenhagen. He received his MA and his Gold Medal (equivalent to the PhD) in psychology and psycholinguistics from the University of Aarhus. He was a Fulbright visiting scholar at Emory University in 1984. He is currently Docent (Senior Associate Professor) and deputy chair at the Institute of Psychology, University of Aarhus. His research interests focus on memory in naturalistic and applied settings, including autobiographical memory, memory for mass media events, and flashbulb memory. These interests extend more broadly to the study of literary fiction, schizophrenia, depression, and aging.

John J. Skowronski is currently Associate Professor of Psychology at the Ohio State University and he resides at the Newark Campus. His MA and PhD are from the University of Iowa. His research specialty is social cognition. In addition to his research into autobiographical memory and event dating, his recent work includes the study of spontaneous social inferences using an implicit memory paradigm, differences in social information processing and impression formation between mild depressives and nondepressives, and the possible memory and impression differences produced by implicit versus explicit social information processing.

Charles P. Thompson received his BS from Wisconsin State College, Eau Claire, in 1958 and his PhD from the University of Wisconsin in 1962. He began his professional career at the University of Wyoming, where he learned to appreciate mountains and trout fishing. In 1965, he moved to Kansas State University and currently has the title of Professor of Psychology. His research specialty is memory, with recent emphasis on autobiographical memory, voice identification, and memory expertise.

Theory and Overview

For the last 15 years, we have collected diaries to study autobiographical memory. The diaries typically consist of one personal event recorded each day over periods ranging from one month to 2½ years. We now have more than 400 such diaries. This book presents the data garnered from those diaries along with our view of autobiographical memory. It should come as no surprise that our view is heavily influenced by our diary data but, of course, we also draw on the rich vein of research on autobiographical memory carried out in other laboratories.

AUTOBIOGRAPHICAL MEMORY AS A SUBSET OF EPISODIC MEMORY

The last 30 years has produced an ever-widening gap between the view of memory held by the general public and that held by those who do research on memory. There is now general agreement among memory researchers that it is appropriate to think of memory as a collection of distinctly different types of memories rather than one undifferentiated memory. One of the major problems in memory research has been the division of the memory system into conceptual components that can be experimentally dissociated.

To place autobiographical memory in context, we first discuss some of the differing types of memory that have been proposed to exist in the general declarative memory system (as contrasted with procedural memory, e.g., Squire, 1992) or the explicit memory system (as contrasted with implicit memory, e.g., Schacter, 1992). We begin with the distinction between episodic and semantic memory first made by Tulving (1972) more than 20 years ago. The validity of the distinction between episodic and semantic memory has been hotly debated (e.g., McKoon, Ratcliff, & Dell, 1986), and the initial proposal has been modified (e.g., Tulving, 1983). Nonetheless, Tulving used the term *episodic memory* to refer to memory for something (an event) that occurred at a specific time and place; it is these kinds of specific episodes that are often thought of as constituting one's autobiographical memory.

However, it may be that there is more to autobiographical memory than a mere collection of episodes. For example, Nelson (1993) argued that we need to distinguish between *generic event memory, episodic memory,* and *autobiographical memory.* In her view, generic event memory refers to a schema that provides the outline for a type of event (e.g., going to a movie) without providing any of the details of the event (e.g., time, place, other people in group, specific film shown). Drawing on Tulving's work, Nelson also argued that episodic memory refers to memory for a specific event occurring at a specific time but that not all episodic memories are autobiographical in nature. She stated that "autobiographical memory as used here is specific, personal, long-lasting, and (usually) of significance to the self-system. Phenomenally, it forms one's personal life history" (p. 8). Thus, meeting a loved one for breakfast for the first time qualifies as an autobiographical event whereas a routine, everyday breakfast would not. In the first case, one would remember the details of the event (such as place and time) and would be able to place the event in the story of one's life. In the case of the routine breakfast, one would be able neither to remember the details nor to place the event in a life narrative. However, the routine breakfast might remain as an episodic memory for a limited time.

THE DEVELOPMENT OF AUTOBIOGRAPHICAL MEMORY

Nelson's argument stems from recent research showing that very young children can have episodic memories (Fivush & Hudson, 1990) and generic memories (Nelson, 1978; Nelson & Gruendel, 1981) but may not have autobiographical memory. That is, the children may be able to remember episodes but may not be able to place them in an autobiographical narrative.

Let us elaborate on this finding in a bit more detail. One of the enduring puzzles in memory has been that of childhood amnesia. Pillemer and White (1989) summarized the results of a large number of studies in which investigators asked adults to recall their earliest memories from childhood. The earliest memory reported is usually at age 3½. Not only are people typically unable to recall any memories prior to age 3, but the number of memories available between the ages of 3 and 6 is markedly lower relative to memories available after that period.

Childhood amnesia is even more puzzling because 3-year-olds are quite good at describing what happens in a familiar situation (e.g., going to Burger King) although they are not particularly good at describing what happened on a specific occasion (Nelson, 1978; Nelson & Gruendel, 1981). More important, children under 3 not only can report details of some isolated specific events but can remember them for as long as 2 years (Hudson, 1986; Ratner, 1980).

One proposed solution to the puzzle has been to suggest that children's schemas change as they age, so that memories from an early age have no suitable framework from which they can be retrieved (Schachtel, 1947). However, recent developmental research (e.g., Nelson, 1989) suggests that the basic ways of representing events remain unchanged from early childhood through adulthood.

Instead, evidence is mounting that overcoming childhood amnesia may reflect the process of children learning how to talk about memories with others. That is, they learn how to tell their life stories as a narrative. This is the *social interaction* model of autobiographical memory that has been espoused by several investigators (e.g., Fivush & Reese, 1991; Hudson, 1990; Pillemer & White, 1989). Unlike the schema change theory, the social interaction model suggests that children learn how to retain their memories in a recoverable form by formulating them as narratives.

Nelson (1993) discussed some unpublished research by Tessler that provides good support for the social interaction model. Tessler observed differences in mother–child discussions of past events. The discussions were classified as narrative or pragmatic interactions. The narrative conversations focused on what happened when, where, and with whom. Pragmatic interactions used memory as an instrument to retrieve specific information (e.g., "Where did you put your book?"). Tessler found that children of mothers who tended to use the narrative style of conversation remembered more about a trip to a museum than did children of mothers who tended to use the pragmatic style of conversation. Most important, she found that things that mothers and children did not talk about (e.g., objects in the museum) were not remembered.

Based on evidence of this sort, Nelson (1993) constructed a theory of how memory develops in early childhood and how an autobiographical memory system is established. She suggested that memory and learning have the general adaptive functions of guiding present action and predicting future outcomes. The most useful memory for that purpose is generic memory, which describes routines for recurrent situations. However, we can only form a generic memory (schema) on the basis of repeated episodes. Thus, episodic memory is viewed as a temporary holding system for events. If those events recur on several occasions, their common components will be transferred to the more permanent generic memory system.

Her view is that autobiographical memory has a completely different function. In her words,

> The claim here is that the initial functional significance of autobiographical memory is that of sharing memory with other people, a function that language makes possible. Memories become valued in their own right—not because they predict the future and guide present action, but because they are shareable with others and thus serve a social solidarity function. I suggest that this is a universal human function, although one with variable, culturally specific rules. In this respect, it is analogous to human language itself, uniquely and universally human but culturally—and individually—variable. I suggest further that this social function of memory underlies all of our storytelling, history-making narrative activities, and ultimately all of our accumulated knowledge systems. (p. 12)

Although Nelson's view is consistent with the current knowledge about the development of memory in early childhood and makes both biological and sociological sense, we are currently unsure of the utility of distinguishing between autobiographical and episodic memory—that is an issue for future research to decide. We also do not restrict autobiographical memory to events that are (usually) personally significant. At the same time, our data demonstrate (see chapter 5) that self-relevant events are much more memorable than other-events or news events.

Nonetheless, her view ties in nicely with our view of reconstruction and reproduction in memory. Remembering information from Nelson's episodic memory involves reproduction of the event, whereas remembering information from generic memory involves reconstruction of the event. Because episodic memory seems to be rather short-lived, it follows that autobiographical memory should change over time from being reproductive to being reconstructive. That is precisely our view. Further, the research that Nelson cited to support the notion of autobiographical memory has one additional theoretical implication that is important to us and that constitutes one of the major themes of this book: There is no separate temporal trace that accompanies memory. If there were such a trace, then even young children would be able to exhibit evidence of an ability to place events in time or in temporal order, given recall of an event or of several events.

Instead, we argue that event dating (and more generally, discerning the time in one's life at which an event occurred) depends heavily on one or more reconstructive strategies. These reconstructive strategies, in turn, depend on the availability of temporally relevant information in memory. We claim that sometimes, as implied by Nelson's research, this information may take the form of recalled event orders. These orders may come either from generic (or schematic) world knowledge specifying how events are related to one another (as in a script) or from the direct rehearsal and recall of event orders (as suggested by the narrative research). As we argue in later sections, other sources of information from event memory, such as the details of events (e.g., snow on the ground likely indicates a winter event), also contribute to these temporal reconstructions.

SCHEMATA AND INDIVIDUAL DIFFERENCES IN MEMORY

The theme of reconstruction is also one that emerges in our consideration of event memory, and as one might suspect, given the abundant evidence that people use schemata to reconstruct events, we consider such reconstructive processes to be important. However, the evidence for the use of schemata is so overwhelming that the reproductive aspects of memory are sometimes understated. We summarize our view of autobiographical remembering by stating that we believe memory for the content of events changes over time from being largely reproductive (i.e., based on retrieval of a quite detailed memory trace) to being largely reconstructive (i.e., based on knowledge of the structure of the type of event and of the characteristics of the individuals, objects, and places involved). In comparison, as noted earlier, we believe that memory for the temporal location of the event is entirely reconstructive (with some exceptions) almost immediately after the event. Along these lines, we produce convincing evidence that people use schemata to reconstruct dates of events (see chapter 6), and we show that those schemata persist over relatively long periods of time.

We also assume that individuals vary in the degree to which they use schemata as well as the degree to which the use of any schema is possible. Put differently, people undoubtedly differ both in their ability (or inclination) to use schemata and in the usefulness of their schemata. The usefulness of a schema is probably related to the amount of detail in and the accuracy of the schema under consideration. In support of our general proposition, we show that individual differences in ability to date events is strongly related to the degree to which individuals use temporal schema in reconstructing the dates of events (see chapter 6).

REMEMBERING WHAT AND REMEMBERING WHEN

We make a central distinction between memory for the content of an event and memory for the temporal location of an event. We present evidence (see chapter 3) for our contention that memory for the content of the event changes over time from being largely reproductive to being largely reconstructive. The central core of an event (e.g., where the event occurred and who we were with) is forgotten quite gradually, whereas peripheral details fade rather rapidly. Thus, memories of very recent events may be entirely reproductive. Memory for slightly older events usually involve reconstruction of peripheral details but reproduction of central details. Finally, memories of old events typically involve reconstruction of both central and peripheral details.

We emphasize that this change in memory from mostly reproduction to mostly reconstruction holds for the vast majority of events, but not all. We believe that there are numerous events that, because they are unimportant and little attended, are primarily reconstructed even if recall occurs soon after the event. Similarly, there are events that, because they are striking or important, are rehearsed frequently, with rehearsal starting soon after they occur (Conway et al., 1994). Those events are largely reproduced from memory. We argue that those personally important events tend to be recalled quite accurately, but the memory literature (Larsen, 1992a; Neisser & Harsch, 1992) shows quite convincingly that errors can occur. However, research also shows a marked difference between memory for important or striking events that are not personal and memory for important personal events (Neisser, Winograd, & Weldon, 1991).

In contrast to the change from reproduction to reconstruction in memory for events, we contend that memory for the temporal location of events is reconstructive from the outset. To make the point absolutely clear, our view is that there is no temporal trace in autobiographical memory. That is, we believe that a temporal trace is not recorded automatically or routinely attached in some other way to an event. We do not mean that people cannot choose to note the date or time of an event but we expect deliberate noting that creates a symbolic time label to occur rather infrequently.

We believe that when individuals attempt to locate an event in time, they use several possible reconstructive procedures. These procedures may be used alone or in combination with any number of the other procedures to zero in on the correct temporal location. With the caveat that we do not intend to create an exhaustive list, five of the major procedures used by individuals are outlined here.

First, individuals may rely on temporal information contained in the event to place the event in time. The time of the event might be inferred (with varying degrees of precision) from such things as the weather (e.g., snow), the location (e.g., traveled to Malaysia only one summer), or the people (e.g., knew Jim during graduate school). The more detailed the memory for the event, the more likely it is that the event will contain information useful for placing it in time.

Second, people may rely on temporal information about that class of events to date the specific event. Temporal information about the class of events includes specific dates (e.g., birthdays, holidays such as Christmas), specific day-of-week knowledge (e.g., bowl on Thursdays, church on Sundays), approximate dates (e.g., spring break is about mid-March), and approximate week schedules (e.g., golfing on the weekend, graduate research meetings are usually early in the week).

Third, the vast majority of event memories are easily placed in categories with temporal boundaries. For example, we have memories that can be categorized as occurring during college, elementary school, military service, marriage, graduate school, or while living at a particular residence. Many of those categories have overlapping temporal boundaries so that the potential temporal location of an event can be narrowed by knowing that, for example, the event occurred in graduate school before marriage.

Fourth, many events occur as related chains that aid in locating them in time. One campaigns for political office before serving in that office; one does research, analyzes the results, and writes a paper before finally seeing the published report; and so on. We can use these related chains of events to put the events in proper order. Further, our general world knowledge about such things as the dates of elections, dates of office-taking, and publication lags allows us to put the proper spacing between events in a chain.

Finally, people also use landmark events to infer temporal location. Some of those landmark events can be subsumed under the categories noted previously (e.g., ended military service, got married). However, many landmark events are unique and cannot be placed in the categories mentioned earlier. The best-known example is the eruption of Mount St. Helens, which Loftus and Marburger (1983) showed could be used to sharpen the temporal estimates of subjects drawn from the area affected by the eruption.

AN EMPIRICAL EXAMPLE:
THE LONG-TERM DIARY STUDY

The data from our long-term diary study illustrate some of the major points made in these first few pages. Our typical study has students keep a diary for one semester (about 3½ months). However, in the long-term study, six undergraduates at Kansas State University kept diaries of personal events for as long as 2½ years. It is worth noting that these long-term diaries more than double the number of long-term diaries in existence prior to this study.

At the end of the data collection period, the subjects were individually tested on the content of their diaries. During testing, they rated how well they remembered the event on a 7-point scale ranging from *not at all* (1) to *perfectly* (7). They then tried to recall the location of the event and who was with them when the event occurred. Finally, the subject estimated the date of the event. As an aid to date estimation, the subject was given a calendar for the general period in which the diaries were kept. The calendar contained no extraneous date-related information; only the month, day of the week, and the date were included (for more details on the collection and testing of diaries, see the Appendix).

Memory for the Content of the Event

This summary of the long-term data shows two points. First, memory for events changes over time from being largely reproductive to being largely reconstructive. Specifically, we show that memory for central details of an event is lost gradually, whereas memory for more peripheral detail is lost relatively rapidly. The point is that, over time, it becomes more and more necessary to reconstruct the details of an event. Second, we believe that the temporal location of an event is almost always reconstructed. That reconstruction should be aided by the amount of detail available in the memory for the event. Other things being equal, the more detail available, the more accurate will be the reconstruction of the temporal location of the event. Thus, we show the relation between memory for detailed content and memory for temporal location of an event.

We begin by looking at how well subjects could recall the central details of events. Those data are shown in Fig. 1.1. In this figure, we have plotted the retention interval in 100-day blocks. The subjects' ability to recall the location and who they were with when the event occurred decreased quite gradually as the retention interval increased.

A second measure of memory, the subjects' rated memory for events, is shown in Fig. 1.2.

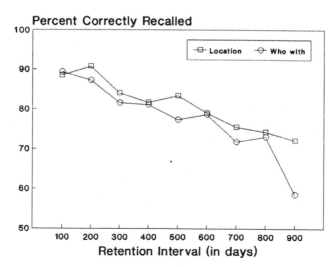

FIG. 1.1. Percentage of core details (*who with* and *location*) recalled at each retention interval.

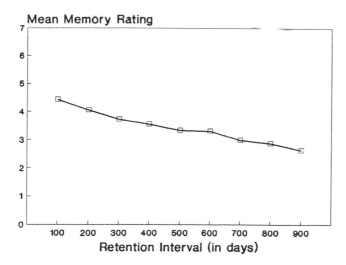

FIG. 1.2. Mean memory rating at each retention interval.

As you can see, memory ratings also decreased quite gradually over the retention interval. Both memory ratings and the recall of core details show a decreasing linear function over time. We speculated that the linear function for memory ratings might be reflecting the forgetting of core details and that forgetting of peripheral details might show a different picture. As a first approximation to examining forgetting of peripheral details, we looked at the proportion of events for which the subject claimed to have a perfect or almost perfect memory (i.e., ratings of 7 and 6, respectively). Those data are shown in Fig. 1.3.

When we look at the proportion of events given perfect or almost perfect ratings, we see the classic Ebbinghaus forgetting curve. The proportion of events given those ratings drops sharply over the first 300 days and then levels off. These data support our view that memory for the content of the event changes systematically over time from reproductive to reconstructive. At first, individuals are able to retrieve both core and peripheral components of the event. As time passes, however, more and more components of the event have to be reconstructed, with reconstruction of peripheral components preceding the reconstruction of core components.

Memory for the Temporal Location of the Event

We believe that the temporal location of the event is almost always reconstructed. Further, we believe that the reconstruction of temporal location is achieved through the use of both temporal schema and critical information retrieved from the memory. One implication of this belief is that, generally

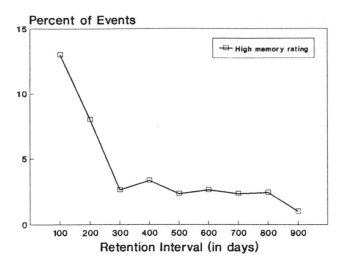

FIG. 1.3. Mean percent of events for which subjects claimed to have perfect (memory rating of 7) or almost perfect (memory rating of 6) memory plotted by retention interval.

speaking, the more information retrieved from the event memory, the more accurately the individual will be able to place that event in time.

Our look at memories rated as perfect or almost perfect showed a dramatic drop over the first 300 days, with a leveling off thereafter. We suggested that those data represent a good first approximation of the loss of peripheral information. To the extent that peripheral information is used to place events in time, dating accuracy should show a similar decline. We reasoned that, aside from special cases like holidays and birthdays, dating events exactly requires retrieving a great deal of information from the memory. Further, that information often is peripheral to the core content of the event. Thus, we looked next at the proportion of events dated exactly.

As Fig. 1.4 indicates, memory for temporal location also resembles Ebbinghaus's classic memory function. The subjects' ability to date events exactly decreases dramatically over a retention interval of 300 days. Their performance then levels off over the rest of the retention interval.

The data on the proportion of events rated as remembered perfectly or almost perfectly, taken together with the data on the proportion of events dated exactly, paint a picture supporting our view that the more details one can recall about an event, the more likely one will be able to accurately reconstruct when the event occurred. Note that the information needed to recall the exact date of an event is forgotten more quickly than the other details of the event. It is clear that the ability to date events exactly often depends upon a clear memory of the event.

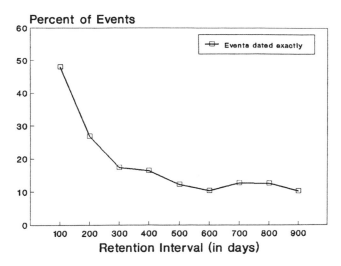

FIG. 1.4. The percent of events dated exactly at each retention interval.

Temporal Schema in Memory

We turn now to the use of temporal schema in reconstructing the dates of events. Events often contain information that can be used to place the events in time. For example, if an event involved scraping ice from a windshield, one might assume the event occurred in the winter. Consider a second example of a person remembering when he bowled a 250 game for the first time. He knows that he only bowls on Thursdays, and his attempt to date the event will reflect that knowledge. His date estimate may be several weeks off, but the day of week will be correct.

That last example was chosen deliberately because our data have forced us to focus on the use of various kinds of day-of-week information. Some time ago, we plotted the distribution of the errors individuals made in dating events and found they produced a fascinating pattern. Each of our studies reproduces this pattern, and Fig. 1.5 shows the data collected in a recent study. The figure presents all errors of 52 days or less normalized to total 100%. Note that 1% of all errors were greater than 52 days.

As Fig. 1.5 shows, peaks in these errors occur at regular 7-day intervals. These data show that people are using day-of-week information to help make date estimates. Although they may not guess the right date, they often identify the correct day of the week.

The figure also shows the percentage of events dated exactly (i.e., the zero error point). About one third of all events were dated exactly, but it must be recognized that there are three sources for exact dates. The first source, of course, is those events for which the exact date is remembered. Except for

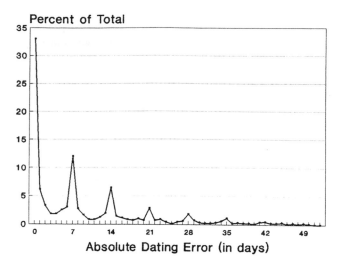

FIG. 1.5. The normalized distribution of dating errors (in days). Errors greater than 42 days are not included in the distribution.

very recent events, we expect the number of such events typically to be very small. The second are those recurring events whose dates are known (e.g., birthdays or holidays such as Christmas). Finally, exact dates can be approximated through relational (e.g., it was the Wednesday before spring break) or schematic (e.g., bowling league meets on Monday evenings) knowledge. Such approximations result in a number of hits. For example, if a subject knows that the event fell on a Thursday during February, a random pick of a Thursday in that month has a 25% probability of being correct.

Because the day-of-week effect is so obvious in our data, we have focused on day-of-week errors and have ignored whether our subjects picked the correct week or were several weeks in error. Because exact dates include both schematic and episodic knowledge, we plot the data in two ways. One plot includes all the data (i.e., includes exact dates). The other plot focuses only on the use of schematic information by excluding errors from the correct week. That is, the second plot excludes exact dates and errors within three days of the exact date. In both plots, the data are normalized to sum to 100%. Figure 1.6 shows both plots of the data from Fig. 1.5 transformed to reflect day-of-week error.

An error of 0 means that the person picked the correct day of week. An error of +1 or −1 means that they were either a day short or a day over in their estimate, and so on. The solid line includes all data, whereas the dotted line excludes exact dates and errors falling within the correct week. As Fig. 1.6 shows, people often picked the correct day of the week (i.e., an error of 0). That is true both when exact dates are included in and when they are excluded from the data. In chapter 6, we describe how the use of partial

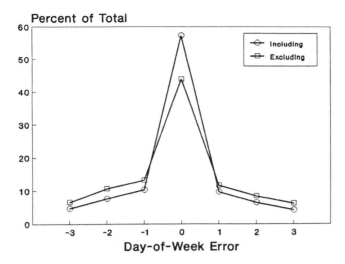

FIG. 1.6. The normalized distribution of day-of-week errors plotted separately for all data and for the data excluding all errors within 3 days of the correct date (i.e., excluding the correct week data). In this plot, a score of zero means that the subject gave the correct day of week when dating the event (although the date could be one or more weeks in error). The negative scores represent date estimates that were short of the correct day of week, whereas positive scores represent date estimates that overshot the correct day of week.

temporal information (e.g., knowledge that the event occurred on a week-end) results in errors decreasing symmetrically around the correct day-of-week. That is, next to getting the correct day-of-week, subjects are most likely to be a day short or a day long—and so on.

The Durability of Schematic Information

Given that subjects use day-of-week information to date events, we wondered whether day-of-week information was used over extended periods of time. Day-of-week information may be readily available over a period of 3 months but it may be forgotten over longer periods of time. When starting to investigate this issue, we saw evidence for other schematic effects as well. In our six very-long-term diaries, subjects could have made errors of over a year in dating events. The distribution of dating errors for those diaries produced the very interesting pattern of errors shown in Fig. 1.7.

Subjects sometimes got the correct day of the year but placed it in the wrong year. Obviously, every person has a memory store of several well-known yearly events such as birthdays and public holidays. These data also show that there is a marked day-of-week effect even when the individual misses the correct week by as much as 50 or 51 weeks. Also, the day-of-week effect appears to be more erratic when errors are greater than 365 days.

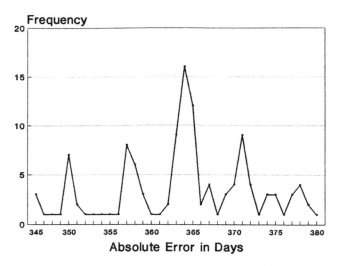

FIG. 1.7. The number of dating errors between 345 and 380 days in error made by the 6 long-term subjects. These data show both a day-of-year effect (i.e., the subject got the right date but the wrong year) and day-of-week effects at 50 and 51 weeks.

That apparent irregularity is produced because the day-of-week usually shifts one day each year. That is, if January 3 is on a Monday this year, it will be on a Tuesday next year. Thus, if subjects are a year in error, they will be either a day long or a day short in hitting the correct day of week, depending on whether their error is a year long or a year short. Of course, a different adjustment holds for leap years.

Next, we looked at the day-of-week error for events falling within the most recent year. To focus on schematic reconstruction, we used the procedure previously described and eliminated exact dates by considering only those responses with errors greater than 3 days. Put differently, we removed responses that were within the correct week. Those data are presented in Fig. 1.8.

Even when events that have been dated exactly are removed, it is evident that the subjects were using day of week when making date estimates for events that occurred in the most recent year. In fact, the subjects picked the correct day of the week on about a third of those events.

If we consider events that are more than a year old, we still see a peak at the 0 error point. Once again, subjects were picking the correct day of the week when making their date estimates even when events that were dated exactly were removed. Indeed, the subjects were still picking the correct day of the week about a third of the time. These data clearly show that our subjects were using day-of-week information to date events.

If day-of-week information is important in locating events in time, then individual differences in dating accuracy should occur as a result of differ-

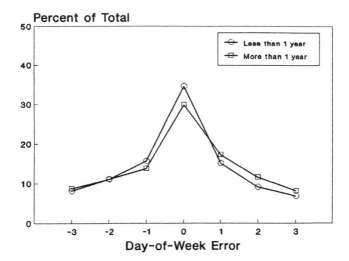

FIG. 1.8. The normalized distribution of day-of-week errors for the 6 long-term subjects plotted separately for events from the most recent year and events more than one year old.

ential ability in the use of day-of-week information. As a first step in assessing individual differences, we looked at the proportion of events that each subject could date exactly. We speculated that *good daters* made effective use of temporal information such as day of week to reconstruct the exact date of an event whereas *poor daters* did not.

Table 1.1 shows how long each of our subjects kept a diary and the accuracy in dating events for the most recent year (the names have been changed to preserve the anonymity of our subjects). There were large differences in the subjects' ability to date events exactly. For example, Mary was able to date approximately 40% of her events exactly, whereas John dated less than 10% of his events exactly. Based on their performance, we consider Mary an

TABLE 1.1

Diary Duration and Percent of Events Dated Exactly During the Most Recent Year for the Six Subjects in the Long-Term Diary Study

	Recent-Year Accuracy	
Name	*Duration*	*% Dated Exactly*
Mary	2 yr., 6 mo.	38.4
Bob	2 yr., 6 mo.	28.8
John	2 yr., 6 mo.	9.7
Sue	2 yr., 1 mo.	15.7
Ann	1 yr., 7 mo.	20.5
Tom	1 yr., 6 mo.	26.5

example of a good dater and John an example of a poor dater. We focus on these two subjects to examine how they used day-of-week information.

We plotted the absolute error distributions as a way of examining use of day-of-week information. We look first at Mary's absolute errors for events occurring in the most recent year (see Fig. 1.9. Note that in Fig. 1.9 through Fig. 1.12, the values do not sum to 100% because many errors were greater than 42 days). Her data produce a distribution with clear peaks at 7-day intervals. Indeed, Mary made relatively few errors that did not correspond to the correct day of the week.

When we plot Mary's dating error distribution for events that are greater than a year old, we still see those peaks occurring at 7-day intervals (see Fig. 1.10. Note the scale change). These peaks indicate that she knew the day of the week on which the event occurred even though the event may be 2 years old. Note that her ability to date events exactly (i.e., 0 error) has dropped from about 38% to about 16%.

In contrast to Mary, our best dater, John's performance was more erratic. Plotting John's dating error distribution for the most recent year (see Fig. 1.11), we see peaks at 7-day intervals, but we also see a relatively high proportion of errors for other days of the week. It appears that John was not using day-of-week as efficiently as Mary. Also, John could only date about 10% of the most recent events exactly. John was not good at estimating when events occurred.

If John was not efficient at using day of week in the most recent year, one may wonder what happens to his performance for the preceding year

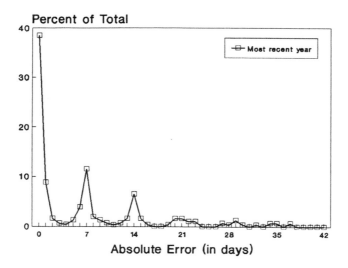

FIG. 1.9. The normalized distribution of dating errors (in days) for events from the most recent year for Mary. Errors greater than 42 days are not included in the distribution.

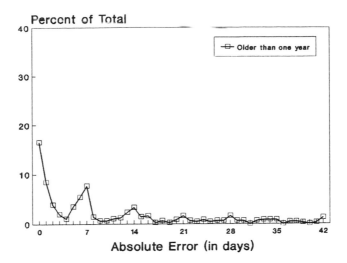

FIG. 1.10. The normalized distribution of dating errors (in days) for events more than one year old for Mary. Errors greater than 42 days are not included in the distribution.

and a half. As illustrated by Fig. 1.12, John's performance became more chaotic as the retention interval increased. Evidence of day-of-week information is still there, but John certainly was not using it efficiently.

Let us summarize the important points from this brief examination of our long-term diaries. First, our data support the view that memory for the

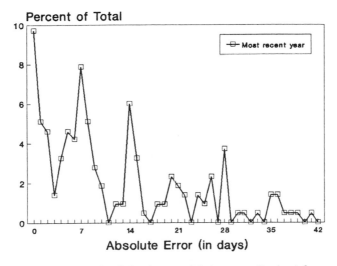

FIG. 1.11. The normalized distribution of dating errors (in days) for events from the most recent year for John. Errors greater than 42 days are not included in the distribution.

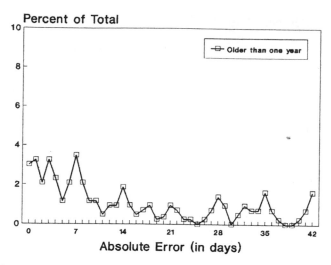

FIG. 1.12. The normalized distribution of dating errors (in days) for events more than one year old for John. Errors greater than 42 days are not included in the distribution.

content of the event changes over time from being largely reproductive to being largely reconstructive. The central core of an event (for example, where the event occurred and who one was with) is forgotten quite gradually, whereas peripheral details fade rather rapidly. Thus, memories of very recent events may be entirely reproductive. Memory for slightly older events usually involve reconstruction of peripheral details but reproduction of central details. Finally, memories of old events likely involve extensive reconstruction of both central and peripheral details.

Second, our data show that people use schemata to reconstruct dates of events. In contrast to the change from reproduction to reconstruction in memory for events, memory for the temporal location of events is reconstructive from the outset. The use of temporal schemata is apparent over relatively long periods of time. We emphasize that our theoretical view proposes that there is no temporal trace in autobiographical memory.

Finally, our data show that individual differences in ability to date events is strongly related to the degree to which individuals use temporal schemata in reconstructing the dates of events. We expect individual differences in the use of schemata is widespread. That is, we expect similar differences occur in the reconstruction of events.

SUMMARY

In this introductory chapter, we have briefly discussed the place of autobiographical memory in the general memory system, the possible development of autobiographical memory (according to Nelson, 1993), and the use of schemata as well as the role of individual differences in memory. We then used our long-term data from Kansas State University students as a convenient vehicle to illustrate the difference we propose between *remembering what* and *remembering when* in autobiographical memory. Those data also served to illustrate the role of individual differences in the effective use of strategies for remembering when.

With the exception of chapter 2, the book elaborates and extends the basic theoretical view and empirical base that we have presented. To keep the initial presentation brief, we did not cover in this initial chapter the important roles of the emotion (i.e., pleasantness or unpleasantness) attached to events and the degree to which the event is seen as (or becomes) part of the self-schema. Those topics are covered in detail in subsequent chapters.

OVERVIEW OF THE REMAINING CHAPTERS

In chapter 2 we describe the methodological issues connected with diary research, the contents of the diaries, the procedures used in collecting and testing the diaries, and the rationale for the statistical methods used to analyze the data. Many readers may prefer to skip over chapter 2, which is intended for those who are interested in methodological issues or who wish to examine our methods in some detail. Together with the appendix, it is also intended as a reference whenever readers wish to remind themselves of the exact procedure in diary collection or exactly how subjects were to respond to a particular measure.

Following chapter 2, the book is divided into two major sections describing memory for the content of the event and memory for the temporal location of the event. The final chapter is an overview and summary of our research. The book ends with an appendix that describes in detail all the measures used in the diary studies.

Chapter 3 focuses on forgetting and demonstrates the contrast between forgetting core events and forgetting peripheral events. That chapter also documents the validity of the self-report (i.e., the memory rating) we use to assess memory. Finally, in chapter 3 we explore the relation between event memory and such variables as retention interval, event rehearsal, personal involvement in the event, and event type (or content). In chapter 4 we assess the effect of emotional content on memory for the event. Briefly put, we show that the intensity of affect has a strong effect on memory with events with strong affect (either positive or negative) being remembered much better than events with neutral affect. In addition, there is a small but consistent pleasantness effect, with pleasant events remembered better than unpleasant events. The section on memory for content concludes with a chapter on the effectiveness of the self schema (chapter 5). In that chapter, we use diaries in which individuals recorded events both for themselves and for either news events or events for another person. Tests of those diaries provide convincing data that events encoded with the self-schema are remembered much better than either news events or other-person events.

The section of the book on memory for temporal location opens with a chapter on schematic reconstruction of dates of events (chapter 6). In that chapter, we begin with a discussion of the cognitive representation of time and alternative theories of memory for time. Then we consider subjective reports of the strategies that people employ to date past events. Such reports suggest that reference to schemata and landmark events are the most common strategies, even at short retention intervals. We develop a model of the week schema in order to indicate how schema use can account for the objective accuracy of dating, which is observed in distributions such as those in Fig. 1.8. Chapter 7 focuses on forgetting of temporal location, with an emphasis on the data showing that reconstruction of exact dates is strongly related to forgetting peripheral details of the event. We also discuss such issues as telescoping and gender differences in event dating. In chapter 8, we present data showing that event memory and dating accuracy are related: Well-remembered events are well-dated events. However, some event characteristics (e.g., event pleasantness) continue to predict dating accuracy, even when recall is controlled. We argue that these two effects suggest that the details of events are used to reconstruct event dates but that other sources of temporal information are also used for that purpose.

The section on remembering when ends with a chapter on the effectiveness of the self-schema (chapter 9). Events related to the self-schema are dated more accurately than news events or other-person events. For other-person events, the inferior datings are almost entirely due to lower memory of the events. For news events, however, dating accuracy is even more inferior to self-events than can be explained by the lower level of memory for news. We suggest that, because of *source amnesia*, news memories are often dissociated from the self-related schemata that support temporal reconstruction.

Chapter 10 is an overview and theoretical summary of our research. In that chapter, we integrate all of our findings into a systematic picture with our theoretical interpretation of those results.

CHAPTER TWO

The Diaries

In this chapter, we discuss the major methodological issues that are at issue in many studies of autobiographical memory—including, of course, our diary memory studies. We also describe the content of the diaries, how they were collected, and the general procedure used during the testing session. For the reader interested in the exact procedure used in these experiments, we have provided an appendix with a detailed description of all the measures used in these diary studies, along with tables summarizing which of the measures were used in each of the studies. We end the chapter with a brief discussion of the multiple regression procedures that we used to analyze many of our data sets, including the rationale underlying, and inferential consequences of, their use.

METHODOLOGICAL ISSUES

The Conflict Between Control and Ecological Validity

The laboratory study of memory has historically emphasized experimental control. In our view, this is perfectly sensible. After all, the laboratory study of memory is oriented toward theory testing, and theory-testing demands control over as many aspects of the situation and the stimuli as possible. However, this emphasis on control often comes with costs. One such cost is that subjects in laboratory experiments are frequently asked to remember stimuli that are not structured, organized, or personally meaningful. For example, the early research of Ebbinghaus stimulated the development of a large body of laboratory research that used c-v-c nonsense syllables as the stimuli to be learned. The c-v-c experiments were perfectly sensible within the theoretical context of associationism; it was thought that the use of c-v-c stimuli allowed assessment of associations without the potentially confounding effects of stimulus meaningfulness. Ironically, later research (Archer, 1960; Glaze, 1928) demonstrated that the nonsense syllables actually varied in meaningfulness.

The stimuli used in these experiments were undeniably artificial. The widespread use of such artificial stimuli led to concerns that experimental cognitive psychology was seriously misguided. In real-world contexts, most stimuli encountered by people are meaningful. That is, they can be related to a large body of stored knowledge that people develop over time. Because of this, some of the more extreme critics even implied that the experimental cognitive psychologists' efforts on memory research had been substantially wasted (e.g., Neisser, 1982). Worse, these critics claimed that experimental psychologists' conclusions about human memory could be misleading or even totally incorrect (for an opposing position, see Banaji & Crowder, 1989).

We courageously straddle the fence on this issue. In our view, both highly controlled laboratory research and research conducted in real-world contexts have their appropriate uses. They each play appropriate roles in *full-cycle* psychology (Cialdini, 1980). Full-cycle psychology occurs when initial ideas and theories in psychology are derived from real-world research. These ideas are then vigorously tested in the controlled environment of the laboratory. The implications and conclusions from this laboratory research are subsequently investigated in real-world contexts. Finally, the cycle begins anew. It is within this context that we explore autobiographical event memory. We are open to new findings that may possibly be explored more precisely in the laboratory and are interested in learning how well laboratory findings validate when taken back out of the "clean" laboratory into the "messy" real world.

However, despite the fact that we believe that extra-laboratory memory research has a valuable role to play in the pursuit of knowledge about memory, we are aware that such research presents some methodological difficulties. The major methodological issues in our autobiographical memory studies can be grouped into seven categories: (a) the problem of establishing if and when an event occurred; (b) the problem of selectivity (i.e., what events get recorded or remembered, as well as what gets recorded about an event); (c) the effect of recording events; (d) the conceptual classification of the memory measure (cued recall vs. recognition); (e) the validity of the memory measure; (f) the possibility of a calendar artifact; and (g) the validity of the self versus non-self effects. These problems are valid concerns in many other autobiographical memory studies as well. We deal with each issue in turn.

Establishing If and When an Event Occurred

In many autobiographical memory studies, participants are asked to report and to date life events. One type of study asks participants to report their earliest memories (e.g., Dudycha & Dudycha, 1941; Kihlstrom & Harackiewicz, 1982). In another type of study, participants are asked to respond to cue words with whatever recollections come to mind and to date those recollections (e.g., Crovitz & Schiffman, 1974; Galton, 1879; Robinson, 1976; Rubin, Wetzler, & Nebes, 1986). A third type of study asks people to report their memory for *flashbulb memories*, events that are thought to be of high personal or historical importance (e.g., Brown & Kulik, 1977).

There are two serious problems with the studies just described. Except for some of the flashbulb memory studies, which sometimes involve widely known historical events, there is simply no way to verify the date of most of the generated memories. Diary studies (in which the exact dates of life events are known) clearly show that estimated dates of events can be greatly in error (e.g., Linton, 1975; Thompson, 1982). The second problem is perhaps more important. We now have impressive evidence that people who attempt to recall past events sometimes generate accounts that are either grossly inaccurate or that didn't happen at all (e.g., Lindsay, 1993; Linton, 1975; Loftus, 1993; Neisser & Harsch, 1992; Thompson & Cowan, 1986).

Because we are provided with a summary of the event shortly after the event occurred and the date of the event, the diary procedure solves these problems. In short, we know both *that* the event occurred and *when* it occurred. However, diary procedures like the present one, as well as those used in studies of flashbulb memories and randomly selected events (Brewer, 1988; Brown & Kulik, 1977; Neisser & Harsch, 1992), do not solve all the problems of verification. For one thing, there will always be a difference between the original event and the diary record, even when the record is required to be made on the spot (Brewer, 1988). Therefore, verification of recall by reference to a diary record is in principle an assessment of consistency between two accounts of the events, not an assessment of veridicality in a more absolute sense. A potentially more serious problem is that, at the time of recollection, the subject may recall a different part of the event (or a very similar but distinct event) from that recorded in the diary. The recall may thus differ from the diary account, although it corresponds to something that actually happened. A good example of this kind of recall error is the *time slice error* pointed out by Brewer (1988), in which the subject seems to be remembering an event that occurred a while earlier or later in the event chain as the diary record. Such time slice errors may account for some of the inconsistencies in flashbulb memory studies (Neisser & Harsch, 1992; Larsen, 1992a). Because we, as experimenters, cannot ever attain full knowledge about the events that occur in our subjects' lives, the risk of misclassifying recollections as erroneous because they do not fit the limited information we have cannot be fully alleviated. However, the requirement that subjects in our studies should strive to identify the events uniquely in the diary records is believed to keep this problem to a minimum (see Bahrick & Karis, 1982, for a useful topology of techniques for the study of ecological memory, graded by the degree to which ecological memories can be verified).

In addition to this verification problem, inherent in all diary procedures, our procedure leaves one other potential source of error. Because we collect event records once each week, subjects could record events with a lag of 6 days from the date of occurrence. Although we can be sure that the event did occur, there is room for slight error regarding the date of occurrence.

Selection and Encoding of Events

When subjects record events for later testing, they must select the event to be recorded as well as the components of the event that constitute the record. The issue is whether the selection process produces some systematic bias in our memory measures. We speak to the problems of event selection and selection in encoding (and recording) the event in separate sections.

Selecting the Event. In many autobiographical memory studies, the events are deliberately selected on the basis of some criteria. For example, in his long-term study of his own memory, Wagenaar (1986) deliberately selected only extremely memorable events for inclusion in his diary. However, Linton (1975) and White (1982) selected events in a fairly random manner for their long-term diaries. As another example of events selected on the basis of some criteria, we have already mentioned the studies that ask participants to report their earliest memories (e.g., Dudycha & Dudycha, 1941; Kihlstrom & Harackiewicz, 1982). Reason and Lucas (1984) suggested that such procedures can introduce a recording bias into the data. The concern here is that data based on events selected for special characteristics may not represent the characteristics of ordinary autobiographical memory. This is particularly troublesome in studies (e.g., Wagenaar, 1986) that are intended to describe long-term autobiographical memory.

The studies that come closest to alleviating these concerns are the diary study by Brewer (1988) and our diary studies. In an ingenious study, Brewer used an alarm device that sounded at random intervals. When the alarm sounded, participants were to record whatever they were doing at that moment. At first glance, this procedure appears to be the perfect way to produce a random and representative sample of events from individual's lives. However, even Brewer's clever procedure doesn't solve the problem completely—often people did not respond because they were doing something private.

We approached the problem in a different way: In most studies, we asked participants to give us a variety of events from their lives. We specifically asked them to give us events that were memorable and events that were not very memorable as well as events that were pleasant and events that were unpleasant. We emphasized that the greater the variety of events that they gave us, the better would be our measure of their memory. Participants in our diary studies responded with a wide variety of events, and it appears that those events mirrored the variety of events in their lives. We asked participants not to give us events that would be so personal as to be embarrassing. However, the requirement to exclude embarrassing events did not prevent the inclusion of extremely important personal events. We have several entries that reported the deaths of parents or siblings, entries that reported the occasion of engagements, weddings, and births, and entries that described the break-up of close personal relationships (e.g., "Someone who was in my life in a very special way told me they no longer wanted to be").

Here, we need to include the caveat that our two Danish studies (collected at Aarhus University) asked participants to record memorable events with no restriction regarding embarrassing events. This minor change in procedure did not seem to affect the pattern of our results.

In short, both our approach and Brewer's (1988) approach probably produced a variety of events that closely approximate the variety of personal events in everyday memory. One can get some sense of the range of events by considering some events from our initial study that were rated extremely memorable or not very memorable. The nonmemorable events included "Found an earring on the apartment shuttle bus," "Saw prisms in physics class," and "Played football with Ed and Kirk." By contrast, the events rated as extremely memorable included "Someone who was in my life in a very special way told me they no longer wanted to be," "Got elected to the house disciplinary board," and "Lori stood me up, then came over and picked me up."

Although we have no formal data to back up this statement, we were struck with the impression that, taken together, the events provided by each person during the typical 3-month collection period often provided a clear outline of a unique personality. Most impressively, that personality emerged even though our instructions clearly suggested that the participants need not include any extremely personal events.

Encoding the Event.   In a laboratory study, the encoding conditions for the material to be recalled (e.g., a list of words, a short story) are carefully controlled, and the materials are known exactly. In a diary study, there is no way to control the encoding conditions or to know the exact characteristics of naturally occurring personal events. Selection is a necessary component in encoding a memory from the rich fabric of a personal event. Indeed, initial observation of the event involves the processes of attention and encoding, with both processes focusing on selected aspects of the event.

When a written record is made of the event, producing the record necessarily involves abstraction and memory, thus further selecting from the
initial event. The selection process is not restricted to written records. If the
event is tape recorded, visual context cues are not included. If a video
recording is made, there can be significant action taking place off-screen.

We think that the three most important points to be kept in mind when
considering the theoretical and methodological implications of recording an
event are that (a) any record will abstract and condense the event; (b) any
attempt to systematically control the abstraction process will make assumptions about what should be remembered, and given our present state of
knowledge about memory, such assumptions are probably not warranted;
and (c) our everyday memories are also based on components extracted
from the original event.

Effect of Recording Events

One of the major concerns about the diary memory procedure is that the
act of recording the event may modify memory for the event. That is, recording an event may change the event's representation in memory (cf,
Zajonc, 1960). There are many laboratory phenomena that lead us to predict
that recording the event should facilitate memory for the event. People who
record events in a diary memory study know that they will be tested on
their memory for those events. Thus, they have the advantage of intentional
recall, whereas recall for most events from one's life is incidental. The typical
advantage of intentional over incidental recall (presumably as a result of
elaborative rehearsal) has been well documented in laboratory studies (e.g.,
Craik & Watkins, 1973). In addition, the act of recording the event produces
additional rehearsal and, it can be argued, may produce a generation effect
as well. Both elaborative rehearsal (e.g., Rundus, 1971) and the act of gen-
erating a to-be-remembered item (Slamecka & Graf, 1978) have been shown
to increase memory in laboratory studies. Finally, participants select the
events to record and, once again, there are numerous studies (e.g., Underwood, Ham, & Ekstrand, 1962) attesting to the positive effects of item selection on memory.

Given the data from the laboratory, the most reasonable prediction is that
one or more of these processes operate to produce superior performance
for individuals recording events for subsequent test. Obviously, if that prediction is correct, some adjustment must be made to take into account the
inflated memory produced by the processes enumerated previously. The
point of diary studies is, after all, to produce an account of everyday memory,
not memory enhanced as an artifact of the procedure. However, if the impact
of event recording results only in a quantitative alteration in the memory
(e.g., strengthens the trace), then the problem is probably not a significant

one. In such a case, one would expect the memory to exhibit the same kinds of effects (e.g., forgetting patterns, etc.) exhibited by unrecorded memories, except that recorded memories may simply be a bit stronger.

More serious is the possibility that the act of recording an event may change the relations between preratings and postratings qualitatively. Recording an event may change the way in which the event is represented in memory (e.g., the form of the representation, connections to other ideas and events, etc.). This is a far more serious problem than a mere quantitative shift, for it suggests that memories derived from a diary methodology may exhibit entirely different characteristics than those from other methods.

Fortunately, our data suggest that recording the event does not substantially facilitate later recall and does not seem to produce qualitative shifts in memory. We arrive at that conclusion using two types of data. The first is from studies comparing the recall of people who recorded their own events with people whose events were recorded by others (Thompson, 1982, 1985b). People whose events were recorded by others did not know which events were recorded until the memory test. In these studies, rated recall of events was equivalent for those who recorded their own events and those who did not. The second type of data is from a study (Skowronski, Betz, Thompson, & Shannon, 1991) in which people recorded events for themselves and for another person (usually a close friend with whom they had daily contact). At the end of the recording period, recorders were tested on both diaries. Despite the fact they recorded events from both self and other, the recorders remembered self-events better than other-events. Taken together, these data suggest that it is the personal relevance of the event that determines how well it will be remembered and not the act of recording the event.

The Memory Rating Measure: Recognition or Cued Recall?

There is considerable confusion regarding the classification of our memory rating test. This can be clarified by considering the comments of Tulving and Watkins (1973). They make the point that free recall, cued recall, and recognition are on a continuum. As an example, we may present the word *graph* during study and, in separate conditions, present the following cues in a memory test: graph, grap-, gra--, gr---, g----, and -----. The condition with "graph" is called a recognition test, the condition with all blanks is called a recall test, and all the others are called cued recall tests.

In our diary memory studies, we explicitly instruct our subjects to "be sure to rate your recall for the event and not for writing it down." With that in mind, consider the following typical description of an event: "I picked up Mary at the bus station." That short description does not indicate whether

Mary is a relative or a sweetheart, whether the initial greeting was formal or emotional, whether there was much excitement and bustle (or lack thereof) at the bus station, or any of the other components of what quite possibly is a very rich memory. Yet that short simple statement may elicit the memory for all the encoded characteristics of the event. Clearly, we must regard each event description as a cue for a potentially complex and rich memory. We ask the subject to rate the extent to which all this information is actually elicited. It follows that the diary memory procedure should be regarded as cued recall.

It is worth noting that the memory rating procedure avoids a problem implied by the previous discussion: The original diary record almost certainly will not contain a description of everything that was committed to memory. With a standard recall procedure, recalled material that is beyond the original record cannot be scored, and actual memory therefore will be underestimated.

The Validity of the Memory Measure

Some investigators are concerned that our subjects do not engage in an objective memory task but instead simply provide us with a subjective self-report of the clarity of their memory for an event. This concern is entirely reasonable, given the research suggesting that people often do not have exact insight into their cognitive processes (e.g., Nisbett & Wilson, 1977).

However, there are at least three reasons to place more than minimal faith in the memory data that we have collected. First, recent evidence from other paradigms suggests that memory measures of the type we used in these studies are strongly correlated with more traditional measures of memory. For example, work in metacognition suggests that subjects' judgments of knowing are typically highly related to other, more typical measures of memory (e.g., Leonesio & Nelson, 1990). Thus, when people say that they recall something well, they typically perform well on other measures of memory. A good example from our data is the comparison of the subjective memory rating and objective accuracy data of Larsen and Thompson (in press) described in chapter 5. In that study, both cued recall and rated memory clarity declined reliably over time, and the decrease in recall was quite comparable for the two measures. Although the correlation is not perfect, it is strong enough to suggest that our memory ratings have considerable validity as a measure of the "goodness" of memory.

A second reason to be comfortable with our memory outcomes is that those outcomes tend to be quite sensible, replicating the results obtained from research using other methodologies. Indeed, if we were not to tell anyone about our memory method but instead simply say that we had done some research indicating that memory for events decreases with lengthening retention interval, is a combination of both memory for gist and memory for peripheral detail, is slightly better for pleasant than unpleasant events, is much better for emotional and extreme events than unemotional and unextreme events, and is better for atypical than for typical events, we would be met with a resounding "so what's new?" The fact that the data from the memory ratings tend to duplicate results obtained using other memory measures is impressive and adds to confidence in both the findings and the measure (by the principle of convergent validity). Moreover, there is an additional benefit in these outcomes, one that pertains to the continuing "real-world" versus "controlled research" debate. Despite the claims of many that laboratory research in memory is irrelevant to remembering in the real world (e.g., Neisser, 1982), it should be quite comforting to experimental cognitive psychologists that many of the outcomes obtained in laboratory studies, with standard memory measures, also appear in our memory rating data.

The third reason to believe that the memory rating data is actually indexing memory is the strong relation between rated memory and event dating accuracy (or error). That is, even though dating accuracy is affected by numerous factors, one would expect that well-remembered events should also be accurately dated events. As indicated in chapter 8 (see Table 8.2), this relation occurred, and occurred strongly, in every data set that we collected. The event date provided by the subject is not a self-report but is instead a reproduction or a reconstruction from memory, and one whose accuracy can be objectively assessed. Hence, objectively-determined dating accuracy should be subject to some of the same biases that supposedly beset the subjective memory ratings (although, as we document in this book, event dates may be subject to other biases as well). Because of the strong relation between the two measures, the event dating data provide additional convergent validity for the memory ratings.

Another important methodological concern is that subjects might have been basing their memory ratings during the test, and their metamemory ratings at the time of recording, on the quality of the description of the event rather than their memory (or, at recording, metamemory) for the event. However, we explicitly instructed subjects to rate their memory for the event, not for the cue they had recorded. More important, we present data showing that subjects' memory ratings changed in the classical Ebbinghaus fashion as retention interval increased; that is, memory ratings dropped rapidly at first and then more slowly as retention interval increased. Furthermore, memory ratings increased as metamemory ratings increased, but when separate retention interval curves were plotted for each initial metamemory rating, those curves produced parallel Ebbinghaus functions.

Clearly, if memory ratings were based solely on the quality of the description of the event, there would be no effect of retention interval. Even if we were to put aside that strong claim, it would strain the imagination to propose that memory ratings based on the description of the event, rather than memory for the event, would conform to the classical Ebbinghaus forgetting function with parallel functions produced for each initial metamemory rating. In short, we find it entirely safe to conclude that the memory ratings in our experiments were based on memory for the events.

The Data Speak. Another concern is that the self-report memory ratings used to assess event memory simply reflect subjects' views about how well they should remember the event. The previous section should do much to allay that concern. In this section, we demonstrate that our data provide a very powerful argument against the idea that the relations between subjects' ratings of event characteristics and their memory ratings reflect their pre-conceptions about memory and not their actual memories. To appreciate these data, the reader must be aware of the logic behind regression analyses (which is described in a later section of this chapter).

In many of our studies, we asked subjects to predict how well they would remember each event. It is certainly the case that these memory predictions should reflect subjects' theories about memory. By the logic of regression, if the relation between a predictor and subjects' final memory ratings is a really merely a reflection of their ideas about memories and not their actual memories, then adding their memory predictions to the regression model should eliminate the relation between the predictor and subjects' final memory ratings.

To explore this possibility, we conducted a series of pooled within-subject regression analyses. Each analysis examined the extent to which subjects' final memory ratings were predicted by one of the individual predictors (i.e., affective intensity, valence, person-typicality, frequency, initial mental involvement) that we assessed at the time that subjects' entered events into the diaries. The memory predictions were collected at this time, so they would not apply to variables collected during test, such as rehearsal. Our standard set of predictors (i.e., the linear and quadratic effects of retention interval and a dummy vector representing subjects) were included in each model, as were subjects' initial memory ratings (i.e., their prediction of how well they would remember each event).

One would suspect that the pre-ratings, which are provided at about the same time as the initial memory predictions, would be most prone to ex-pectation effects. In a series of analyses, we evaluated whether subjects' initial memory predictions eliminated the relation between five variables (i.e., event valence, affective extremity, emotionality, frequency, and per-son-typicality) and the memory ratings.

Before getting to the results, we point out that this procedure is strongly biased in favor of the hypothesis that subjects' memory ratings are caused by their hypotheses about memory. The reason is this: We show in our analyses (reported in chapter 3) that these pre-ratings are strongly related to subjects' memory predictions. However, it is unclear whether this relation is caused by subjects' expectations about memory (so that the expectations are driving the predicted memory ratings) or whether the relation reflects an incidental (i.e., noncausal) relation between the characteristics of memorable events and the pre-ratings.

The data are clear and compelling on this issue. The relation between four of the predictors and the final memory ratings is not rendered insignificant when the relation controls for subjects' memory predictions. We have nine data sets containing both the memory predictions and the affective intensity variable; the relation between affective intensity and subjects' final memory ratings was significant in seven of the data sets and approached significance in the other two (80KS yielded the largest $F(1, 2407) = 35.63$, $p < .0001$, $\beta = .103$; 91KS yielded the smallest $F(1, 1628) = 1.97$, $p < .17$, $\beta = .031$). We have four data sets containing both the memory predictions and the emotionality variable, and the relation between emotionality and subjects' final memory ratings was significant in all four (92KS yielded the largest $F(1, 3254) = 28.70$, $p < .0001$, $\beta = .094$; 91KS yielded the smallest $F(1, 1628) = 4.60$, $p < .04$, $\beta = .060$). We have four data sets containing both the memory predictions and the frequency variable, and the relation between frequency and subjects' final memory ratings was significant in all four (90KS yielded the largest $F(1, 3677) = 138.89$, $p < .0001$, $\beta = .192$; 91KS yielded the smallest $F(1, 1628) = 29.91$, $p < .0001$, $\beta = .119$). We have one data set (88OH) that contains both the memory predictions and the person-typicality variable: Both the linear ($F(1, 3222) = 17.14$, $p < .0001$, $\beta = -.064$) and the quadratic ($F(1, 3221) = 16.74$, $p < .0001$) effects of person-typicality were significant.

The sole variable that was not consistently related to the final memory ratings when the data controlled for the initial memory predictions was the event valence variable. We had nine data sets that contained both the valence and memory predictions variables, and event valence was positively related to the final memory ratings in seven of the nine analyses. However, this relation was statistically reliable in only one analysis (88OH, $F(1, 3230) = 5.15$, $p < .03$, $\beta = .033$) and approached significance in two others (91KS, $F(1, 1628) = 3.23$, $p < .08$, $\beta = .036$; 89KS, $F(1, 2850) = 3.60$, $p < .06$, $\beta = .027$). Because event pleasantness was the variable that was most weakly related to event memory in our analyses (see chapter 4), it is not surprising that the predictive relation between pleasantness and memory was rendered nonsignificant when the initial memory ratings were controlled. In our view, it is likely that the initial weakness of this relation is ultimately responsible for its demise in the face of procedures that control for subjects' expectations about what they would recall. However, despite this control, the data still tended toward better recall of positive events than negative events in seven of the nine data sets.

Because rehearsal was not evaluated in the pre-ratings but was collected during testing, it is intuitively less likely that the rehearsal ratings were subject to the kinds of expectation effects that have been discussed with respect to the pre-ratings. Nonetheless, it is conceivable that peoples' preconceptions about the relations between event rehearsal and event memory were reflected in both the memory predictions and the memory ratings. Thus, we conducted a series of analyses in which we assessed the relation between subjects' rehearsal ratings and the final memory ratings, controlling for subjects' memory predictions. All five data sets that containing both the rehearsal ratings and the memory predictions evinced a significant relation between the rehearsal and the final memory ratings (80KS yielded the largest $F(1, 2407) = 914.00$, $p < .0001$, $\beta = .464$; 91KS yielded the smallest $F(1, 1628) = 110.12$, $p < .0001$, $\beta = .239$).

It should be emphasized that the significant effects that we report for all of these analyses were occurring despite the fact that the initial memory ratings were relatively strong predictors of the final memory ratings (88OH yielded the largest $F(1, 3230) = 522.60$, $p < .0001$, $\beta = .351$; 80KS yielded the smallest $F(1, 2407) = 68.41$, $p < .0001$, $\beta = .464$). As we point out in chapter 3, people have some ability to predict what they will later be able to remember. Thus, the best conclusion from these analyses is that the ability of subjects' event ratings to predict their memory ratings is not due to subjects' expectations about how their ratings should be related to memory. Instead, subjects' memory ratings likely reflect their judgments about how well they remember each event, and subjects' event ratings reflect those factors that have an actual impact on event memories.

However, we do not consider memory ratings to be perfect reflections of memory. These ratings are subjects' judgments about their own event memories, and as such, they can be prone to the same kinds of biases and distortions that beset other judgments. For example, in chapter 3 we review evidence suggesting that the slope of the forgetting curve produced by these memory judgments is affected by the length of the retention interval. This does not make sense if the memory ratings are thought to be a direct reflection of memory, but it makes perfect sense if one considers the possibility that the memory judgments can be affected by judgmental anchoring processes.

The Calendar Artifact

As we show in chapter 6, subjects are very good at estimating the day of week on which an event occurred even when they are wrong about the week during which the event occurred. The effect is quite striking, and we have dubbed it the day-of-week effect. Some people have posed the following question: Given that subjects use a blank calendar as an aid to event dating and that the calendars included day-of-week information, isn't the day-of-week data "artifactual?" Although this is a reasonable concern, recent data collected by a colleague (Jeff Gibbons) shows that our use of a calendar does not produce an artifact but rather allows our subjects to make use of their day-of-week information. In his study, half of the subjects were not given a calendar, but they were allowed to specify the day of the week (or group of days) on which they thought the event might have occurred. Those subjects produced day-of-week effects completely comparable to the subjects using calendars. Again, the calendar simply allows subjects to use information they have available.

Although our calendar procedure is valid, it is only one of the several ways in which people may be asked to make retrospective temporal judgments. For example, people may sometimes be asked how long ago the event occurred (as in studies by Huttenlocher and her colleagues; Huttenlocher, Hedges, & Bradburn, 1990; Huttenlocher, Hedges, & Prohaska, 1992) and may be expected to answer without any dating aids (e.g., a calendar) available. In other circumstances, people may be asked to reconstruct the exact date of events and may have the luxury of access to a wealth of information, such as calendars, diaries, and notes (as apparently happened in John Dean's Watergate testimony). We argue that none of these event dating or temporal judgment situations are any more or less valid than any other situation. Instead, we suspect that each situation has its own unique features but that the different temporal judgment situations share some common characteristics.

Indeed, the data from both the Huttenlocher et al. (1990; 1992) paradigm and from our diary paradigm indicate that subjects make extensive use of reconstructive strategies in their attempt to reproduce temporal information. This supports one of the major claims of this book—that there is no temporal trace embedded in memory. Instead, temporal information is reconstructed from one or more of the potential sources of temporal information available in memory (e.g., specific event details, temporal tags, temporal schemata) and in the environment (e.g., the days of the week, months, years that may appear on a blank calendar).

Validity of the Self Versus Non-Self Effects

As we describe later (see chapters 5 and 9), we sometimes compared memory and dating performance for self-events and non-self-events. We have to consider the possibility that the self versus non-self effects reported in this book may reflect the fact that the self-events recorded were qualitatively different from the non-self-events. This concern reflects the possibility that there is some consistent confound between the self and non-self categorization and some other unspecified variable. For example, it may be that recorded self-events were predominantly positive and other-events were predominantly negative, so that the self versus non-self difference that emerged in our studies reflects this pleasantness effect rather than the self versus non-self distinction.

In two studies (Betz & Skowronski, 1995; Skowronski et al., 1991) we attempted to address this issue by conducting a content analysis on the events that were collected. This content analysis categorized the events listed in the diaries along multiple dimensions and into multiple categories that were organized hierarchically (see Skowronski et al., 1991, for further details). Inclusion of the content coding scheme into the regression analyses used in those studies generally had little effect on the results that emerged from the analyses. For example, as reported by Skowronski et al. (1991) a self-other difference in event recall occurred, controlling for the category content (which itself was significant, indicating that the content coding scheme had some validity) as well as for the other effects that were included in the regression models employed in that study. Examination of means in the individual content categories bears this out. Of the 69 content categories in which there were memory ratings from both self and other diaries, 60 produced differences in the expected direction (i.e., self-memories being better recalled), and the reversals tended to occur in cells with very few observations. A similar outcome was recently reported by Betz and Skowronski (1995) for both memory ratings and dating error and accuracy.

An examination of self-other differences in the sources of information used to specify dates leads to a similar conclusion. In the Betz and Skowronski data, subjects reported the various sources of information that they used to reconstruct event dates. As Betz and Skowronski (1995) noted, the pattern of source use is fundamentally similar for the self and other events, as is the relation between source use and dating accuracy. Again, this suggests that there are not substantial qualitative differences in event dating for self-events and for other-events.

In general, then, the self versus non-self data cannot be easily explained by claiming that the events recorded in the self and other diaries are somehow different, or that these events are differentially involving, or that the information available in the self and other memories is qualitatively different. Instead, it is much more likely that the differences are merely quantitative: There is simply more information available in the memory traces for self-events than for other-events.

THE DATA SETS

This book is based on almost 450 memory diaries collected at three different locations (Aarhus University, Kansas State University, The Ohio State University at Newark) from 1979 to 1992. Most of the diaries were collected from students during a term (semester or quarter) and are, therefore, from 10 to 15 weeks in duration. Six of the diaries were collected in conjunction with a 3-year research project (Thompson, Cowan, & Frieman, 1993; Thompson et al., 1991); they range from 18 months to 30 months in duration. The long-term diaries more than double the number of such diaries in existence prior to their collection. Furthermore, all of the diaries (both short-term and long-term) are from ordinary students, whereas the other long-term diaries were kept by professional memory researchers. It is a troubling possibility that their expertise in and knowledge about the processes of memory modified their performance in recalling their diaries.

The individual data sets are summarized in Table 2.1, which shows the date of collection of the data set, where the data was collected, the number of diaries in the set, the length of the (longest) retention interval, and the major purpose of the study. The data sets described in Table 2.1 are very rich and have been used in previous publications. To assist the reader, Table 2.2 lists previous publications about diary memory and the data set (or sets) used in each publication. Note that some of our publications on autobiographical memory (e.g., Larsen & Plunkett, 1987) used procedures other than diary memory.

Collecting and Testing the Diaries

In all cases, the diaries were collected once a week. In most of the studies, the exception to that rule occurred once each semester whenever a short break (e.g., Thanksgiving) or a long break (e.g., spring break) fell on the day for collecting events. In those cases, 2 weeks' worth of events were

TABLE 2.1
Data Sets and Major Purpose of the Studies

Data Set	N	RI	Major Purpose
79KS	32	16	Roommate-recorder study
80KS	30	14	Pleasantness study
81KS	42	8	Present-absent study (self-other)
83KS	23	14	Participant-observer study
86KS	35	13	Pleasantness study
86AU	1	48	Personal vs. news events study
87KS	43	14	Calendar study
88OH	62	11	Self-other study
89KS	33	15	Dating accuracy judgment study
89OH	30	10	Boundary effects study
90KS	6	129	Long-term diary study
90AU	12	60	Personal-news: Memory and Dating
91KS	25	15	Time-of-week study
91OH	47	11	Self-other study
92KS	38	15	Time-of-week study
Total	428		

Note: The data sets were collected at Kansas State University (KS), The Ohio State University at Newark (OH), and Aarhus University (AU). They are identified by year of collection and location (e.g., 80KS). The number of participants (N) and maximum retention interval in weeks (RI) are also included for each study

TABLE 2.2
Previous Publications and Data Sets

Publication	Data Set(s) Used
Betz, A. L., & Skowronski, J. J. (1995)	91OH
Larsen, S. F. (1988)	86AU
Larsen, S. F. (1992a)	86AU
Larsen, S. F. (1992b)	90AU
Larsen, S. F., & Thompson, C. P. (1995)	90AU, 91KS
Skowronski, J. J., Betz, A. L., Thompson, C. P., & Larsen, S. F. (1995)	91KS
Skowronski, J. J., Betz, A. L., Thompson, C. P., & Shannon, L. (1991)	88OH
Skowronski, J. J., Betz, A. L., Thompson, C. P., Walker, W. R., & Shannon, L. (1994)	Review chapter
Skowronski, J. J., & Thompson, C. P. (1990)	79KS, 80KS, 83KS, 86KS
Thompson, C. P. (1982)	79KS
Thompson, C. P. (1985a)	80KS
Thompson, C. P. (1985b)	81KS, 83KS
Thompson, C. P., Skowronski, J. J., & Betz, A. L. (1993)	89KS, 89OH
Thompson, C. P., Skowronski, J. J., & Lee, D. J. (1988a)	Tabor College data
Thompson, C. P., Skowronski, J. J., & Lee, D. J. (1988b)	80KS, 83KS, 86KS

collected the following week. There were some special problems in collecting the events for the six long-term diaries because the participants were gone during holiday breaks and over the summer. We instructed them to mail the diaries to us and provided them with stamps and envelopes for that purpose. However, the students varied in the diligence with which they performed that task, and even the most diligent did not always remember to provide us with their events.

In most studies, recording of events continued up to the day before the test. Events were collected at a specific time each week (often a Wednesday) and, at the time of test, participants provided events for the period from the last collection date to the day before testing.

During the test session, the event descriptions were read to the participants in a random order. As each event was presented, the participant first determined whether or not the event was unique. That procedure was used because participants obviously could not accurately date events that had occurred more than once during the recording period. It was an easy task for the participant (and usually the experimenter) to determine when an event was not unique. Such events were usually something like "went to a movie" or "went out for a drink." If the event was not unique, it was deleted, and the participant went on to the next event. When the event met the requirement of being unique, the participant made a series of ratings or estimates about the event. Although the exact judgments varied from study to study, they always included a rating reflecting how well the event was remembered and an estimate of when the event occurred.

Analyzing the Data: Multiple Regression

We often used multiple linear regressions, rather than ANOVA, in our inferential analyses. The ANOVA framework requires that, to avoid missing values, we collapse across observations within each subjects' data. In contrast, the regression framework more easily accommodates missing values, thus facilitating the use of multiple observations from each subject in the analyses.

The use of multiple observations from each subject was also facilitated by the use of dummy coding for each subject. That is, to conduct each regression analysis, a dummy coding vector was constructed for each subject and was entered into the analysis. This vector essentially has the effect of causing subjects to serve as a categorical variable in the regression model. Conceptually, this technique is similar to partitioning the variance in a within-subject ANOVA to between-subjects variance and within-subject variance so that the effects of interest are tested against an error term that does not contain any between-subjects variance. By using this pooled within-subject regression technique, the problem of non-independence of observations is circumvented, and each data point can be validly treated as a separate observation in the regression analysis (for elaboration of this technique, see Cohen & Cohen, 1983). Because of the large number of degrees of freedom that accumulate in the error term, another important consequence of this technique is the production of considerable analytic power.

In addition, the regression framework allows us to investigate and control for factors that may moderate the relation between a predictor and a dependent measure. For example, one of these factors is event age. To control for the possibility that recall, dating accuracy, and dating error may vary both linearly and quadratically over time (see chapter 3), and that important variables such as an event's event emotional intensity and valence (i.e., pleasantness-unpleasantness) may be related to event age, terms for the linear effects of event age and the quadratic effects of event age were included as covariates in all regression models. Hence, all statistically reliable effects that we report control for possible effects due to the linear age and quadratic age of events and hence are independent of those potentially confounding factors.

Similarly, in our studies we typically collect other ratings of events, such as ratings of the frequency with which events of the types reported in the diaries occur or ratings of the level of mental involvement that subjects experienced with each event. The regression analyses allow us to examine the relation between event memory, event dating accuracy or dating error, and any specified variable, controlling for the effects of other variables in each regression model. This is an important procedure: One of the interpretive difficulties with many earlier diary studies is that it is always possible that a relation between a predictor and a dependent measure could be due to a third, unmeasured variable that is correlated with the predictor. For example, prior autobiographical memory research has generally demonstrated that pleasant events are better recalled than unpleasant events (see Rapaport, 1942). However, this relation may occur for a number of reasons unrelated to event pleasantness. For example, the pleasant events obtained in the earlier research may have been more intense than the unpleasant events, and the intensity, rather than the affective direction, may have been responsible for the supposed pleasantness effect in event recall. If both event affective direction and event intensity measures are obtained, the regression analyses allow examination of the possible effect of event affect on event recall, uncontaminated by (or controlling for) the effects of event intensity (in fact, we have conducted such analyses; see chapter 4). Although this procedure cannot control for all possible mediating variables, it is certainly better than simply ignoring the possible mediators, as most prior research has done.

Finally, one of the issues that is encountered when using these multiple regression techniques is that there are a large number of regression models that are appropriate to the data. For this book, to maintain a degree of consistency across studies, we took on the task of reanalyzing the data from most of our relevant data sets. In these reanalyses, we attempted to maintain as much consistency in the regression models used across studies as possible. One consequence of these reanalyses is that data previously examined and published using ANOVA are now reexamined using regression (e.g., see Thompson, 1985b). A second consequence is that the results from these new analyses may differ slightly from the results of analyses that employed the regression technique reported in earlier papers. For example, the self and other Betas that we report in chapter 4 (e.g., the Skowronski data collected in 1988) differ slightly from the Betas that we previously reported in Skowronski et al. (1991). Gratifyingly (and thankfully!), the interpretation of the results of any of the previous papers does not change as a result of these reanalyses (although the compilation of results presented herein may have differing implications than the result of a single paper; see Thompson, 1985b).

Memory for
Everyday Events

As we discussed in chapters 1 and 2, the studies described in this book assess memory for the content of events that occurred in the lives of our subjects. In many of these studies, event memory was assessed by asking people to provide a memory self-report. That is, people were asked to remember the event cued by the event description recorded in their diaries and to report how well they remembered the event (see the Appendix for the exact form of the self-report measure).

In this chapter, we review the results of various analyses of our event memory data. Specifically, we explore the relations between self-reported event memory and such variables as retention interval, event rehearsal, involvement, and event type (or content).

These analyses serve two functions. First, they provide information about the characteristics of real-world event memory. Such information is important, and it may lead to conclusions about memory that differ from those derived from the laboratory. For example, in chapter 1 we noted that the memory ratings that we obtained from subjects seemed to decrease relatively slowly across retention intervals, especially compared to the expectations that may be derived from the forgetting work of Ebbinghaus. In this chapter, we review the results of numerous studies that explore how personal memory, as reflected in our memory ratings, decreases with the passage of time. Furthermore, we explore how personal event memory is related to a number of other event characteristics, such as the level of involvement that people have in the events.

Second, our analyses of the memory data help to establish the validity of these data. They do so by allowing comparison of our data with memory data generated in the laboratory, with data collected using more typical memory measures, or both. The event memory data collected using our self-report measure compares favorably to these other data.

CHARACTERISTICS AND PREDICTORS OF MEMORY FOR PERSONAL EVENTS

The Impact of Retention Interval on Event Memory

One of the well-documented effects in laboratory research is the relation between retention interval and memory. The study of such effects dates to Ebbinghaus (1885/1964). Ebbinghaus studied lists of material, waited for specified (and varying) periods of time, and attempted to remember the material using free recall. Ebbinghaus found a characteristic curvilinear relation between recall and retention interval. Recall decreased rapidly with lengthening retention interval, but eventually a floor was reached such that no additional forgetting seemed to occur. This negatively accelerating forgetting curve has been replicated numerous times in laboratory-based experimentation using a variety of objective memory measures such as free recall and recognition. We investigated whether our highly meaningful event memories would evince similar effects.

Memory Ratings. To explore this possibility, we subjected the final memory rating for each event to pooled within-subject regression analyses (see chapter 2). The memory rating for each event was the dependent measure, and subjects (through dummy coding), retention interval, and quadratic retention interval (i.e., the test for significant curvilinearity in the memory rating-retention interval relation) were the predictors. Table 3.1 presents the betas and significance levels of both the linear retention interval and the quadratic retention interval effects for all studies. Without exception, the linear and quadratic effects are statistically significant, all p's < .0001. Thus, these analyses indicate that the memory ratings decrease both linearly and curvilinearly with lengthening retention interval.

The form of these linear and curvilinear relations is illustrated in Fig. 3.1, which depicts the data from four of the studies. These studies were selected to provide a sense of the range of the forgetting functions in our short-term (10–15 week) studies, from the flattest to the steepest. The form of these functions is always the same: There is a relatively sharp decrease in recall at short retention intervals with a slower decrease at longer intervals. In

TABLE 3.1
Betas From Pooled Within-Subject Regressions (all betas $p < .0001$)

Study		Memory Ratings		Perfect Memory	
		Retention Interval	Quadratic Retention Interval	Retention Interval	Quadratic Retention Interval
Self-Events					
79KS	β	−.327	.144	−.201	.193
$F(1, 2571)$	F	409.59	52.12	140.38	85.13
	p	.0001	.0001	.0001	.0001
80KS	β	−.303	.121	−.219	.099
$F(1, 2409)$	F	367.83	48.19	176.50	29.60
	p	.0001	.0001	.0001	.0001
83KS	β	−.324	.155	−.274	.193
$F(1, 1607)$	F	218.37	40.74	150.15	61.21
	p	.0001	.0001	.0001	.0001
86KS	β	−.299	.153	−.222	.169
$F(1, 2566)$	F	317.06	67.00	161.24	75.09
	p	.0001	.0001	.0001	.0001
87KS	β	−.286	.192	−.231	.196
$F(1, 3295)$	F	412.06	148.37	281.76	163.15
	p	.0001	.0001	.0001	.0001
88OH (self)	β	−.290	.148	−.266	.154
$F(1, 3249)$	F	367.48	77.59	306.97	83.99
	p	.0001	.0001	.0001	.0001
89KS	β	−.318	.143	−.241	.186
$F(1, 2852)$	F	505.07	83.21	251.92	123.00
	p	.0001	.0001	.0001	.0001
89OH	β	−.319	.214	−.293	.208
$F(1, 1589)$	F	250.79	88.47	207.89	81.80
	p	.0001	.0001	.0001	.0001
90KS(long-term)	β	−.312	.057	−.115	.083
$F(1, 3631)$	F	377.67	18.26	42.68	32.02
	p	.0001	.0001	.0001	.0001
91OH (self)	β	−.201	.112	−.142	.124
$F(1, 2256)$	F	121.21	30.64	62.08	38.56
	p	.0001	.0001	.0001	.0001
91KS	β	−.252	.220	−.223	.226
$F(1, 1630)$	F	160.31	94.89	115.28	90.66
	p	.0001	.0001	.0001	.0001
92KS	β	−.317	.146	−.286	.200
$F(1, 3256)$	F	486.20	85.08	388.09	155.88
	p	.0001	.0001	.0001	.0001
Other-events					
.88OH(other)	β	−.235	.164	−.197	.145
$F(1, 2724)$	F	221.85	84.68	146.94	62.65
	p	.0001	.0001	.0001	.0001
91OH(other)	β	−.249	.136	−.116	.122
$F(1, 1947)$	F	163.97	41.28	34.69	32.34
	p	.0001	.0001	.0001	.0001

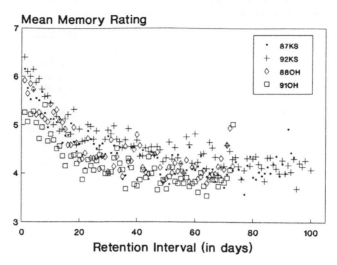

FIG. 3.1. Memory ratings: the form of the forgetting function obtained in four selected studies.

short, these forgetting functions are generally Ebbinghaus-like (cf., McCormack, 1979; Rubin, 1982; Rubin et al., 1986).

However, as noted in chapter 1, the decrease in memory ratings with increasing retention interval does not precisely match Ebbinghaus' forgetting functions. In particular, the rapid decrease in recall evident at short retention intervals is much less pronounced in our data than in the typical list-learning experiment of Ebbinghaus, in which vast amounts of information are apparently lost quite rapidly. By comparison, our memory rating data suggest a somewhat slower rate of information loss, especially for short retention intervals.

This difference in the shape of the forgetting functions may be due to general differences in meaningfulness between our real-life memory stimuli and many laboratory stimuli. For example, Ebbinghaus wanted to minimize interference effects in his studies of forgetting, so he often used meaningless nonsense syllables as his stimuli. The use of such stimuli was widespread in later laboratory research. In comparison, in our studies the memories that subjects recorded in their diaries were always meaningful. In chapter 1, we speculated that the relative stability in our memory ratings may reflect this meaningfulness. In particular, we suggest that the memory ratings may reflect people's recollection of the gist of their listed events as well as their recollection of the exact event details. This presumes that gist recall is longer lasting than recall of exact event detail (see Bransford & Johnson, 1973, for research documenting the importance of gist for recall). This gist recall phenomenon may be one important characteristic of real-world memory research: In the real world, people can encode and store the gist of events meaningfully, and this meaningful encoding may decrease the apparent rate of forgetting. This may be especially true when people are themselves selecting the events used in the memory test by including those events in their diaries.

However, we reasoned that under some circumstances we should be able to gain some sense of the rate of decrease in the recall of specific event details, independent of the gist of the item. We investigated this possibility by converting the memory rating to a binary measure: We assigned a 1 to memory ratings of 6 and 7 and a 0 to all other ratings (for convenience, we call this the *perfect memory* measure). This procedure follows from our suspicion that higher memory ratings reflect recall of event details as well as gist, whereas lower memory ratings do not reflect as much detail (but may still reflect memory for gist). Figure 3.2 presents the perfect memory data from the same four data sets used to construct Fig. 3.1. A comparison of the data from those two figures indicates that the decrease in memory in the early retention intervals is much more pronounced for the perfect memory measure than for the memory ratings. We also conducted regression analyses of the perfect memory data. As one might expect, both the linear and curvilinear decrease in the frequency of reporting memory ratings of 6 or 7 with lengthening retention interval were significant in all data sets (see Table 3.1).

The results of the analyses that we have presented so far present us with one additional complication, revealed by a comparison of the forgetting functions produced by the memory ratings from the long-term study (Figs. 1.2 and 1.3) with the forgetting functions from the 10–15 week studies (Figs. 3.1 and 3.2). Although the decrease in the memory ratings with lengthening retention interval is curvilinear in all cases, the long-term study does not

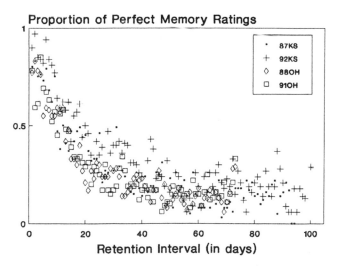

FIG. 3.2. Perfect memory measure and the form of the forgetting function obtained in four studies.

show as rapid a decrement in memory for the recent events as do the short-term studies.

At least two factors may explain this difference. One possibility is that the difference is due to the subject population that was employed in the studies. The subjects in the short-term studies were volunteers recruited from introductory classes, typically receiving only minimal experimental credit for their participation. By comparison, the subjects in the long-term diary study received direct compensation for their participation. This direct compensation may be responsible for greater task diligence. The compensated subjects may have more deeply encoded their events and later may have searched their memories more thoroughly at testing than the subjects drawn from the introductory psychology pool.

A second possibility, which we think is more reasonable, focuses on the fact that our memory measure is a rating scale. It is possible that the ratings provided by subjects reflect relativistic ratings. That is, individual memories may be rated in comparison to the set of memories contained in the diary. For example, those events that are most memorable are given a 7, those that are least memorable are given a 1, and appropriate adjustments are made for the others that are in between.

This possibility naturally implies that the steepness of the forgetting function produced by memory ratings depends on the length of the retention interval. The logic is as follows. Assume that time is the only factor affecting memory. Further assume that the most recent events are best recalled and given ratings of 7, whereas the oldest events are most poorly recalled and given ratings of 1. The other events will be dated relativistically and will be placed somewhere between the two extremes. If the retention interval is only 7 days long, then the forgetting function will appear quite steep, dropping from 7 to 1 in a period of 1 week. However, if the retention interval is 7 years, then the forgetting function will appear quite flat. This example is, of course, exaggerated. Nonetheless, the logic of relativistic rating implies that retention interval affects the apparent steepness of the forgetting function for memory ratings.

However, that a memory rating scale may affect the apparent steepness of the forgetting function is not a serious problem. The reason is that, regardless of the retention interval, the data clearly and consistently show that memory decreases as time passes. Moreover, it decreases curvilinearly— that is, it decreases with some rapidity in recent retention intervals and somewhat more slowly in later retention intervals. This is exactly the pattern to expect based on laboratory studies of memory, strongly suggesting that at least some of the characteristics of memory as studied in the laboratory transfer to the study of memory in the real world. Furthermore, by the principle of convergent validity, this outcome increases our confidence that memory self-report measures are actually reflective of subjects' actual memories. However, the possible relativistic nature of the memory ratings suggests that one must be cautious not to confuse the memory ratings with the actual strength of the underlying memory trace or with actual memory clarity. Instead, the overall pattern of the memory ratings and how that pattern is affected by various factors are more informative than the absolute ratings themselves. At the same time, most of our studies cover comparable retention intervals; that reduces the problem of comparing ratings between studies.

The Content of Events and Event Memory

Event Samples. A second approach to validation of the memory measure examines the relation between a sample of the actual events and the associated memory ratings assigned by the subjects. In our view, such an examination certainly suggests that the memory ratings are reasonable. We obviously do not have the space to provide a complete listing of all events recorded. We specifically asked our subjects to provide a variety of events (i.e., events that were pleasant and unpleasant, events that were memorable and not very memorable, etc.), and they generally complied with our request. Furthermore, we asked our subjects to provide a unique set of events, defined as events that were potentially discriminable in memory from other similar events. During the memory test session we asked subjects to report on the uniqueness of each event, and if it was not unique, it was discarded.

A sense of the memory ratings provided by our subjects for various types of events can be gleaned from the examples presented next. All the examples listed below are for events that were remembered 10 to 15 weeks after they were listed in the diaries.

This first group of events were given memory ratings of 1: Subjects thought they remembered them quite poorly.

- Did homework almost all day because the weather was bad.
- Watched movies at Jim's house on the VCR from 8:00 p.m. to 3:45 a.m.
- Watched the Superbowl and lost $5 in a bet with Doug's dad.
- Skipped my study skills class and stayed in my dorm room by myself.

This second group of events were given memory ratings of 4: Subjects thought they had moderate memory for these events.

- Received a new couch for the apartment from the landlord.
- Mark and I started to make caramel corn but we soon found out that we were out of baking soda. We were able to borrow some.

- I received a test back that I had taken. I received the highest grade in the class.
- My roommate left to go on a ski trip for a week. I felt anxious about staying by myself.

This third group of events were given memory ratings of 7: Subjects thought that they had extremely good memory for these events.

- I lied to my Physics teacher and said that I had to leave class because of a doctor's appointment. I felt like he could see right through me.
- Hit a deer with my car while driving to town with Rachael. Dented my front fender.
- Jake (my boyfriend) and I broke up. As I was leaving, Jake and I ran into my ex-boyfriend (Joe). It was very uncomfortable.
- My brother was out of control and was shaking a lot because of dad's death. He finally passed out.

Content Analyses. Obviously, a method other than event sampling is desirable. After all, if we were unscrupulous, we could intentionally select events that could mislead about the extent to which subjects' memory ratings were reasonable. One way to avoid this possibility is via a content analysis of the data (other memory studies have used this approach; see Goldsmith & Pillemer, 1988). We conducted just such a content analysis, in which we categorized the data in several different ways—by type of person(s) involved in the event, by location, by activity type, and so on. The results of two of these content analyses are presented in Table 3.2.

Because each event could be placed into several categories, we report the results of descriptive analyses—the mean memory rating for events in each category and the percentage of events in each category that were given memory ratings of 6 or 7—but no inferential analyses. As the tables show, there were substantial memory rating differences among the various categories. However, these rating differences fail to coalesce into any interpretable pattern. Furthermore, the pattern of memory ratings was dissimilar for the two studies, leading us to doubt the utility of these analyses.

Originally, we had hoped to find some systematicity between the event content and the corresponding ratings. In retrospect, this was perhaps an overly optimistic assumption. First, idiosyncratic differences are likely among our subjects. Different people focus on different aspects of their lives, and averaging over these perspectives certainly obscures these individual differences. Second, our content categories are probably too broad to capture all of the complexity involved in diary events. To illustrate these points, consider the following two hypothetical events:

TABLE 3.2
Mean Memory Ratings and Percentage of 6 and 7 Ratings
by Content Categories, 88OH and 91OH Self-Event Data

Content	Ohio State 1988			Ohio State 1991		
	N	Mean FMR	%FMR 6/7	N	Mean FMR	%FMR 6/7
I. Others in event						
A. Family						
mother	81	4.70	.308	88	4.39	.193
father	56	4.57	.286	46	4.50	.152
sister	28	5.61	.643	31	3.90	.000
brother	30	5.03	.333	13	4.62	.385
husband	24	5.04	.417	45	5.09	.444
wife	0	.	.	16	4.56	.125
son	25	5.52	.560	73	4.25	.164
daughter	30	5.27	.433	37	4.03	.054
nonimmediate family	123	5.31	.512	47	4.51	.234
family group	27	5.85	.667	97	4.74	.320
B. Friends						
same sex	155	4.77	.400	117	4.40	.179
opposite sex	23	5.04	.478	67	4.27	.134
old	40	4.93	.400	8	5.13	.375
new	2	6.00	.500	0	.	.
unspecified	35	5.14	.457	36	4.53	.306
group of friends	111	4.91	.441	133	4.51	.180
C. Love related						
boyfriend	133	4.62	.406	141	4.74	.269
girlfriend	44	4.34	.205	1	6.00	1.000
ex-boyfriend	15	5.40	.467	19	4.47	.263
ex-girlfriend	6	6.33	.667	0	.	.
unspecified	73	5.41	.507	38	4.82	.263
D. Acquaintance						
same sex	4	4.75	.250	21	4.38	.143
opposite sex	1	5.00	.000	32	4.41	.156
old	.	.	.	1	5.00	.000
new	1	5.00	.000	0	.	.
unspecified	8	5.50	.625	23	4.57	.391
group	2	4.50	.000	18	4.61	.333
E. Strangers						
same sex	2	5.00	.500	10	5.80	.700
opposite sex	4	5.75	.750	15	5.00	.467
unspecified	1	1.00	.000	11	4.27	.455
group	4	3.50	.000	10	4.60	.300
II. Activities						
sports related	148	4.80	.331	124	4.27	.250
party activities	101	5.22	.525	73	4.72	.233
music related	39	4.67	.308	15	4.87	.200
food related	284	4.85	.394	226	4.43	.208
media	127	4.40	.276	108	4.03	.120

(Continued)

TABLE 3.2
(Continued)

Content	Ohio State 1988			Ohio State 1991		
	N	Mean FMR	%FMR 6/7	N	Mean FMR	%FMR 6/7
sexual	6	4.67	.333	2	6.50	1.000
rest/relaxation	74	4.46	.338	74	3.81	.108
socializing/commun.	92	4.77	.348	226	4.43	.221
holiday/special occasions	202	5.85	.663	108	5.34	.481
holidays/entertainment	8	5.63	.500	127	4.40	.220
health related	51	5.12	.471	54	4.48	.148
law	19	5.42	.474	11	5.55	.455
shopping/purchasing	178	4.62	.315	167	4.22	.168
home improvements/chores	105	4.60	.343	79	4.04	.203
car/vehicle related	68	4.49	.309	99	4.68	.283
school related	463	4.47	.317	477	4.05	.149
work related	167	4.30	.263	154	4.33	.273
family related	15	5.00	.333	80	4.41	.212
personal appearance/fitness	66	4.80	.394	44	4.07	.136
volunteer/civic work	14	4.50	.286	9	4.56	.222
pet related	35	5.23	.429	27	4.78	.370
financial	35	5.34	.486	41	4.71	.268
personal favors	83	4.61	.313	60	4.25	.200
church	47	4.11	.191	20	4.50	.200
other	51	5.10	.412	91	4.62	.253
III. Unforeseen						
health	124	4.62	.387	64	4.56	.266
car/vehicle	80	5.06	.425	38	4.76	.289
conflicts	38	4.97	.421	39	5.08	.385
birth/death	11	5.73	.727	15	5.07	.333
home	12	4.92	.333	12	5.67	.500
emotional	34	4.74	.324	64	4.64	.281
weather	32	4.84	.438	41	4.15	.220
school	142	4.45	.324	57	4.05	.158
sports	16	4.63	.375	6	5.67	.667
love related	33	6.06	.758	21	5.10	.429
work	167	4.81	.365	41	4.44	.268
other	48	4.69	.354	32	5.06	.312
IV. Location						
home	50	4.62	.400	272	4.04	.195
school	31	4.61	.290	130	4.34	.185
work	13	5.00	.385	40	4.13	.275
church	2	5.00	.000	11	4.73	.364
public	309	4.91	.392	305	4.44	.233
other	123	5.02	.447	115	4.43	.235

48

- Did homework with my girlfriend late into the night and worked until 2 a.m.
- Went dancing with my girlfriend until 2 a.m.

It is unclear how the content of these events consistently relates to memory. For example, memory may be related to salience or novelty. Yet which was more novel, homework or dancing? From our perspective, one cannot know. Memory may be related to personal importance. Which was more important, homework or dancing? Again, from our perspective, one cannot know. Moreover, even if one did know, our content analysis would still obscure important memory differences. For example, if homework was important and dancing unimportant, placing these two in the "girlfriend" category would ignore differences in importance.

Initial Memory Ratings

Subjects' Predictions of Event Memory. The failure of the content coding analysis to relate consistently to event memory emphasizes the difficulty external observers have in gaining insight into others' event recall. However, the subjects themselves should certainly be highly familiar with the idiosyncrasies of their diary events and should know which events were personally meaningful and which were not. This suggests that subjects should have an ability to predict which events they would recall well and which events they would recall poorly. In fact, in his own long-term diary, Wagenaar (1986) obtained just such a relation between predicted and actual recall (p. 247). However, Wagenaar was a very sophisticated subject, so there still is reason to be skeptical of subjects' ability to predict their own memories.

Further skepticism can be generated by extrapolating the research of Wilson and his colleagues, which suggests that people do not have much insight into their own cognitive processes (e.g., Nisbett & Wilson, 1977; Wilson, Hull, & Johnson, 1981). Hence, people generally may not be very good at knowing what they will and will not remember.

In several of our studies, we explored these ideas by asking our subjects to predict their own level of event recall (for a similar idea, see Wagenaar, 1986). These *initial memory ratings* (see the Appendix for the exact measure) were made at the time that the events were recorded into the diaries. To determine whether initial memory ratings predict final memory ratings, a series of analyses was conducted using the pooled within-subject regression technique described in chapter 2. The initial memory rating was the primary predictor of interest. Other terms in the regression model included retention interval and quadratic retention interval (and, of course, a term to control for between-subject effects). As displayed in Table 3.3, the betas showed that the initial memory ratings were always strongly and positively related

TABLE 3.3
Betas From the Pooled Within-Subject Regressions Investigating Whether
Initial Memory Ratings Predict Final Memory Ratings

Study		Memory Ratings
	Self-events	
79KS	β	.285
$F(1, 2570)$	F	299.24
	p	.0001
80KS	β	.290
$F(1, 2408)$	F	331.65
	p	.0001
83KS	β	.342
$F(1, 1606)$	F	243.90
	p	.0001
86KS	β	.369
$F(1, 2565)$	F	477.86
	p	.0001
87KS	β	.283
$F(1, 3294)$	F	343.20
	p	.0001
88OH(self)	β	.354
$F(1, 3234)$	F	534.53
	p	.0001
89KS	β	.279
$F(1, 2851)$	F	348.19
	p	.0001
89OH	β	.344
$F(1, 1579)$	F	281.62
	p	.0001
90KS(long-term)	β	.302
$F(1, 3627)$	F	378.06
	p	.0001
91KS	β	.272
$F(1, 1629)$	F	158.17
	p	.0001
92KS	β	.322
$F(1, 3255)$	F	489.77
	p	.0001
	Other-events	
88OH(other)	β	.284
$F(1, 2707)$	F	301.09
	p	.0001

to the final memory ratings (all p's < .0001). As subjects' initial estimates of event memorability rose, their final memory ratings rose as well. Clearly, subjects are capable of predicting how well they will remember events.

However, these data also suggest that there is considerable room for error in subjects' predictions. One index of this error is the percentage of variance in the final memory rating accounted for by the initial memory rating. The percentage of total variance in the final memory ratings accounted for by the initial memory ratings ranged across studies from 2.60% to 11.00%, with a mean of 7.05%. This relatively small percentage of variance in the final memory ratings accounted for by the initial memory ratings suggests that, though it is statistically reliable, the ability of people to predict their own memories should not be overstated. That is, even though people were able to predict their own memories, there was still plenty of imprecision in their predictions.

This imprecision in prediction is itself potentially misleading. Some of this imprecision may simply result from "slop" (e.g., random error) in the measures. But 90% unaccounted variance is an awful lot of slop. Thus, our data suggest that there may be something for every theoretical perspective in these memory ratings: Those who claim that people are not aware of their cognitive processes (e.g., Wilson et al., 1981) can gleefully point to the imprecision of the predictions; those who claim that people have some sense of what they will remember can point out that, in these studies, initial memory ratings are always highly significant predictors of final memory ratings.

One other aspect of subjects memory predictions was of theoretical interest. We considered the possibility that subjects' predictive efficacy varies across retention interval. On reflection, this possibility makes some intuitive sense. After all, people should remember recent events quite well, regardless of the memorability of the events. Hence, at short retention intervals, subjects' predictions of event memorability may only moderately predict final memory ratings. At short retention intervals, nearly everything is well recalled, so the initial memory rating is relatively powerless as a predictor. However, at longer retention intervals, not everything is well recalled. Thus, at longer intervals, one would expect subjects' initial ratings to be more strongly predictive of their memory ratings. This reasoning suggests that there should be a Retention Interval × Initial Memory Rating interaction in predicting final memory ratings—the ability of initial memory ratings to predict final memory ratings should be better as retention interval lengthens.

We explored this possibility by conducting another set of regression analyses. The pooled within-subject regression model used the final memory rating as the dependent measure and included subjects, retention interval, quadratic event retention interval, initial memory rating, and the interaction of retention interval and initial memory rating as predictors. The results were of these analyses were mixed but were generally consistent with our reasoning. In about a third of the studies, the interaction between retention interval and

Framingham State College
Framingham, Massachusetts

initial memory rating was significant. To understand these interactions further, the data were reanalyzed by breaking each study into 35-day blocks. Thus, the 10-week studies have two such blocks, and the 15-week studies have three such blocks. Table 3.4 reveals that, for those studies with significant interactions, the initial memory ratings better predicted the final memory ratings at the longer retention intervals than at the shorter intervals.

The Relation Between Initial Memory Ratings and Final Memory Ratings Is Not Causal. The use of initial memory ratings in many of our studies raises the possibility that the final memory ratings in these studies are epiphenomenal. Specifically, subjects may report an initial memory rating and later use this initial rating (rather than their actual recall of the event) to derive the final memory rating given during memory testing. However, there are several lines of reasoning that argue against this possibility. First, as we have

TABLE 3.4
Interaction Data and Betas for the Relation Between Initial
and Final Memory Rating by Study and 35-Day Block

	IMR Betas		
Study	*Block 1*	*Block 2*	*Block 3*
	Self-events		
79KS			
$F(2, 2566) = 4.88$, $p = .008$	.286	.321	.308
80KS			
$F(2, 2404) = .39$, $p = .678$	.300	.315	.302
83KS			
$F(2, 1602) = 3.14$, $p = .043$	.291	.384	.397
86KS			
$F(2, 2561) = 1.09$, $p = .338$	.320	.434	.433
87KS			
$F(2, 3290) = 3.60$, $p = .028$	.308	.344	.249
88OH(self)			
$F(1, 3175) = 6.91$, $p = .009$	.333	.389	–
89OH			
$F(1, 1577) = .31$, $p = .577$	.374	.364	–
89KS			
$F(2, 2847) = 4.22$, $p = .015$	.243	.323	.317
91KS			
$F(2, 1625) = 1.12$, $p = .327$	.273	.329	.258
92KS			
$F(2, 3251) = .06$, $p = .947$	.315	.363	.345
	Other-events		
88OH(other)			
$F(1, 2654) = 4.94$, $p = .026$	.257	.319	–

argued, the predictive relation between initial memory ratings and final memory ratings strengthens across retention interval. This suggests that people were not remembering their initial memory ratings and using this information to construct their final memory ratings. Were people doing so, the predictive ability of the initial memory ratings would have been stronger at short retention intervals (when the initial ratings would probably be well-remembered) than at longer retention intervals (when the initial ratings would likely have been forgotten). As we noted earlier in this chapter, the actual interaction pattern was exactly opposite of this, suggesting that people were basing their rated recall for the events on event recall, not on their prior memory ratings.

A second aspect of the data also suggests that initial memory ratings were not used to derive final memory ratings. We reasoned that if the initial memory ratings were used to derive the final memory ratings, then all other predictors (e.g., retention interval, event affective intensity [i.e., extremity], event pleasantness [i.e., valence]) would be unrelated to the final memory ratings once the initial memory ratings had been taken into account. Because the regression analyses that we conducted included the linear and quadratic retention interval terms as well as a term for the prediction of memory, we can use those analyses to evaluate this hypothesis. Despite the finding that the initial memory prediction was a strong and significant predictor of memory, for all the studies both the linear and quadratic terms for retention interval were significant in these analyses, all p's < .0001.

That retention interval predicts memory, even with initial memory ratings controlled, is illustrated in Fig. 3.3. In this figure, the final memory ratings from the 88OH data set are plotted as a function of both retention interval and initial

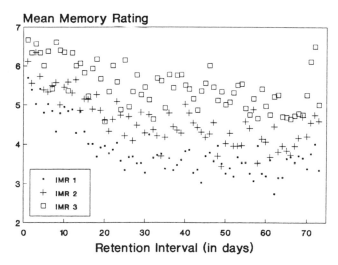

FIG. 3.3. Final memory ratings from 88OH plotted as a function of both retention interval and initial memory rating.

memory rating. This illustrative figure typifies the outcome of such plots across our studies. Memory for events clearly decreased across time, regardless of the initial memory rating assigned to the event. Hence, these data suggest that although the initial memory ratings were a predictor of event memory, they probably had no causal impact on subjects' final memory ratings.

A cross-tabulation of initial and final memory ratings also helps to dispel the idea that the initial memory ratings causally affected the final memory ratings. If such causal impact occurred, there should be little distributional overlap in these cross-tabulations, regardless of event age. Such lack of overlap could be seen if an initial memory rating of 3 has final memory ratings almost exclusively of 6 and 7, an initial memory rating of 2 has final memory ratings between 3 and 5, and an initial memory rating of 1 has final memory ratings of only 1 and 2. Table 3.5 plots the cross-tabulations of initial and final memory ratings for the first, fifth, and tenth weeks of all our studies. As that table reveals, such nonoverlapping does not occur. Even at short intervals, events with initial memorability of 2 are associated with final memory ratings of 7. At long intervals, initial memorability ratings of 1 are associated with final memorability ratings as high as 6. This is simply inconsistent with the argument that initial memory ratings are somehow causing of final memory ratings.

Predicting the Predictor: What Is Related to the Initial Memory Ratings? As we noted earlier, it is difficult for outside observers to make judgments about the final memorability of subjects' events. There is simply no way for an external observer to know the specific event attributes that cause a subject to experience heightened memory for a specific event. From the subject's view, however, the events are likely to differ greatly in personal

TABLE 3.5
Cross-Tabulation of Initial and Final Memory Rating by Age
(in Weeks) at Weeks 1, 5, and 10

Initial Memory Rating	Final Memory Rating						
	1	2	3	4	5	6	7
Week 1							
1	9	19	50	104	262	221	255
2	3	7	25	70	192	262	275
3	1	4	8	19	72	143	240
Week 5							
1	22	123	214	288	159	56	43
2	7	76	130	305	236	122	81
3	3	18	38	104	164	139	124
Week 10							
1	29	185	206	197	124	39	33
2	14	106	183	328	235	68	51
3	4	44	62	116	150	117	77

meaning and can likely be differentiated on many dimensions. We have capitalized on subjects' ability to make these ratings (e.g., pleasantness, intensity, emotionality, frequency, initial mental involvement) and demonstrate later in this chapter and in subsequent chapters that many of these factors are related to the final memory ratings. However, we wondered which of these characteristics was also predictive of subjects' initial memory ratings.

To answer this question, the factors of subjects, retention interval, quadratic retention interval, event intensity, and event pleasantness were regressed onto the initial memory ratings. The pleasantness (or unpleasantness—i.e., valence) and the intensity of events were included in all models. Other factors, such as emotionality ratings, person-typicality ratings, event frequency ratings, and mental involvement ratings were included if available.

The largest corpus of results that we have pertain to the relation between both rated event intensity and rated event pleasantness and predicted memory. Table 3.6 displays the results of these analyses, and they uniformly indicate that event intensity and event pleasantness reliably predict the initial memory ratings. The results of the analyses that include other ratings of the events show similar outcomes. Analyses with event typicality find that atypical events are assigned high initial memory ratings, although this pattern is qualified by a quadratic typicality effect: Highly typical events are also assigned elevated initial memory ratings.

The high consistency of the predictive relation between event pleasantness and event intensity that we see in the initial memory ratings is not observed for the final memory ratings (see chapter 4). This can be taken as evidence that people's prior theories about memory do not necessarily map well onto later recall. Because of this, the notion that initial memory ratings are causally related to final memory ratings is further weakened.

A purist may argue that the observed relations between event pleasantness and initial memory ratings and event intensity and initial memory ratings are consistent with the naive intuition our subjects bring to the study. Specifically, the pattern of results matches what one would expect were the initial memory ratings themselves derived from the pleasantness and intensity ratings. Such a view, therefore, requires argue that final memory ratings are derived from initial memory ratings, which are in turn derived from the characteristics of the event itself (e.g., pleasantness, intensity). This is impossible to rule out, although it seems quite implausible, and we have outlined in detail the arguments against this position in chapter 2. For now, we return to describing the relations between event memory and possible predictors, in this case, event rehearsal.

Event Rehearsals

Event Rehearsals and Event Memory. So far, the evidence that we have presented in this chapter indicates that the diary procedure and the memory ratings yield data that are sensible and are highly similar to data

TABLE 3.6

Pooled Within-Subject Regression Analyses Investigating Predictive
Relations Between Pleasantness, Intensity, and Emotionality
and Initial Memory Ratings

Data Source & Year		Valence of Event Affect	Derived Evaluative Intensity of Affect	Direct Emotionality Rating	Other Predictors in Model
			Self-events		
80KS	β	.059	.389		
F(1, 2407)	F	9.89	395.51		
	p	.0017	.0001		
86KS	β	.087	.428		
F(1, 2564)	F	27.07	609.65		
	p	.0001	.0001		
87KS	β	.062	.401		
F(1, 3293)	F	18.00	625.73		
	p	.0001	.0001		
88OH	β	.070	.333		Person typicality
F(1, 3218)	F	20.58	428.04		
	p	.0001	.0001		
89KS	β	.064	.182	.360	Event frequency
F(1, 2848)	F	19.27	101.74	337.04	
	p	.0001	.0001	.0001	
89OH	β	.053	.365		
F(1, 1577)	F	5.74	221.05		
	p	.0167	.0001		
90KS(long-term)	β	.096	.119	.368	Event frequency
F(1, 3677)	F	58.48	58.96	433.32	
	p	.0001	.0001	.0001	
91KS	β	.099	.167	.393	Event frequency
F(1, 1626)	F	28.30	51.65	197.51	
	p	.0001	.0001	.0001	
92KS	β	.085	.166	.356	Event frequency
F(1, 3252)	F	37.12	90.67	366.44	
	p	.0001	.0001	.0001	
			Other-events		
88OH	β	.059	.321		Person typicality
F(1, 2715)	F	11.54	317.61		
	p	.0001	.0001		

produced by laboratory experiments. This impression is further strengthened when one examines the relation between some of the other ratings given to the events and the final memory rating. For example, in some studies we asked subjects during the diary test session to rate the extent to which they rehearsed each of the events (see the Appendix for more detail on the rehearsal measure). There is extensive laboratory evidence that rehearsal generally improves recall. Consequently, we expected subjects' rehearsal ratings to predict recall.

There are some potential problems with this prediction. First, it is entirely possible that subjects make major mistakes in estimating event rehearsal. After all, to estimate past rehearsals, subjects must review the entire diary period, estimate the number of times they rehearsed an event, and translate this estimation into an appropriate response. Error can enter into a response to our rehearsal question at any of these points. Furthermore, although we asked subjects to restrict the diary items so that they were unique, it is certainly possible that subjects may have experienced similar events either within or prior to the diary recording period and simply confuse or integrate their rehearsals of these events. Finally, Conway (1990; Rubin et al., 1986) noted another concern with rehearsal estimates: There is the possibility that subjects simply forget their rehearsals. If this were the case, the relation between reported rehearsals and final memory ratings would be suppressed, with a theoretical limit of no relation. This would be a difficulty for studies that reported weak or nonexistent relations between rehearsal and memory.

Despite these problems, the real-world memory literature generally suggests that we ought to obtain a relation between rehearsal and memory. This outcome has been true for both cross-sectional designs (Bahrick & Karis, 1982) and longitudinal designs. The exceptions are mostly in the flashbulb memory literature (e.g., Pillemer, 1984), a type of autobiographical memory that some theorize differs from most autobiographical memories, particularly because of the extreme emotionality associated with the events (cf., Conway, 1990).

Our own research always shows a relation between event rehearsal and event memory. The betas for the studies that have included rehearsal as a measure are shown in Table 3.7. The betas indicate that higher rehearsal ratings are associated with higher memory ratings. As often happens, our regression models contained numerous other predictors, and the effects described indicate the predictive relation between rehearsal and final memory rating, controlling for all other terms in the model. All betas are significant at $p < .0001$. In Fig. 3.4, we illustrate this relation graphically using three data sets: the one with the strongest relation, the one with the weakest relation, and one with a typical relation.

The Rehearsal Ratings and Retention Interval. As mentioned earlier, measuring event rehearsals is difficult, and the validity of the rehearsal ratings may themselves be subject to several biases. Most important, event rehearsals

TABLE 3.7
Pooled Within-Subject Regression Analyses Investigating Predictive
Relations Between Reported Rehearsal Ratings and Final Memory Ratings

Data Source & Year		Rehearsal Rating	Other Predictors in Model
		Self-Events	
79KS	β	.393	
$F(1, 2570)$	F	589.17	
	p	.0001	
80KS	β	.491	Event pleasantness, event intensity
$F(1, 2406)$	F	1085.67	
	p	.0001	
83KS	β	.609	
$F(1, 1606)$	F	747.04	
	p	.0001	
90KS	β	.184	Event pleasantness, event intensity,
$F(1, 3499)$	F	119.67	direct emotionality rating,
	p	.0001	initial event frequency
91KS	β	.253	Event pleasantness, event intensity,
$F(1, 1625)$	F	124.05	direct emotionality rating,
	p	.0001	initial event frequency
91OH	β	.267	Event pleasantness, event intensity,
$F(1, 2262)$	F	214.96	initial mental involvement
	p	.0001	
		Other-Events	
91OH	β	.494	Event pleasantness, event intensity,
$F(1, 1949)$	F	688.30	initial mental involvement
	p	.0001	

may be forgotten over time. All other things being equal, the forgetting of rehearsals will lead to a decrease in the estimate of rehearsals for older events relative to younger events. But of course, things are not equal: The opportunities to rehearse events increase over time. Again, all other things being equal, this increase in opportunity implies an increase in rehearsal estimates with increasing retention interval. It is possible for either effect or both effects to occur.

A series of regressions were conducted on the data sets that included the rehearsal measure. In these pooled within-subject regressions rehearsal estimates were the dependent measure, and subjects (dummy coded), event retention interval, and quadratic event retention interval were the predictors. The results were mixed but generally favor the idea that people forget their rehearsals. The impact of age is significant in three studies, marginal in one study, and not significant in two studies. With one exception, the direction of the effect was uniformly in favor of subjects forgetting rehearsals. Table 3.8 displays the betas for these effects.

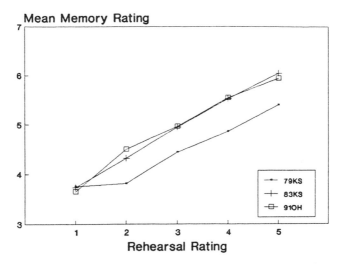

FIG. 3.4. Relation between rehearsal and event memory using three data sets: the data set with the strongest relation, the one with the weakest relation, and one with a typical relation.

It appears that, although the rehearsal rating predicts the memory rating, the rehearsal rating can be, at best, thought of as a rating that indexes rehearsal relative to events within the same approximate time period. That is, one may be most easily led astray if comparing the ability of the rehearsal ratings to predict recall if two rehearsal ratings were from disparate time periods. In this regard, we again note that our regression technique investigated the rehearsal–memory relation while controlling for retention interval effects, so the significant effects that were obtained should be independent of the biasing effects of time.

The Role of Involvement in Event Memory

One of the other ways to explore personal memory is to look at the relation between memory and the subject's level of involvement in the event. However, the notion of involvement can have different definitions. For example, consider three possible ways in which a person can obtain information about a basketball game. One can actually play in it, one can watch it, or one can read about it in the newspaper. These three methods of information gain vary on at least two dimensions, the level of mental involvement in the event and the level of physical involvement in the event. High physical involvement suggests that one has access (at least temporarily) to many of the peripheral cues involved in the event. Furthermore, one often takes responsibility for and has a personal commitment to actions in which one has participated. These factors should work to heighten event memory.

TABLE 3.8
Pooled Within-Subject Regression Analyses Investigating
Whether Retention Interval Predicted Rehearsals

Data Source & Year		Retention Interval	Quadratic Retention Interval
		Self-Events	
79KS	β	−.049	−.061
$F(1, 2571)$	F	7.52	7.72
	p	.0061	.0055
80KS	β	−.092	.037
$F(1, 2409)$	F	25.86	3.41
	p	.0001	.0650
83KS	β	−.113	.026
$F(1, 1607)$	F	31.16	1.34
	p	.0001	.2480
90KS	β	.000	−.024
$F(1, 3509)$	F	0.00	3.28
	p	.9944	.0702
91KS	β	−.011	.022
$F(1, 1630)$	F	0.23	0.81
	p	.6294	.3685
91OH	β	−.037	.003
$F(1, 2266)$	F	3.56	0.02
	p	.0594	.8916
		Other-Events	
91OH	β	−.035	.000
$F(1, 1953)$	F	2.74	0.00
	p	.0983	.9944

However, physical presence at an event does not necessarily guarantee mental involvement. As those of us who are instructors know, a precious few of our students attend lecture in an active and involved state; too many others are passive and uninvolved. Thus, a second aspect of involvement refers to mental involvement—an individual's tendency to be mentally active and engaged during an event. We collected data on both of these types of involvement and related the involvement measures to event memory.

Heard, Participated, and Observed Ratings. An obvious prediction is that the higher the level of physical involvement, the better the memory for the event. After all, physical involvement in an event is likely to provide the subject with a wider range of memory cues than event knowledge that was obtained vicariously. In one of our diary studies (88OH), during the diary test we asked subjects to record their level of involvement in events that they were recording for another person. Specifically, subjects were asked to indicate whether the event that was recorded was one that they themselves had participated in, had observed, or had merely heard about second hand.

We were interested in investigating two ideas. The first of these was the obvious one: Increasing degrees of event participation should be associated with higher reported event memory. A second idea of interest was how these ratings behave over retention interval. That is, we wondered if there would be only a main effect of degree of event participation on recall or if events in which people participated directly "stayed with them" differently (e.g., more persistently) than events that were only encountered secondhand.

A pooled within-subject regression analysis (with subjects, linear and quadratic retention interval, and participation rating) of the memory data indicated that increases in the reported degree of event participation were related to increases in reported event memory, $F(2, 2653) = 66.36$, $p < .0001$. Events in which subjects directly participated were better remembered ($M = 4.66$) than events observed ($M = 4.32$), which were in turn were better remembered than events that were merely communicated to the diary-keepers ($M = 3.84$).

To assess whether this effect was altered over time, a second regression was conducted, this time including an interaction term representing the Retention Interval × Degree of Event Participation interaction. This latter measure was nonsignificant, $F(2, 2651) = .24$, $p = .79$. Figure 3.5 displays the final memory ratings as a function of both retention interval and degree of initial event participation. Clearly, reported memories based on the three types of participation do not differentially decay over the retention interval.

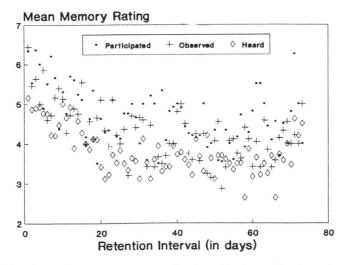

FIG. 3.5. Final memory ratings as a function of both retention interval and degree of initial event participation.

Level of Initial Mental Involvement. In a second study (91OH, self and other), we asked subjects to indicate, at the time an event was entered into the diary, the degree of initial mental involvement they experienced in the event. Numerous laboratory studies indicate that attention and active processing facilitate memory for events, and we were expecting the same types of effects to emerge in our real-world data. We began by running a model that included the final memory rating as the dependent measure and subjects, linear and quadratic retention interval, pleasantness, intensity, diary type (self or other), and mental involvement as predictors. In a second analysis, we added the interaction of diary type and involvement to the model. Of main interest in these analyses was the relation between involvement and final memory rating and whether this relation differs for the two diary types (as indicated by the interaction).

The results showed that the relation between event involvement and memory was generally as expected: the higher the involvement, the better the memory. However, the results suggested that this relation depends on whether the events were self-events or other-events, $F(1, 4264) = 13.66$, $p < .001$. To explore this interaction, subsequent regressions were conducted at levels of diary type. Final memory rating again served as the dependent measure, and subjects, age, quadratic age, pleasantness, intensity, and mental involvement served as predictors. The results showed that the interaction occurs simply because the slope of the line describing the relation was somewhat steeper for self-events; that is, differences in mental involvement were associated with larger memory changes for the self-events, $F(1,2263) = 46.45$, $p < .0001$, $\beta = .137$, than for the other-events, $F(1,1950) = 19.16$, $p < .0001$, $\beta = .105$.

The Novelty of Events and Event Memory

Event Frequency. Several studies included a pre-rating of event frequency. This measure asked people to assess how often the events recorded in their diary happen, with higher ratings indicating greater infrequency. This event frequency effect was tested regressing subjects, age, quadratic age, and event frequency onto the final memory rating. In all cases, these ratings were significant, 89KS $F(1,2849) = 158.63$, $p < .0001$, $\beta = .191$; 90KS $F(1, 3678) = 404.55$, $p < .0001$, $\beta = .297$; 91KS $F(1,1629) = 79.85$, $p < .0001$, $\beta = .191$; 92KS $F(1,3255) = 165.51$, $p < .0001$, $\beta = .193$. As expected, people generally reported better memory for infrequently-occurring than for frequently-occurring events.

Person Typicality and Person Atypicality. Event frequency is not the only index of an event's novelty. The novelty of an event is also determined by how unusual an event is for a specific person. Two of our studies, 88OH and 91OH, explored this idea by obtaining pre-ratings of person typicality.

These ratings indicate how typical the event was for the person for whom the rating was made. For example, if a person got an A on an exam and the person often received A's, then this would be a typical event. On the other hand, if the person usually got C's on exams, then the A would be atypical.

The impact of event typicality was first tested by running regressions with final memory rating as the dependent measure and subjects, age, quadratic age, diary type, and event typicality as the predictors. The results for the two studies clearly show an atypicality effect. Specifically, atypical events were rated as more memorable than typical events in 88OH, $F(1, 6010) = 95.51$, $p < .0001$, $\beta = -.116$, and in 91OH, $F(1, 4267) = 63.26$, $p < .0001$, $\beta = -.119$. Another regression was conducted including the interaction term of diary type and typicality; the results showed that the impact of event typicality on final memory ratings did not differ for self-events and other-events, $F(1, 6009) = .00$, $p = .95$ for 88OH; $F(1, 4266) = .02$, $p = .89$ for 91OH.

Laboratory data from social cognition researchers show an interesting finding: Events that are either atypical or typical are better remembered than events of middling typicality. This means that the pattern of final memory rating means may be U-shaped across rated typicality. This U-shape was investigated by running a regression including final memory rating as the dependent measure and subjects, age, quadratic age, diary type, typicality, and quadratic typicality as predictors. The results indicate that the quadratic typicality effect was significant for both 88OH and 91OH, $F(1, 6009) = 73.57$, $p < .0001$, $\beta = .104$ for 88OH; $F(1, 4266) = 20.77$, $p < .0001$, $\beta = .078$ for 91OH. The means for final memory rating as a function of event typicality for both 88OH and 91OH are shown in Fig. 3.6. In the 88OH study we

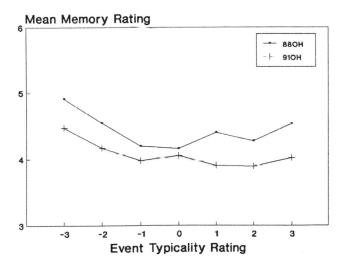

FIG. 3.6 Means for final memory rating as a function of event typicality for the 88OH and 91OH data sets.

found evidence for increased memory for typical events, but in the 91OH study we did not. Thus, the jury remains out on whether typicality effects found in the laboratory will manifest in real-world studies.

CONCLUSIONS AND IMPLICATIONS

The data that we present in this chapter lead to several conclusions about the characteristics of personal memories. First, our data consistently showed that the rated recall of events declined with retention interval. As one would expect from laboratory research, the rate of this decline was faster for short retention intervals and slower for longer intervals. However, in contrast to much of the laboratory research, subjects' memory ratings generally declined relatively slowly with lengthening retention intervals. Our subsidiary analyses of the data suggested that some of this gradualness can be accounted for by the fact that subjects' memory ratings involve two important components of memory: memory for gist and memory for detail. It is the memory for gist (as in Bransford & Johnson, 1973) that seems partly to account for the relative gradualness of forgetting: Memory for the gist of an event seems to be quite long-lasting. In comparison, memory for the other details of events seem to fade with relative rapidity.

A second conclusion from the data that we present in this chapter is that rated recall for events is consistently related to several characteristics of the events. Events with higher rehearsal ratings were better recalled than events with lower ratings. Events in which subjects physically participated were better recalled than events that subjects merely encountered secondhand. Events stimulating high levels of initial mental involvement were better re-called than events with lower mental involvement. Atypical events (defined in terms of event frequency) were better recalled than typical events. Person-atypical events (defined in terms of unusualness for the person) were better recalled than person-typical events, and there is a hint in the data that person-typical events may be better remembered than events that are neither particularly person-typical or person-atypical.

A third conclusion from the data reported in this chapter is that people have some awareness of how their memories work and of the factors that affect personal memory (see Leonesio & T. O. Nelson, 1990). In our studies, subjects' predictions of their own memories were always statistically significant; in fact, relatively speaking, this was one of the more potent predictors of memory. However, this awareness is imperfect: In absolute terms, the proportion of variance accounted for by subjects' predictions of their memories was relatively small.

The notion that subjects' do have insight, albeit imperfect insight, into their own memories is supported by the results of our analyses of the factors that predicted subjects' predictions of memory For example, subjects thought that they would remember events that were affectively extreme and that were positive. As we note in chapter 4, these two event characteristics do indeed predict actual memory for personal events. However, subjects' predictions clearly are not always correct. Subjects predicted that they would better remember positive events that pertained to others, and as the data in chapter 4 demonstrate, that prediction does not seem to hold true.

In addition to providing evidence about subjects' memories, in this chapter we also addressed concerns about the validity of our data. As we discussed in chapter 2, research using a diary methodology is fraught with potential problems. These concerns include subjects being paid for recording events (i.e., compensation bias), what events are selected for inclusion in the diary itself (i.e., recording bias), and even concerns about verifiability of the events themselves. The results that we obtained in this chapter should serve to allay many of those concerns. In particular, we argue that the proof is in the pudding: Most of the findings that we report are quite consistent with existing experimental data in both the social psychology and cognitive psychology literatures. In general, the remarkable aspect of these results is their unremarkability. They duplicate well the results obtained elsewhere and extend those outcomes in sensible ways.

Even those rare occasions in which there appears to be some difference between the laboratory research and our own, are, on closer examination, not a problem. For example, the relatively slow loss of information across retention intervals is likely a gist-related phenomenon, one that has been verified in the laboratory. Indeed, by exploring the data in more detail, we found evidence that non-gist detail was lost relatively quickly whereas recall for event gist seemed to persist.

Because of our concerns about the validity of our memory measure, we conducted and discussed in this chapter numerous analyses designed to allay some of these validity concerns. For example, the initial memory rating results indicate that subjects were capable of predicting how well they would remember an event in the future. This would be uninteresting if the initial memory ratings were causally related to the final memory ratings, that is, if subjects derived their final memory ratings from their initial memory ratings. However, the data reveal that this is just not the case. Subjects' memory predictions were far from perfect. Sometimes, events that were predicted to be poorly recalled were actually rated as well recalled, and vice versa. Furthermore, other factors were predictive of subjects' event memory, even when the initial memory ratings were taken into account. This should not occur if the initial memory ratings were being used to generate the final ratings. Our analyses all yielded a similar conclusion, that subjects' predictions of memory seemed to play little role in their later event recall.

Additional analyses investigating other artifactual method-based explanations for our results yielded similar negative outcomes. We note, however, one place where method may have played some role. That is, there is some reason to believe that the memory rating procedure contributes to the apparent slowness of forgetting across retention intervals. It does so in two ways. First, as we have already discussed, the gist information reflected in the rating is forgotten slowly, and this slow decay probably causes the relatively slow forgetting rate observed in the memory ratings. Second, the length of the retention interval seems to have an impact of the forgetting function—the longer the retention interval, the slower the apparent rate of forgetting. We have speculated that this effect may occur because subjects make their memory judgments relatively, that is, they use the best recalled and worst recalled items to anchor the response scale. These outcomes suggest that the memory rating should not be taken as an absolute index of memory trace strength or clarity. However, this problem does not appear to alter the general characteristics of the memory data (e.g., curvilinear forgetting function, relations to event characteristics, etc.). These characteristics generally remained constant across all of our studies, despite variations in the retention intervals employed.

The general parallel between our data and the data produced elsewhere, both in the lab and in other personal memory studies, is quite impressive. In fact, by the principle of *convergent validity* (e.g., Campbell & Fiske, 1959), this parallelism reflects on both the laboratory research and on our research. In contrast to recent speculation, the results of laboratory research are valid for everyday memory, and our memory measure indeed provides a reasonable measure of memory, one that we contend is likely to be especially valuable in studies of real-world personal memory.

In the spirit of full-cycle psychology, though, we believe a more thorough investigation into some of our findings may be warranted in the laboratory. For example, we obtained a result in which event intensity and event involvement both predicted final memory when regressed simultaneously. Exactly how are these two measures different? Further research may begin with qualitative data collection—specifically, asking subjects what they believe the different pre-ratings mean. From there, parallel manipulations in the laboratory may uncover similar differences and a need for theory building.

For now, however, we continue with our examination of the memory data. One of the pre-ratings that we have not yet discussed assessed the emotional content (both pleasantness or valence and intensity) of events. Because the relations between pleasantness, intensity, and memory have a long and rich history in the memory literature and are of considerable contemporary interest, we decided that they deserved a chapter all their own. That chapter follows.

CHAPTER FOUR

Emotional Pleasantness
and Intensity

One question that has been of longstanding interest to philosophers, psychologists, and laypersons concerns the relation between the evaluative or affective nature of an event and event recall. At least two independent factors need to be taken into consideration in addressing this question. The first is the affective intensity (or evaluative extremity) of events: Is recall better for events that are intense or for those that are not intense? The second concerns the evaluative direction (or valence) of events: Is recall better for events that are pleasant or for those that are unpleasant?

There are no easy answers to these questions. The empirical study of the relation between the affective nature of events and event recall has continued for many years, and the results of these empirical studies have often yielded contradictory results (for useful reviews and summaries, see Banaji & Hardin, 1994; Holmes, 1990; Meltzer, 1930; Rapaport, 1942). Although the overall trend in the research favors recall for pleasant rather than unpleasant events and for affectively extreme events rather than affectively moderate events (e.g., Matlin & Stang, 1978), numerous exceptions and qualifications exist.

Consider the relation between evaluative intensity and event memory. One might generally expect evaluatively intense events to be better recalled than less intense events; this outcome occurs with a high degree of consistency. However, Clark and her colleagues (e.g., Clark, Milberg, & Ross, 1983) have demonstrated that an individual's arousal level can produce a state-dependent memory effect that may moderate the relation between evaluative intensity and event memory. That is, the results of several studies suggest that material learned at high levels of arousal is best remembered when high arousal levels are reinstated at the time of retrieval; materials learned at low arousal levels

67

are best remembered when arousal levels are also low at the time of retrieval. Thus, evaluatively intense events may not be well remembered if the events produced high levels of arousal at encoding but the arousal level at the time of retrieval is relatively low.

Another exception to the idea of a simple relation between the evaluative intensity of an event and event recall may be seen in clinical studies of memory repression. Although there is a continuing debate over whether people repress memories that are extremely threatening to them, clinical psychologists frequently report such cases. That is, patients undergoing therapy appear to have forgotten severely traumatic events, events that, to the rest of us, seem difficult to forget (for varying perspectives on this issue, see Ceci & Loftus, 1994; Cohler, 1993; Lindsay & Read, 1993; Pezdek, 1993).

Similar inconsistency plagues the investigation of whether affectively pleasant events are better recalled than unpleasant ones. Although a fair amount of evidence suggests that the former are better recalled (e.g., Bower & Gilligan, 1979; Brewer, 1988; Holmes, 1970; Linton, 1975; Robinson, 1980; Wagenaar, 1986; see also Matlin & Stang, 1978), numerous exceptions to this outcome exist. Many of the studies that do not find evidence for a valence effect (e.g., Banaji, 1986) simply fail to obtain a difference in memory between pleasant events and unpleasant events. However, some studies find a reversal of the usual valence effect (e.g., Kreitler & Kreitler, 1968; Skowronski & Carlston, 1987). As with the intensity data, the inconsistency in the outcomes of these studies may be due to a number of factors. For example, at least some of the studies that find evidence for the memory superiority of unpleasant information are studies of other-perception (e.g., Dreben, Fiske, & Hastie, 1979; Skowronski & Carlston, 1987). This outcome ties in nicely with the finding that the superior recall of positive information seems to occur most strongly when the information is highly self-relevant or self-important (e.g., Hardin & Banaji, 1990).

EFFECTS OF VALENCE AND INTENSITY ON MEMORY: A BRIEF THEORETICAL REVIEW

The diversity in the empirical findings suggests that a number of specific mechanisms may ultimately be involved in explaining the relation between the affective reaction to an event (both intensity and valence) and event recall. Indeed, a brief perusal of the memory literature suggests that a number of causal mechanisms potentially apply to the affective nature of events on event memory, and not all of these mechanisms work toward the same memory outcomes.

A Freudian View: Repression

One of the earliest propositions concerning the relation between the evaluative nature of events and event recall was articulated by Freud (1900/1965; for a useful overview, see B. M. Ross, 1991). In outlining his psychodynamic view of the mind, Freud suggested that information that threatens the self can be repressed. That is, an ego-threatening event may be entered into the unconscious component of mind, from which it can not be easily retrieved. Freud also suggested that this mechanism is not limited to ego-threatening events that were severe threats: Repression can also operate for ordinary, everyday events that are only mildly ego-threatening.

The implications of this theory for memory are straightforward—ego-threatening events should be poorly recalled (for various perspectives on this issue, see Singer, 1990). Some researchers have translated this prediction into a more general statement about unpleasantness. That is, some have extended this Freudian prediction to include all unpleasant events, suggesting that unpleasant events should be more poorly recalled than pleasant events (e.g., Davis, 1987). However, as Holmes (1970) pointed out, this is an overgeneralization. Not all unpleasant events are ego-threatening. Nonetheless, many unpleasant events are ego-threatening whereas few pleasant events are. This asymmetry may lead one to suspect that, across events, positive information will have a memory advantage over unpleasant information.

An Information Processing View

More recent speculation on the relation between the affective nature of events and event recall has adopted the information processing metaphor and has attempted to address how event valence and intensity may affect event acquisition, rehearsal, storage, and retrieval processes. For example, some theorists (e.g., Matlin & Stang, 1978) have suggested that pleasant events may be acquired more efficiently and accurately than unpleasant events and that this heightened efficiency may be able to account for valence effects in memory.

Factors Affecting Encoding Efficiency and Accuracy. The acquisition efficiency for pleasant events can be produced by a number of factors. One mechanism leading to the easier acquisition of pleasant events than unpleasant events comes from ideas about schema-driven processing. In theory, one of the benefits of schema-driven processing is that it allows easier processing and storage of information that is congruent with the schema. Hence, if people generally have a positive conception of themselves or the world around them, positive information will be more easily assimilated than negative information.

Another factor that may have an impact on the efficiency of information processing at acquisition is the frequency (or expectedness) of events. Pleasant events tend to be more common than unpleasant events, and familiarity should allow those pleasant events to be processed more easily. This theoretical position (as well as the schema mechanism discussed earlier) implies that the processing of negative information takes more cognitive work than the processing of positive information. Several studies suggest that this is the case (see Peeters & Czapinski, 1990; Taylor, 1991).

Matlin and Stang's (1978) claim that pleasant events are processed more accurately than unpleasant events also can be tied to the operation of specific cognitive mechanisms. One factor that may serve to promote heightened accuracy for pleasant events is that people may simply be more receptive to positive information than to negative information. Consider the response that a typical child may have when faced with an upcoming injection from a physician. The child may close his or her eyes in an attempt to block out the pain-causing stimulus. This behavior differs from the heightened mental receptiveness that is usually present when the same child encounters a pleasant event (e.g., watching a children's show on TV). Openness to pleasantness and defensiveness to unpleasantness seems to occur in adults as well. One of the lessons of the research on the utility of fear appeals in persuasion is that appeals that promote too much fear are ineffective, in part because such messages cause audience members to cease processing the message (e.g., McGuire, 1969; but see Jepson & Chaiken, 1990). Thus, pleasant events may be better recalled than unpleasant events simply because, at the time that the events occur, people are more mentally involved when processing positive events than when processing negative events.

Another view on the issue of heightened accuracy for the recall of positive information can be derived from the literature on the self. Of particular interest is the empirical outcome that information relevant to or referring to the self is better recalled than non-self-referent information (e.g., Bellezza & Hoyt, 1992; Rogers, Kuiper, & Kirker, 1977). This outcome is often attributed to the fact that self-referent information is subjected to more extensive processing than non-self-referent events, resulting in a deeper, more elaborated memory trace (e.g., Brown, Keenan, & Potts, 1986).

The relevance of this work to the present issue is straightforward. Because the self-concept of many individuals is positive, it is more likely that pleasant events rather than unpleasant events are self-relevant. Positive information should be processed more extensively and encoded more thoroughly or distinctively than negative information. An extension of this idea is that the relation between the evaluative direction of an event and event recall is moderated by the evaluative direction of the self-concept. That is, although those with positive self-concepts should recall pleasant events better than unpleasant events, those with negative self-concepts should recall unpleasant events better than pleasant events. Indeed, there is some research that is consistent with this idea: One of the characteristics of depressives is a tendency to recall unpleasant ideas and events (Dalgleish & Watts, 1990).

This depressive thought research has been an exception to the general tenor of our discussion of information acquisition mechanisms; we have focused on the mechanisms that favor memory for pleasant events. However, as indicated by the depressive thought research, in some circumstances information acquisition may favor unpleasant events. In particular, there may be a tendency to pay increased attention to, and perhaps devote increased processing capacity to, unpleasant, threatening, or unexpected events. For example, in research on person perception, Fiske (1980) noted that perceivers tend to pay more attention to negative than to positive information (and to extreme information than to moderate information). Similarly, Hansen and Hansen (1988) noted that, when presented in the context of a crowd of people, people with threatening faces seem to be especially salient. This enhanced attention suggests heightened memory. However, enhanced attention to negative (and extreme) stimuli probably does not, by itself, enhance recall for negative and extreme information.

Factors Affecting Elaboration. One of the implications of the results of recent research into factors affecting memory is that, although attention may be necessary for event recall, enhanced attention is not sufficient. This is indicated by the well-known distinction between maintenance and elaborative rehearsal. Simply focusing on information and passively considering it (e.g., by mentally repeating it over and over) leads to poor memory; focusing on information and elaborating on it (e.g., by tying it into existing knowledge structures) produces better recall (see Bower & Winzenz, 1970).

These elaborative processing mechanisms may operate to encode negative and extreme information in memory. Hastie (1984) noted that unexpected events often trigger information processing that helps a person to better understand and explain the unexpected event. One of the consequences of this heightened processing is enhanced memory. This research can be straightforwardly extended into the event evaluation–event recall issue. Because intense events are less expected than moderate events, intense events may be thought about more deeply and should be better recalled. Because unpleasant events are less expected than pleasant events, unpleasant events should be thought about more deeply and should be better recalled.

Some theorists and researchers have also considered the potential role that negative emotional reactions play in information processing. Results indicate that negative emotional reactions tend to lead people to narrow and focus their attention, particularly to the events or to the features of events that produced the negative emotional reactions (Schwarz, 1990; Wegner & Vallacher, 1986). These findings are congruent with the mobilization–minimization theory of Taylor (1991), who suggested that the threatening nature of negative stimuli generally evokes strong cognitive responses to those stimuli. This response may lead to heightened initial memory for the negative stimuli.

Factors Affecting Rehearsal. It is relatively easy to construct arguments suggesting that the relation between event affect and memory may be produced by differential event rehearsal. For example, it is reasonable to assume that some events are spontaneously rehearsed more frequently than other events and that these well-rehearsed events will be better recalled. If this rehearsal is related to the affective nature of events, then a relation between event affect and memory will result.

This mechanism applies well to extreme events. Evidence from our labs indicates that extreme events are thought about more frequently than less extreme events (e.g., Betz & Skowronski, 1995). However, despite this confirmatory evidence, it is useful to recall the clinical evidence suggesting that some extreme events, such as extremely unpleasant or threatening events, may be repressed (e.g., Lewis, 1990) or simply not rehearsed and thus not well recalled at all.

Because repression is thought to occur primarily with unpleasant events, a natural follow-up question is whether there are general differences in the rehearsal of pleasant and unpleasant events. We have already noted the research suggesting that unpleasant events engender heightened cognitive activity, and we speculate that some of this activity undoubtedly involves rehearsal of the unpleasant event. Indeed, some research (Klinger, Barda, & Maxeiner, 1980) demonstrates that people are more likely to think about unpleasant events than about pleasant events. Although some of this mental effort is likely directed toward explaining the unpleasant event or to problem-solving activity, at least a portion must involve elaborative rehearsal of the original event. Hence, given these data, the rehearsal mechanism seems to imply heightened recall for unpleasant events.

However, there is another view. Research on the mood repair hypothesis (see Isen, 1984) suggests that, in order to maintain a positive mood, individuals should (if they can) resist recalling and rehearsing negative information. Matlin and Stang (1978) provided direct evidence favoring this proposal. In laboratory experiments using positive and negative words as stimuli, Matlin and Stang found that positive words were rehearsed more frequently than negative words. Hence, the mood repair hypothesis and the Matlin and Stang data suggest that differential rehearsal may be one cause of valence effects in event memory (also see Taylor, 1991). Obviously, given the conflicting data on the relation between affect and rehearsal frequency, it is not yet possible to discern whether rehearsal makes a substantive contribution to the relation between the affective nature of events and event recall.

Factors Affecting Memory Search and Retrieval. How may the memory search and retrieval process affect and bias recall of affectively toned events? Again, there are several possibilities. The cuing potential of mood may operate to favor the recall of positive and moderate events. That is, the mood-congruity effect is thought to occur because mood serves as a cue, directing memory search. Because people's moods are generally moderate and positive, one may expect enhanced recall for moderate and positive events. In addition, positive moods and negative moods appear to differ in their ability to cue mood-relevant memories. More specifically, some research suggests that negative moods do not facilitate the recall of negative material to the same degree that positive moods facilitate the recall of positive material (see Isen, 1984; Mayer & Salovey, 1988, for reviews). Thus, positive moods may be more frequent than negative moods (and hence, more often cue pleasant events), and may be more reliable elicitors of mood-congruent memories. These processes favor the recall of pleasant events.

It is possible that the same kind of cuing occurs for the self-concept. This idea is consistent with theories that suggest that self-knowledge is stored in schemata (e.g., Markus, 1977) or associative networks (e.g., Cantor & Kihlstrom, 1987). In these models, autobiographical information is linked to or organized around concepts important to the self. Activation of the concept may activate the individual events linked to the concepts. Thus, assuming that the self is positive or that many of the individual concepts that are central to the self are positive (as is likely to be the case for most people), then the self-concept will serve as a directive cue, aiding the retrieval of pleasant events.

However, recent research suggests that such cuing may not occur (Klein & Loftus, 1993). Using a priming paradigm, Klein and his colleagues found that making a self-descriptive judgment generally does not facilitate recall of autobiographical memories relevant to the self-judgment. Klein and Loftus speculated that the reason underlying this absence of facilitation is that summary information (e.g., traits) and autobiographical event information about the self are located in different storage systems. If this is the case, then positive self-concepts can not likely serve as recall cues for positive events.

Still another perspective on the potential impact of retrieval mechanisms on memory and how these may be related to the affective nature of events can be derived from the research on state-dependent memory (e.g., Bower, Montiero, & Gilligan, 1978). This area of research indicates that, although the effects may be quite weak, recall of information is best when an individual's mood at retrieval matches an individual's mood at encoding (see Bower & Mayer, 1985). To explain the usual pleasantness advantage in event recall, one merely has to assume that it is more likely that people will be in a good mood than in a bad mood, an assumption that seems to have some justification (see Brown & Taylor, 1986). More specifically, if positive moods are more frequent than negative moods, the conditions that promote state-dependent memory (e.g., a match between state at acquisition and state at retrieval) will more likely be in place for positive moods than for negative moods. Presumably, the events that are present during positive moods are positive, leading to enhanced recall for those positive events.

It should be clear from our brief overview and review that a number of possible cognitive mechanisms can operate to affect the recall of pleasant and unpleasant events. It is possible that the somewhat inconsistent data that have emerged with respect to the relations between recall and an event's valence and evaluative intensity can be explained by the interplay among these mechanisms. This reasoning suggests that, in order to understand the relation between an event's affective direction and recall for that event and between an event's evaluative intensity and recall for that event, one must be very cognizant of the factors that affect the processing of these events and of the cognitive processes involved in that processing. In the following section, we use our diary data to assess how the evaluative nature of events is related to event recall and to investigate the external and cognitive factors that may be involved in the relations between event affect and memory.

EFFECTS OF VALENCE AND INTENSITY ON MEMORY: THE DIARY STUDIES

In our autobiographical memory studies, when subjects recorded an event, they rated its pleasantness on a scale ranging from *very unpleasant* (−3) to *very pleasant* (+3). The relation between these pleasantness ratings (and variables derived from these ratings) and self-rated event recall was examined in several analyses.

The Relation Between Event Pleasantness and Event Memory

Consider the purely descriptive relation between rated pleasantness and memory. A representative plot of this relation, taken from the self-event condition of Skowronski et al. (1991; the 88OH data set), is presented in Fig. 4.1. The most striking characteristic of these data is the U-shaped function

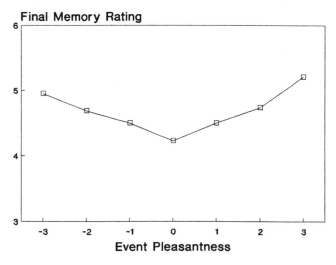

FIG. 4.1. Relation between rated pleasantness and rated recall (from Skowronski et al., 1991).

that emerges. Specifically, as pleasant or unpleasant events become increasingly intense, recall for those events increases. However, the U-shaped function is not perfectly symmetric. Instead, in these data there is a slight tendency for the U-shape to be unbalanced, with the pleasant items receiving slightly higher recall ratings than the unpleasant items. This asymmetry is more noticeable if the data are plotted in terms of intensity, directly comparing pleasant and unpleasant event recall at equal extremes. Such a plot is presented in Fig. 4.2.

After visual examination of data such as these, the impression that one is left with is that the relation between the evaluative intensity of an event and recall for the event is quite robust, whereas the relation between the valence of an event and recall for the event is much more modest (and, at least for self-events, favors recall of pleasant events). As we elaborate shortly, these are the conclusions that emerge from our statistical analyses.

Before proceeding to a review of the results of these analyses, we clarify the method by which we typically assess each event's evaluative direction and evaluative intensity. Obviously, the pleasantness rating that subjects provide for each event contains both event valence and evaluative intensity information. This is not particularly unusual. Indeed, research suggests that, in general, the emotional tone of events can be abstracted into two orthogonal components, valence and intensity (Diener, Larsen, Levine, & Emmons, 1985; see also Reisberg, Heuer, McLean, & O'Shaughnessy, 1988; Thomas & Diener, 1990).

In accord with this idea, we calculated an evaluative intensity measure by taking the absolute value of the pleasantness rating. The valence (i.e.,

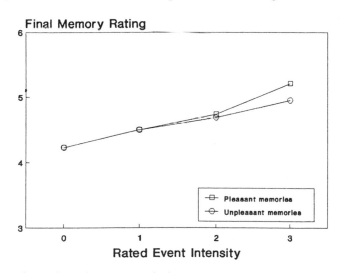

FIG. 4.2. Relation between rated pleasantness and rated recall by event valence (from Skowronski et al., 1991).

pleasant or unpleasant) measure was taken from the original pleasantness rating. Subsequently, we used both the intensity and valence measures as predictors in all the regression analyses that contributed to this chapter. Thus, any conclusions that we draw about event valence control for event evaluative intensity and vice versa. Given that Banaji and Hardin (1994) recently claimed that the overall valence effect obtained in previous research (particularly nonexperimental, real-world memory research) may have been due to an inability to control for event evaluative intensity, it is particularly important to keep this control in mind when considering our data examining the relation between the valence of an event and event recall.

Valence and Intensity Effects on Memory

We turn now to the results of our regression analyses. Regression betas, F-test results, and probability values for all the studies that we have con-ducted using event valence and evaluative intensity as predictors are pre-sented in Table 4.1. These betas control for the linear and quadratic effects of event age as well as for several other descriptive ratings of the events, described later in the chapter. As the data in that table reveal, across studies there is a high degree of consensus concerning the relation between evalu-ative intensity and recall. As indicated by the positive slopes to the betas for the derived evaluative intensity, the more extreme the event, the higher the reported recall (remember that the evaluative intensity measure was derived from the absolute value of the pleasantness score, so that higher numbers index greater intensity).

A second noteworthy finding is that the relation between intensity and recall seems to hold for both self-event recall and for other-event recall. That is, in two studies we asked participants to keep a diary of the events in the life of one other person as well as in their own life. These others were people that the diary keepers saw on almost a daily basis and were typically immediate family members, close relatives, close friends, room-mates, or paramours. (One sad cautionary note: For our second self-other study we asked our diary keepers to avoid paramours, if possible. The breakup frequency we obtained in Study 1 was relatively high, causing significant subject attrition.) The subjects provided the same pleasantness ratings (and other ratings such as person typicality) for others' events as they did for their own events. These other-event pleasantness ratings were also used to derive evaluative intensity ratings. As indicated in Table 4.1, evaluative intensity significantly predicted recall for 8 of the 10 self-event data sets and for both of the other-event data sets.

This self-other similarity does not appear to hold for the relation between event valence and event recall. As indicated by the positive betas, the self-event data indicate a small but fairly consistent positive relation between

TABLE 4.1
Regression Betas, *F*-test Results, and *p* Values Describing the Relation
Between Self-Rated Event Recall and Event Evaluative Intensity,
Event Emotionality, and Event Valence

Data Source & Year		Valence of Event Affect	Derived Evaluative Intensity of Affect	Emotional Involvement Training	Other Predictors in Model
			Self-Events		
80KS	β	.007	.071		Rehearsal
$F(1, 2406)$	F	.25	22.99		
	p	.6172	.0001		
86KS	β	−.007	.246		
$F(1, 2565)$	F	.17	195.73		
	p	.6767	.0001		
87KS	β	.029	.159		
$F(1, 3293)$	F	3.98	98.33		
	p	.0461	.0001		
88OH	β	.058	.151		Person typicality
$F(1, 3219)$	F	15.92	92.26		
	p	.0001	.0001		
89KS	β	.047	.059	.136	Event frequency
$F(1, 2848)$	F	10.40	11.04	48.64	
	p	.0013	.0009	.0001	
89OH	β	−.008	.182		
$F(1, 1577)$	F	.14	62.97		
	p	.7034	.0001		
90KS(long-term)	β	.027	.006	.075	Event frequency
$F(1, 3499)$	F	3.35	.12	12.37	Rehearsal
	p	.0675	.7250	.0004	
91OH	β	.033	.105		Person typicality
$F(1, 2262)$	F	5.43	34.95		Rehearsal
	p	.0199	.0001		Mental involvement
91KS	β	.069	.008	.075	Event frequency
$F(1, 1625)$	F	12.87	.12	6.77	Rehearsal
	p	.0003	.7247	.0093	
92KS	β	.038	.092	.147	Event frequency
$F(1, 3252)$	F	7.11	26.85	59.54	
	p	.0077	.0001	.0001	
			Other-Events		
88OH	β	−.002	.143		Person typicality
$F(1, 2720)$	F	.01	70.99		
	p	.9312	.0001		
91OH	β	−.042	.058		Person typicality
$F(1, 1949)$	F	4.08	7.89		Rehearsal
	p	.0436	.0050		Mental involvement

77

event valence and event memory—pleasant events were rated as being better recalled than unpleasant events. This positive relation is not a universal in the self-event studies: the beta value is positive in 8 of the 10 self-event studies in which we have assessed valence–memory relations but is significantly positive in only 6 of those studies. The beta is nonsignificantly negative in the other 2 studies.

Despite the minor inconsistency in the self-event study outcomes, the overall pattern of data seems to be fairly clear. That is, the best conclusion from these data is that for self-events, pleasant events have a slight recall advantage over unpleasant events. This result replicates the results of numerous other studies both from highly controlled laboratory settings and from less controlled studies of autobiographical memory (see Linton, 1975; Matlin & Stang, 1978; Wagenaar, 1986). In fact, it is curious (and likely coincidental) that the valence hit rate of 60% (6 significant outcomes out of 10 studies) obtained in our studies of autobiographical memory is close to the valence hit rate (roughly 67%) reported in Matlin and Stang's (1978) comprehensive review of the valence–memory literature.

In contrast to this persistent (positive) valence effect for the self, the data for other-event recall certainly do not show such an effect and may be indicative of an unpleasantness effect. Admittedly, this conclusion is very tenuous, given that we have only looked at two studies examining this issue and that in one of those studies, the beta value was nonsignificant (see Table 4.1). Nonetheless, the fact that the repetitive trend toward a valence effect in recall is apparently eliminated when recalling other-events is noteworthy; the possibility that this trend may be reversed in other-event recall is absolutely intriguing. Certainly, the elimination of positive valence effects in other-event recall suggests that nothing about the events themselves may predispose preferential recall of pleasant self-events; instead, the critical causal factor in the event valence–event recall relation lies in how the events are processed.

Some Possible Mediators of Valence and Intensity Effects

It is noteworthy that the significant effects obtained for the relation between evaluative intensity and event recall, and for event valence and event recall, emerged despite the presence of several other event ratings in the regression models. In theory, if the relation between intensity and memory or valence and memory were due to some other factor (such as event frequency), then inclusion of this other factor in the model would work toward eliminating the significant relation. This did not seem to occur.

Emotional Involvement. Four of the data sets (i.e., 89KS, 91KS, 92KS, and 90KS) included an emotional involvement pre-rating. Subjects indicated the extent to which an event produced an emotional response. As the results reported in the far right-hand column of Table 4.1 show, this emotionality rating always significantly predicted memory. The more emotionality an event produced, the better the event was recalled.

As we noted previously, some researchers have speculated that emotionality plays a crucial mediational role, especially in explaining the relation between evaluative intensity and event recall. For example, some theorists have suggested that high emotionality strengthens the distinctiveness of the memory trace (thus enhancing recall for emotionally extreme events), whereas others have suggested that high emotionality can contribute to the production of state-dependent memory effects (potentially interfering with the recall of extreme events). In the context of these ideas, it is noteworthy that the measures of event valence (in the 89KS, 91KS, and 92KS data sets) and evaluative intensity (in the 89KS, 92KS, and 90KS data sets) continued to predict self-event recall despite the presence of this emotionality term in the regression model. It seems unlikely that the effects of event valence and event evaluative intensity on self-event recall can be entirely attributed to the emotionality engendered by the events.

Event Frequency. A similar conclusion, derived from the same four KS data sets cited in the previous paragraph, can be derived for event frequency. As discussed earlier, event frequency may affect processing by causing people to attend to novel stimuli or by causing them to engage in heightened explanatory processing of unexpected events. This appears to be the case. The frequency rating was made on a 1 to 7 scale, on which 1 indicated high frequency (for that class or type of event) and 7 indicated a once-in-a-lifetime event. As expected if low frequency leads to heightened memory, there was a significant and positive predictive relation between perceived event frequency and self-rated event memory in all four studies, β's = .172, .173, .154, and .228, F's = 126.93, 65.43, 106.47, 159.30, all p's < .0001 (see chapter 3). However, the valence and evaluative intensity measures continued to show a significant relation to self-rated memory, despite the inclusion of the frequency measure in the model.

Person-typicality. Similar conclusions can be derived from the two studies that included a person-typicality rating. The person-typicality rating differs from the frequency rating in that the frequency rating is intended to apply to the population as a whole, whereas the person-typicality rating is intended to apply only to the person involved in the event. For example, in the studies asking subjects to provide the person-typicality rating (88OH and 91OH, both self and other), subjects were told that getting a C an a psychology exam was very typical if the diary target usually got C's but was very atypical if the diary target usually got A's. Subjects made this rating on a 7-point scale ranging from –3 for *very atypical* to +3 for *very typical* In all cases, the typicality rating predicted event recall, self β's = $-.124$, $-.114$, other β's = $-.118$, $-.080$, F's = 57.52, 29.30, 47.73, and 10.88, all p's < .001 (see chapter 3). However, as indicated in Table 4.1, the significant predictive relation between evaluative intensity and event recall was significant in all four of these data sets, and the predictive relation between event valence and recall was significant in three of the four (although the direction of the relation was different in the self-event and the other-event studies).

Rehearsal. Using five of our data sets (80KS, 90KS, 91KS, 91OH-self; 91OH-other), we assessed whether rehearsal of the event enters into the relation between event evaluative intensity and event memory or between event valence and event memory. The idea was straightforward: If these processes mediated the significant relations that emerged from our regression analyses, the presence of these process variables in the regression models would render the critical relations nonsignificant.

In all five of the data sets, subjects retrospectively reported how often they rehearsed each of the events. In all cases the rehearsal variable predicted self-reported memory: 80KS β = .458, $F(1, 2406)$ = 1085.67, 90KS β = .184, $F(1, 3499)$ = 119.67, 91KS β = .256, $F(1, 1625)$ = 124.05, 91OH-self β = .267, $F(1, 2262)$ = 214.96, 91OH-other β = .494, $F(1, 1949)$ = 672.03, all p's < .0001 (see chapter 3). Inclusion of the rehearsal variable in the regression model did not eliminate the significant relation (depicted in Table 4.1) that existed between evaluative intensity and self-rated memory in three of the data sets (80KS, 91OH-self, and 91OH-other). In two other data sets (91KS and 90KS), the relation was not statistically reliable.

Similar outcomes were observed when examining the role of rehearsal in the relation between event valence and recall. One of the analyses (80KS) containing rehearsal did not yield a significant relation between event valence and event recall. However, analyses of three other data sets (90KS, 91OH-self, 91OH-other) yielded significant relations, and the fourth (90KS) approached significance.

The results of these analyses suggest that although rehearsal may have a role to play in the relations between evaluative intensity and event recall and between event valence and event recall, it does not appear that rehearsal is the sole mediator of such effects.

Initial Mental Involvement. Analyses including a measure of mental involvement in events yielded similar outcomes. We speculated earlier that one possible explanation for the valence effect observed in event recall was that people were generally more mentally involved in pleasant than in unpleasant events. However, it is clear that, because of the differing direction of the relation between event valence and memory for self and other events, this initial involvement explanation can be a potential mediator only for the enhanced recall of positive self-events.

In the 91OH data sets (both self and other), subjects provided a rating of their level of initial mental involvement in events on a 1 to 5 scale, on which 1 reflected *not at all involved* and 5 reflected *highly involved*. As noted in chapter 3, these initial mental involvement ratings predicted event memory for both self-events and other-events. As noted in Table 4.1, presence of this involvement term in the regression models did not eliminate the relation between event valence and event memory or between evaluative intensity and event memory, either for self-events or for other-events. These data suggest that initial mental involvement does not mediate either of these relations. However, given that we have only one data set examining this variable, the outcome should be viewed with caution.

SUMMARY AND IMPLICATIONS

The data that we report in this chapter document that, using our diary self-report memory methodology, events that are evaluatively extreme are reported as better recalled than less extreme events, events that are emotion producing are reported as better recalled than events that are not emotion producing, pleasant self-events are reported as better recalled than unpleasant self-events, and unpleasant other-events are reported as better recalled than pleasant other-events. These effects generally emerged as significant in our regression analyses despite the simultaneous entry of all effects into the regression models (so that all effects reported control for the effects of other variables) and the entry of numerous other descriptive effects (e.g., the linear effects of event age, the quadratic effects of event age, event frequency, event person typicality). The analyses that addressed the mediational processes of event rehearsal and initial mental involvement suggest that, despite being predictors of memory, these processes are not the sole mediators of the enhanced recall found for self-events and for other-events. The enhanced recall occurred for both evaluatively extreme and pleasant event information in the case of self-events, for unpleasant information in the case of other-events, and for self-events with positive valence.

However, one note of caution about these results must be sounded about the relation between event valence and event recall that emerged in these studies. In conducting the analyses for this chapter, we discovered that the relation between event valence and memory was more likely to emerge after we included some of the other predictors in our regression models than when we ran models with relatively few predictors. For example, in the 92KS data set, there is not a significant valence effect in the model when only the dummy-coded subject term, the linear and quadratic effects of age, event evaluative intensity, and event valence are entered into the model. This stands in contrast to the data reported in Table 4.1, where the same valence effect is reported to be significant. The difference in the outcomes can be explained by the fact that the results for the 92KS data set presented in Table 4.1 are derived from a model that included all five of the effects listed here, plus both the frequency and emotionality rating.

The logic of regression suggests a cause for this phenomenon: The additional variables entered into the model accounted for a significant amount of error relative to the variance shared with the valence term in the model. Thus, the valence effect may be more likely to emerge in cases with a relatively large number of predictors that do not covary substantially with the valence variable but that account for substantial amounts of variance. In this regard, it is interesting to note that the data sets in which the valence term is nonsignificant employed relatively few predictors. In fact, in the results reported in Table 4.1, the 80KS, 86KS, and 89OH-self data sets employed only the five predictors that are common to all our studies. This suggests that the valence effect is one that, although present, is likely to be fairly weak, and it may not be noticed in those cases where there is a large amount of uncontrolled or unaccounted-for variability in the data. The relative weakness of this effect fits with the data suggesting that the positive valence effect does not always emerge in these studies (e.g., Matlin & Stang, 1978).

One other clear suggestion from our studies is that the self-relevant processing of events may be implicated in the valence effects in recall of self-events. When subjects kept diaries about the life of another person, the most memorable events that emerged in the memory test session tended to be unpleasant rather than pleasant. Although this finding needs replication using our methodology, it fits some of the laboratory data on other-perception that also shows the superior recall of unpleasant information (e.g., Dreben et al., 1979; Skowronski & Carlston, 1987).

Finally, it is also relatively clear that these data showed little evidence for the kinds of memory impairment effects that are thought to occur in the face of emotional or evaluatively extreme events. That is, these data provided no evidence favoring explanations including repression as a mechanism for memory impairment claiming that high amounts of arousal serve to reduce recall. One clear finding from these data was that intensity, whether from evaluative or from emotional sources, tended to lead to enhanced recall. That is not to say that some exceptional cases do not exist. The reported research merely suggests that such effects may not typically characterize the relation between intensity and memory.

CHAPTER FIVE

Effectiveness of Self-Schema
in Memory

Memory has become one of the central areas of research in social cognition. One important issue is whether the self provides the sort of elaborate structure that facilitates memory for personal events or for items (e.g., words) related to the self-structure. Another question of general concern is whether self-memory is similar to or different from other-memory (i.e., memory of events happening to others). The answers to these questions are important for other classic issues, such as the effect of the emotional tone of an event on recall for that event. Our diary methodology allows us to examine such important issues in a natural context using real events as the stimulus materials.

The focus of this chapter is on our diary research, but we begin by discussing two somewhat different theoretical views of the self-schema. After this theoretical overview, we briefly review the laboratory research on the self-reference effect, and then we discuss our data examining recall for autobiographical events. In particular, we discuss self-event recall versus recall for nonself-events (i.e., events of others that are known well and news event recall) and how recall for events from these different sources are (or are not) affected by person expectancies and the emotional tone of events.

THEORETICAL VIEWS ON THE FACILITATING EFFECT
OF SELF-SCHEMATA ON MEMORY

The importance of the self as an organizing agent in memory was first discussed in an influential paper by Rogers, Kuiper, and Kirker (1977). After first defining the self, they argued that it should play a major role in encoding personal experiences. The essence of their argument is contained in these quotes from their introduction:

> The self is defined as an abstract representation of past experience with personal data. Phenomenologically, it is a kind of vague idea about who the person thinks he or she is. It probably develops to help the person keep track of the vast amounts of self-relevant information encountered over a lifetime. The self, then, represents the abstracted essence of a person's perception of him or her-self. (p. 677)

> The central aspect of self-reference is that the self acts as a background or setting against which incoming data are interpreted or coded. This process involves an interaction between the previous experience of the individual (in the form of the abstract structure of self) and the incoming material. The involvement of the self in the interpretation of new stimuli imparts a degree of richness and fullness to the input because of the availability of the immense amounts of previous experience embodied in the self. (p. 678)

Obviously, Rogers et al. believe that the self-structure should facilitate the organization of new material in memory and that the rich organization of the self-schema facilitates retention. However, although the focus of this chapter is on the facilitating effects of the self-schema, the self-schema may have other effects on memory, such as distortion (see Greenwald, 1980).

There are two somewhat different views regarding the facilitating effect of the self-schema on memory. The first view argues that the self-schema provides a vehicle for facilitation of memory to a degree not provided by any other organizational or mnemonic scheme. The second argues that the self-schema provides organization that facilitates memory, but it does not provide any more facilitation than any other well-differentiated schema. The second view, however, takes two quite different forms. One (which may be the most widely held position) suggests that the self-schema provides for rich elaborative encoding, which will produce excellent recall. The self-schema is not given special status; rather, other well-developed schemata, such as those generated by the acquisition of expertise, also provide a structure capable of producing superior recall for the events or items encoded using that structure. By contrast, the other approach views the benefits of the self-schema as stemming from the organization provided by the schema rather than the elaboration in encoding (for a recent overview of issues in this area, see Linville & Carlston, 1994).

The Case for Superior Facilitation of Memory by the Self-Schema

Many researchers (e.g., Rogers et al., 1977) have argued that events that can be related to the self-schema are likely to be relatively well recalled. They also suggest that the degree of facilitation produced by the self-schema is superior to that produced by any other schema. Reasons for expecting the self-schema to provide superior facilitation of memory can be found in the cognitive processes of encoding, rehearsal, and retrieval.

Encoding. In 1972, Craik and Lockhart offered the powerful argument that depth of encoding determined the memorability of items. According to Craik and Lockhart, greater semantic involvement (i.e., deeper processing) produces better recall. Strong support for that view was produced in a series of studies by Craik and Tulving (1975). They used structural tasks (e.g., is the word written in capital letters?), phonemic tasks (e.g., does the word rhyme with the target word?), and semantic tasks (e.g., does the word have the same meaning as the target word?) in their experiments. Semantic tasks produced the best recall, structural tasks produced the poorest recall, and phonemic tasks were intermediate. The theoretical explanation was that semantic processing produced much richer encoding, leading to better retrieval.

Given the Craik and Tulving results (together with the theoretical explanation of those data), it follows that the richness of encoding produced by self-reference should result in excellent recall. Indeed, it is difficult to imagine that a richer organizational framework than the self-schema would exist. After all, each of us presumably spends a great portion of our lifetime constructing and elaborating our self-schema.

Interestingly, this suggests that the work on expert performance (e.g., Chase & Ericsson, 1981, 1982; Ericsson & Chase, 1982; Ericsson, 1988; Thompson et al., 1993) is relevant to understanding the self-schema. Given that we have been developing our self-schemata for most of our lives, it can be reasonably argued that, if we are expert about anything, it is about ourselves. That is, we have expert knowledge about the self in the sense that we have an extensive, rich, well-articulated set of information represented in the self-schema. However, although the self-schema has all the characteristics of an expert knowledge base, it is not necessarily accurate. Some of the memories, as well as some of the self-perceptions, contained in the self-schema are probably inaccurate. Note that it is also true that expert schemata need not be totally accurate.

Our expert (although probably flawed) self-knowledge is directly relevant to memory for personal events. The most extensive work on skilled memory has come from the laboratory of Ericsson and his colleagues (e.g., Ericsson & Chase, 1982), who have proposed three general principles for skilled memory. The three principles are meaningful encoding (i.e., the use of preexisting knowledge to store presented information in memory), retrieval structure (i.e., explicitly attaching cues to the encoded material to allow efficient retrieval), and speed-up (i.e., a reduction in encoding time with further practice). The self-schema obviously provides meaningful encoding for personal events and also provides an effective retrieval structure.

In summary, both the work on depth of processing (Craik & Lockhart, 1972) and the work on skilled memory (Chase & Ericsson, 1981, 1982; Ericsson & Chase, 1982) suggest that the use of the self-schema to encode personal events greatly facilitates recall of those events. According to the Craik and Lockhart view, the self-schema provides rich and deep encoding, leading to excellent recall. From the point of view of Ericsson and his colleagues, the self-schema provides both meaningful encoding and an effective retrieval structure, and both of these can facilitate recall.

Selective Rehearsal. The positive effects of rehearsal on memory have been claimed since the time of Ebbinghaus (1885/1964). However, the important distinction between elaborative and maintenance rehearsal made by Craik and Watkins (1973) qualified this view: Elaborative rehearsal facilitates subsequent recall, whereas maintenance rehearsal does not. Selective elaborative rehearsal undoubtedly contributes to superior recall for events encoded with the self-schema. Certainly, it is only natural for us to be more interested in events directly impacting on our lives than we are in events that have great significance for other individuals. It follows that we spend more time retrieving and rehearsing events important in our lives (and presumably encoded with our self-schema) than we spend retrieving and rehearsing non-personal events.

The various types of everyday rehearsal in which we routinely engage include conversing with friends about the past, being reminded of past events (and reviewing them), and reminiscing about the past. These types of rehearsal are inherently elaborative and should produce an increase in recall. Indeed, Linton (1975) repetitively tested some of the events she had recorded and showed that prior testing had a powerful facilitative effect on recall. Obviously, testing of an autobiographical event produces rehearsal of that event.

In the case of selective rehearsal, the contribution of the self-schema is indirect and somewhat circular. The events are rehearsed primarily because they are personal events. However, they presumably can be identified as personal events, in part because they are encoded with the self-schema. Thus, personal events are rehearsed because they are relevant to the self. The rehearsal, in turn, probably also contributes to the continuing development of the self-schema.

Retrieval. We commented earlier about the research on skilled memory by Ericsson and his colleagues (e.g., Ericsson & Chase, 1982). We pointed out that two of the three general principles for skilled memory proposed by Ericsson and Chase clearly apply to the self-schema. Those two principles are meaningful encoding (i.e., the use of preexisting knowledge to store presented information in memory) and an effective retrieval structure (i.e., explicitly attaching cues to the encoded material to allow efficient retrieval).

The self-schema obviously provides an incredibly rich and detailed retrieval structure (e.g., one might try to retrieve the memory of a particular dinner with a female friend by searching under the category of female friends and the subcategory of dinners with same). Because personal events are stored under that structure, they should be easy to retrieve.

Summary. Strong arguments for superior facilitation of memory through the self-schema are found when one considers the processes of encoding, rehearsal, and retrieval. Given the levels-of-processing view (Craik & Lockhart, 1972), the self-schema provides rich and deep encoding, leading to excellent recall. Further, personal events are likely to be given additional elaborative rehearsal, which also facilitates recall. Finally, the self-schema provides a rich and detailed structure that allows the individual to explicitly attach cues to the encoded material, allowing efficient retrieval. Thus, a theoretical analysis of all three processes leads to a prediction of facilitation of memory by the self-schema.

The Case for the Self-Schema as Nothing Special

Some researchers (e.g., Bower & Gilligan, 1979; Klein & Kihlstrom, 1986; Skowronski et al., 1991) have argued that the good recall found for personal events is nothing special. They point out that any event associated with a well-differentiated memory structure will be relatively well recalled. The self-schema is such a well-differentiated structure and will, therefore, produce good recall for personal events.

However, although these researchers agree that the self-schema facilitates recall, their argument that the self-schema is like any other well-differentiated memory structure takes two quite different forms. The arguments put forth by Bower and Gilligan (1979) and Skowronski et al. (1991) are indistinguishable from those given in the previous section except that they do not give the self-schema special status. Rather, these researchers suggest that other well-developed schemata, such as those generated by experts, provide a structure capable of producing superior recall for the events or items encoded using that structure. However, an important focus in their view is that the self-schema provides for rich elaborative encoding, which will produce excellent recall. Indeed, although experts may produce equivalent encoding structures, it is difficult to imagine that a framework richer than the self-schema will exist.

In comparison, Klein and Kihlstrom (1986) viewed the benefits of the self-schema as stemming from the organization rather than the elaboration provided by the schema. They argued that "the effects of self-reference on free recall . . . can be explained by a single principle: the well-documented finding that the organization of stimulus material improves recall" (p. 27).

In short, they argued that the self-schema is no different from any other good organizational scheme.

Further, Klein and Kihlstrom clearly differentiated their position from the elaborative encoding position by arguing that self-reference does not automatically produce organization. They pointed out that the elaborative encoding position is greatly weakened if the dimensions of self-reference and organization can be varied orthogonally. Their view implies that the typical self-reference effect is achieved when self-reference encourages organization but the semantic encoding task does not. More important, it should be possible to reverse the usual results (with self-reference producing better recall of items than semantic encoding) if the semantic encoding encouraged organization and self-reference did not. We discuss the relevant experiments by Klein and Kihlstrom (along with our interpretation of those results) after briefly reviewing the laboratory research on the facilitating effect of the self-schema.

LABORATORY RESEARCH ON THE SELF-SCHEMA

We now turn from our discussion of the theoretical views of the self-schema to a brief review of the plethora of research on the self-reference effect. The research suggests that self-reference facilitates recall but that there are limitations on the effectiveness of that encoding strategy. We finish this section with a review of the Klein and Kihlstrom research.

The Self-Reference Effect

The initial demonstration of the self-reference effect was reported by Rogers et al., (1977). They used a self-reference task together with structural, phonemic, and semantic tasks in their experiments. The subjects rated 40 adjectives representing different personality traits and, in the self-reference task, were asked whether the adjective "describes you?" Rogers et al. replicated the depth-of-processing findings with the structural task (i.e., big letters?) producing the poorest recall, the semantic task (i.e., means the same as . . . ?) producing the best recall, the phonemic task (i.e., rhymes with . . . ?) producing intermediate recall. More important, the self-reference task produced the best performance in recall, approximately doubling the performance achieved for the semantic task.

The self-reference effect is quite robust and has been replicated in a number of studies (Bellezza, 1984; Bower & Gilligan, 1979; Ganellen & Carver, 1985; Halpin, Puff, Mason, & Martson, 1984; Kendzierski, 1980; Klein & Kihlstrom, 1986; Lord, 1980; Maki & McCaul, 1985; McCaul & Maki, 1984; Warren, Chattin, Thompson, & Tomsky, 1983). Of course, each of the studies also added important extensions or restrictions to the self-reference effect.

Generally, self-reference is no better than reference to a familiar other (e.g., Bower & Gilligan, 1979), supporting the view that any event that can be related to any well-differentiated memory structure will be relatively well recalled. Indeed, two investigations (Keenan & Baillet, 1980; Lord, 1980) found that the self-reference effect was no better than reference to unfamiliar others under some conditions. Keenan and Baillet (1980) asked subjects factual or evaluative questions about persons varying in familiarity. Familiarity facilitated memory in a recognition task—but only for evaluative judgments. Finally, Lord (1980) found a reversal of the self-reference effect when he asked subjects to imagine themselves, their fathers, or Walter Cronkite interacting with a variety of objects. Imagining their fathers or Walter Cronkite interacting with the objects produced better recall than imagining themselves with the objects. Note, however, that we need not (and probably don't) tie such interactive images to our self-schema.

In line with those results, several investigators (e.g., Bellezza, 1984; Maki & McCaul, 1985) found the self-reference effect occurred only when the to-be-remembered material involved a relation to the self-schema. In these studies, self-reference facilitated recall when the target words were descriptive adjectives (i.e., traits) but not when they were nouns. For example, Bellezza (1984) looked at the self as a mnemonic device. He compared subject-generated cues composed of personal experiences to cues composed of names of parts of the body. He found that the body-part cues were more easily reconstructed at recall than the personal-experience cues. In spite of the advantage of retrievability for body-part cues, trait words were better recalled after being associated with personal experiences. However, when nouns were used as the to-be-remembered items, the two types of cues produced equivalent recall.

In support of previous results, Maki and McCaul (1985) showed that reference facilitated memory when the to-be-remembered words were part of some other known-person schema. However, the effect of reference decreased as the knowledge of the person decreased. For example, reference to one's self was more effective than reference to one's mother, which in turn was more effective than reference to Ronald Reagan. As with the Bellezza experiments, the facilitation occurred only when the target words were descriptive adjectives (traits); facilitation did not occur for nouns.

There is an important exception to the failure of to-be-remembered nouns to produce a self-reference effect. Warren et al. (1983) used a task in which they asked subjects to report when they had last seen an object. That autobiographical task produced better recall than rating the word for pleasantness. That is fairly impressive performance; Packman and Battig (1978) found pleasantness ratings produced the best recall of seven semantic orienting tasks. The exception occurs, we believe, because the subject must retrieve an event from personal experience. Thus, Warren et al. (1983) clearly demonstrated that retrieving an autobiographical event (i.e., memory for perception of an object) can facilitate recall, presumably because that event was encoded by the self-schema.

In summary, then, the argument put forth by Bower and Gilligan (1979) and more recently by Skowronski et al. (1991) is given considerable support by this research. These researchers argue that the good recall found for personal events is nothing special. They point out that any event that can be related to any well-differentiated memory structure will be relatively well recalled. The self-schema is such a well-differentiated structure and will, therefore, produce good recall for personal events. Their view also explains why the self-reference effect does not appear to hold when the target words are nouns. The presumed reason is that self-reference facilitates memory only when the materials to be remembered are part of or can be easily related to the self-schema. Objects represented by nouns are more difficult to relate to the self-schema than are traits.

Self-Reference: Elaboration at Encoding or Organization?

As noted earlier, Klein and Kihlstrom (1986) argued that the effects of self-reference could be explained by the well-known finding that organization improves recall. In their view, the self-schema is no different from any other good organizational scheme. They differentiated their position from the elaborative encoding position by arguing that the dimensions of self-reference and organization can be varied orthogonally. They suggested that the typical self-reference effect is achieved when self-reference encourages organization but the semantic encoding task does not.

They began by replicating the results of Rogers et al. (1977) using structural, semantic, and self-referent tasks. Each subject was given 48 words (trait adjectives), and each task was performed on a different subset of 16 words. Because they hypothesized that self-reference encouraged organization, Klein and Kihlstrom (1986) measured the degree of clustering produced by each task. They used a measure of clustering similar to the ARC measure (Roenker, Thompson, & Brown, 1971), which sets chance clustering equal to zero and perfect clustering equal to one. They found the usual self-referent effect, with the self-reference task producing better recall than semantic or structural tasks. More important for their hypothesis, the self-reference task produced significantly more clustering ($M = .32$) than the semantic task ($M = -.09$).

In four additional experiments, they showed that self-referent and semantic tasks produced essentially the same levels of recall if they were first matched for the amount of organization that they produce. Even more important, the usual results were reversed (i.e., self-reference produced poorer recall of items than semantic encoding) when the semantic task encouraged organization and self-reference did not.

As we have mentioned, their interpretation of these data was that the self-schema is no different from any other good organizational scheme. We agree that the self-schema promotes organization and thereby facilitates recall. In addition, Klein and Kihlstrom provide convincing evidence that under the right conditions, a semantic task that promotes organization produces better recall than a self-reference task that does not promote organization. That is certainly a nontrivial point. However, it does not preclude the possibility that nonorganizational encoding can be partially responsible for self-reference effects; this outcome simply argues that nonorganizational encoding may not be solely responsible for such effects. This explanation suggests that the processing mechanisms inherent in Chase and Ericsson's (1981) discussion of expert performance are, perhaps, a better way to conceptualize self-reference effects than a depth-of-processing framework. In fact, in his more recent work, Klein seems to agree. Based on the results of several studies, Klein and Loftus (1989) argued that both elaborative processing and organization independently contribute to the self-reference effect.

RECALL OF AUTOBIOGRAPHICAL EVENTS

We believe that while encoding ongoing personal events, the self-schema normally functions as an expert system—that is, it provides a rich context for encoding and retrieving the events of one's life. That rich context is, of course, highly organized. We partition our lives into categorical segments that include temporal (e.g., college years), personal (e.g., good friends), and activity (e.g., sports) classifications. Thus, the organization provided by the self-schema does indeed play an important role in facilitating recall. We also believe that the rich encoding environment that the self-schema provides is important. For example, participation in a sports event may be related to all three of the classifications just named, and probably several other categories as well. Most events can be encoded in a variety of ways and retrieved through multiple routes. It is the rich and elaborate structure of the self-schema that makes it extremely effective for encoding and retrieval.

Our next focus is on our diary studies, several of which investigate the recall for self-events and nonself-events. We have looked at two types of nonself-events, events for a well-known other, such as a spouse or a close friend and news events. We discuss these two types of nonself-events in the two sections that follow.

Memory for Self-Events Compared to Well-Known-Other Events

The first diary data collected using self-events and events from a well-known other was from the roommate study (Thompson, 1982). The subjects recorded events experienced by themselves and by a well-known other (usually a roommate) for a semester. At the end of the recording period, the recorders and the roommates were both tested for memory of their own events (note that there was no self versus other memory comparison in this study). Because recorders and roommates did not differ on any of the memory measures, we concluded that recording events did not affect memory for those events.

There were several a priori reasons to expect that the recorders would show better recall than the roommates: The recorders knew they were to be tested (and thus had the advantage of intentional rather than incidental recall), they recorded the events (thus producing additional rehearsal), and the event records were the exact cues used to describe the event during testing (thus the recorders knew the context for recall). We assume the failure of recorders to show better recall than roommates can be attributed to the self-schema. Generally, we assume that successful storage (and retrieval) depends on the integration of the target material into one or more of the schemata in the individual's knowledge structure. We also assume that the ease with which new information can be integrated into a schema is increased if the degree of familiarity or the richness of the associative structure of the schema is increased. For both roommates and recorders, the materials used in the study were personal events. It follows that both storage and retrieval of personal events should be facilitated by the great familiarity with and the rich associative structure of the self-schema. Thus, we speculate that those facilitating effects overpowered the factors that could have led to lowered memory for the roommates (e.g., incidental learning, less rehearsal, and knowledge of recall context).

Our post-hoc rationale for finding equivalent recall for roommates and recorders has an obvious corollary. We assume that events for a friend or roommate are stored with a less rich and less familiar structure (i.e., one of the schemata for other persons). If that is true, we expect both storage and retrieval of events for a friend or roommate to be less effective than for personal events.

Several predictions for recall follow from these assumptions. First, recorders should remember their own events better than events recorded for roommates. Second, roommates should remember events recorded for them better than the recorders remember those events. Third, the subset of events be classified as both recorder and roommate events (i.e., both persons participated in the event) should be remembered equally well by both the recorder and the roommate (and as well as events experienced exclusively by each individual).

Our assumptions also allow us to make predictions about subjects' predictions about their own memories and their roommates' memories. First, recorders should be equally accurate in predicting their recall of their own events and of their roommates' events. Second, because they cannot be as familiar with the schemata held by their roommates, the recorders should predict their own recall of their roommates' events more accurately than they predict the roommates' recall of those same events. Finally, the recorders should be able to predict that roommates will recall roommate events better than recorders will.

To test our predictions, we did a follow-up study (Thompson, 1985b) in which 21 participants recorded events for themselves and a roommate for 3 weeks. They recorded four events each day (two for themselves and two for their roommates), and the event records were collected twice each week. At the time the events were recorded, the recorder made a metamemory judgment (i.e., predicted the recallability) for the event on a 3-point scale, ranging from *not very memorable* (1) to *extremely memorable* (3). In the case of roommate events, separate judgments about recallability were made for the recorder and the roommate. Recorders also indicated whether they were present during roommate events.

The recorders informed their roommates that they were recording events but were instructed not to let their roommates know what events were being recorded. After a year had passed, we contacted as many roommates as possible (10 of 21) to verify whether the recorders had followed instructions. Nine of the 10 contacted said they had absolutely no knowledge about which events were being recorded. The tenth said that the recorder sometimes made comments that made it possible to guess which events were being recorded. These responses suggest that recorders followed the instructions very closely.

The memory test was given during the seventh week after recording began. Thus, the average retention interval was about 6 weeks. Roommates were tested only on their events, whereas recorders were tested on both their own and their roommate's events. The memory testing procedure generally followed that outlined in the Appendix.

The findings replicated the results of the initial roommate study: Recorders and roommates did not differ reliably in their mean memory ratings of their own events. Again, we interpret that result to mean that the facilitating effects of the self-schema overrode the factors that could have led to lowered self-event memory for the roommates (e.g., incidental learning, less rehearsal, and knowledge of recall context).[1]

More important, recorders recalled their own events better than the events of their roommates—and their metamemory ratings indicated that they were aware it would happen. Specifically, recorders' mean memory rating for their own events ($M = 5.13$) was reliably higher than their mean memory rating for their roommates' events ($M = 3.87$). This difference held when the events were adjusted for the initial memorability rating: At the time of

---

[1]Because these analyses involve only a few data sets, we have not reanalyzed the data. Readers interested in the specific statistical tests should refer to the original publications.

recording, recorders rated their own events as more memorable ($M = 2.03$) than their roommates' events ($M = 1.50$).

As predicted, roommates rated recall of their events better ($M = 4.61$) than the recorders rated their own recall for those events ($M = 3.99$). However, the presence or absence of the recorder was included as a factor in this analysis, yielding a reliable interaction between the recorder-roommate and present-absent factors. Roommates' memory for their events was higher than the recorders' memory for those events only when the recorder was not present at the events. A final analysis comparing recorders' memory of their own events with their memory of roommate events at which they were present showed that the recorders rated recall for their own events as reliably better ($M = 5.13$) than the roommate events ($M = 4.44$).

We thought it was possible that the present–absent dimension was reflecting whether the subject participated in or merely observed an event. Thus, in a second follow-up experiment (Thompson, 1985b; Experiment 2) we asked subjects to record personal events in which they either participated or simply observed. Contrary to our speculation, there were no differences in rated recall for those two types of event (but see the involvement data in chapter 3).

Two findings in these data provide strong evidence regarding the effective retrieval of personal events. First, and most important, roommates' memory for events from which the recorder was absent was better than the memory of the recorders for those events. This occurred even though the recorder selected all the events for recording and had the advantage of additional rehearsal of those events when writing them down. Further, roommates recalled the events recorded for them just as well as the recorders recalled their own events.

Second, recorders recalled roommate events at which they were present better than roommate events for which they were absent. More important, recorders recalled their own events better than the roommate events at which they were present. Thus, an event perceived as one's own (i.e., an event related to the self-schema) clearly has an advantage in recall above and beyond the advantage bestowed by being present at an event.

As we discussed in chapter 4, several other studies focusing on the effect of expectancies and emotional tone on recall also compared the recall of self-events with recall of the events of others (Betz & Skowronski, 1995; Skowronski et al., 1991). In those studies, the subjects recorded one event each day for themselves and another event for a close friend or relative whom they saw on an almost daily basis. Each paticipant made entries for approximately 10 weeks and was tested individually at the end of that period. The procedure for testing was the same in the two studies with the exception that the 67 subjects in the Skowronski et al. study were tested on events from their own diaries first, whereas the order of the testing was counterbalanced for the 49 subjects in the Betz and Skowronski study.

Both studies confirmed that self-events are better recalled than other-events. For example, the Skowronski et al. study showed mean rated recall for self-events was 4.41, whereas mean rated recall for other-events was 3.83. More important, Betz and Skowronski (1995) had subjects evaluate how often they rehearsed each event. During testing, the participants rated rehearsal for each event on a 5-point scale, from *not at all* (1) to *every day or nearly every day* (5). As expected, self-events ($M = 2.11$) were rehearsed more frequently than other-events ($M = 1.73$). Even when rehearsal was statistically partialled out, self-events were recalled better than other-events. Thus, although selective rehearsal clearly facilitates recall, it does not account entirely for the superiority in recall of self-events. Put differently, self-events probably are better recalled because they are selectively rehearsed and because they are stored with the self-schema.

Memory for Self-Events Compared to News Events

Recall of events stored with the self-schema has been compared to recall for events reported in the news (Larsen, 1992b; Larsen & Plunkett, 1987; Larsen & Thompson, in press). The first of those studies (Larsen & Plunkett, 1987) used retrieval of memories prompted by either object words (i.e., nouns) or emotion words (i.e., adjectives). On half the trials, subjects were instructed to retrieve personal memories (i.e., events that were personally experienced) whereas on the other half they were instructed to retrieve events for which they were not present (i.e., events that they had been told about or heard on the news). The instruction to retrieve reported events resulted in a far higher proportion of unsuccessful retrievals ($M = .13$) than did the instruction to retrieve experienced events ($M = .02$). Experienced events also were retrieved faster ($M = 7.2$) than reported events ($M = 10.7$).

In a study of his own memory, Larsen (1992b) recorded one public news event and one personally experienced event every day from January through June of 1986. The motivation for his study was the research on flashbulb memories, which involve unusually clear and vivid recall for the context in which the event is received (e.g., the assassination of President Kennedy). As Larsen (1992) pointed out, it was difficult to know what to make of the vivid recall for context because there had been no investigation of memory for context in ordinary autobiographical memory.

In Larsen's self-study, the events selected were among the most remarkable for the day and were uniquely distinctive at the time of recording. The events were recorded in a format that required entering what, who, where, and when In addition, an event detail was entered in the form of a question and associated answer that uniquely identified that event. For news events, additional information concerning the reception context was recorded: the source from which the news was first received and a context detail (in the form of a question and answer) unique to that situation.

Memory was tested in two sessions, 5 weeks and 5 months after recording had finished, respectively. Thus, the retention interval varied from 1 to 11 months. A random sample of half the events was tested during the first session, and the remaining events were tested during the second session. Memory for each event was tested by cued recall and recognition. The original record of the event (i.e., what, who, when, where) was given as a cue, and the detail question recorded with each event was asked to determine whether it elicited the target answer (also recorded with each event). For news events, Larsen also responded to the query regarding the context of hearing the news. After each recall, the original answer was shown, and a rating of vividness of recognition was made on a 3-point scale indicating no recognition (1), vague recognition (2), and vivid recognition (3).

Recall and recognition measures showed the same pattern of results. The percentage of events recognized (where ratings of 2 and 3 indicated recognition) illustrate the findings. Autobiographical events were recognized best (80%), recognition for news was next (65%), and news context had the poorest recognition scores (33%). Each of the three conditions differed reliably from the other two. Further, when retention interval was considered, these differences were consistent over time.

These findings show that memory of events related to the self-schema is greatly facilitated. It is noteworthy that this occurs despite the finding that the news events were rated as more unusual (i.e., distinctive) than the autobiographical events. However, the very low memory for news context also indicates that personal experience is not sufficient to bestow the advantage of self-reference on memory for a situation. It appears that the content of the situation must be relevant to the self to create that effect.

In the most recent study comparing memory for personal and news events (Larsen & Thompson, in press; Experiment 1), 11 subjects kept parallel diaries of self-events and news events for 12 weeks. The diary format included, for both types of event, the critical details of the event itself and of the circumstances (i.e., context) in which the event occurred. News events of a personal kind (e.g., a call informing the subject of her sister's newborn baby) were excluded from the results.

Memory for the events was tested two times with random samples from each subject's diary. Test 1 took place one week after the diary period had ended, and Test 2 was 5 months later. For each event, a number of cued recall questions were asked, the original description by the subject was presented for recognition, and the subject was given a blank calendar and asked to date the event as precisely as possible. The subjects also gave clarity of memory ratings, which are roughly equivalent to the memory ratings used in the experiments by Thompson and Skowronski.

Analyses of these data showed a very consistent pattern with both memory ratings and recall of details reliably better ($p < .001$) for personal events than for news events. The mean clarity of memory rating was 4.04 (on a 5-point scale) for self-events and 3.29 for news events. Similarly, the mean memory accuracy score was 3.41 (again on a 5-point scale) for personal events and 2.96 for news events. This is a convincing demonstration of the difference in the closeness to the self-schema of the two event types. As in the Larsen (1992b) single-subject study, the effect was obtained despite the greater unusualness of the news events.

Moreover, for both event types, the core events had higher memory measures (i.e., recall and memory clarity) than the personal context of those events ($ps < .001$). This result replicates the very meager memory for news context observed by Larsen. Furthermore, the fact that the core-context difference also holds within autobiographical events suggests that the self-schema does not exert a global effect (like a flashbulb) but rather works selectively on relevant information within each event.

Conclusions Regarding Recall of Autobiographical Events

Memory for self-events is superior to memory for well-known-other-events and memory for news events. The data supporting that conclusion are completely consistent in a series of four self–other studies and three personal event–news event studies. The latter include a study of retrieval prompted by words (Larsen & Plunkett, 1987), a study of personal autobiographical memory (Larsen, 1992b), and a study with paid volunteers (Larsen & Thompson, in press; Experiment 1). The superiority of personal event recall occurred even when specific instructions were given to select events that were among the most remarkable for the day (Larsen, 1992). Unusual and remarkable events occur with considerable frequency in the news but for most people occur in ones' personal life with less frequency. For example, it is relatively rare to experience a personal event with the importance and emotional impact of the assassination of Olof Palme.

We speculate that the superiority of memory for personal events over memory for others' events and memory for news events can be attributed to the efficacy of the self-schema. The self-schema is, we believe, a powerful tool for encoding and retrieving personal memories. Furthermore, the extremely low memory for the personal experience of reading or hearing something in the news shows that being present in a situation is, in itself, not sufficient to explain the self-schema effect. On the other hand, forgetting of the rather fragile personal context (i.e., so-called source amnesia) may explain some of the confusions, which seem common in everyday life, concerning when and by whom something was said.

Effects of Expectancies and Pleasantness

The focus of this section is on our diary studies investigating the effect of person expectancies and emotional valence (i.e., pleasantness or unpleasantness) on recall of self- and other-events. We begin by briefly reviewing the theoretical view of memory for self versus memory for others from a social-psychological perspective. That review serves as an introduction to our diary research.

Self-Other Memory from a Social-Psychological Perspective.   The social psychological literature contains many different views of the self. Many researchers from the social cognitive perspective view self-memory and self-judgment as fundamentally similar to other-memory and other-judgment (for reviews, see Greenwald & Pratkanis, 1984; Kihlstrom & Cantor, 1984; Kihlstrom et al., 1988). This view suggests fundamental similarities in the way that information about the self and others is encoded and retrieved. Because the self-schema presumably is richer than schemata for others, some differences in recall may exist, but those differences should be quantitative rather than qualitative.

Other theorists (e.g., Bem, 1972; Gergen, 1982) do not agree that processing information about the self is essentially the same as processing information about others. Their view is supported by studies demonstrating the fundamental attribution error (i.e., people are much more likely to think in terms of categories when considering other people than when considering themselves; see Ross, 1977). Also, self-judgments tend to be fairly unstable compared to judgments about others (e.g., Salancik, 1974). Hence, these theorists may expect to find qualitative differences in the impact of variables on self-event memory and other-event memory.

Match of Events to Prior Expectancy (Person-Typicality).   As we noted in chapter 3, research in social cognition has generally shown that facts either consistent with or inconsistent with expectancies about a person are recalled better than facts that are expectancy-neutral (e.g., Hastie, 1980). The recall data from the diary studies that we described in chapter 3 provided some evidence that such effects may occur in real-world settings. However, the data from these studies can also be used to investigate whether person-typicality effects in recall are the same for self-events and other-events.

This comparison is important because it provides evidence about the degree to which expectancies are involved in processing and storing information. If the same pattern holds for the recall of both self- and other-information, then expectancies appear to be used for both and, more important, a fundamental similarity exists in the way in which self- and other-information is processed. On the other hand, differences in recall of self- and other-information suggest that self-events may be processed qualitatively differently than other-events.

The Skowronski et al. (1991) data and the Betz and Skowronski (1995) data showed that person-atypical events were recalled better than person-typical events, and the Skowronski et al. (1991) data showed that both extremely typical and extremely atypical events were recalled better than events of intermediate typicality. Importantly, the results of both studies showed that these effects did not vary with the source of the event (i.e., self or other). Thus, person-typicality appears to affect the recall of self-events and other-events in similar ways.

Skowronski et al. (1991) found a three-way interaction between event source, typicality, and pleasantness (i.e., valence) of the event. However, this interaction appeared to have more to do with the conditions under which event pleasantness affects recall than with the differing effects of person-typicality for self-events and other-events. Pleasantness was positively related to recall only for self-events and only when those events were intermediate in typicality—that is, neither extremely typical nor extremely atypical.

Event Pleasantness. The interaction described previously hinted at the possibility that the pleasantness (i.e., positivity) effect in memory holds only for self-events. In fact, there are both logical and empirical reasons to doubt that one would find better recall of pleasant other-events than unpleasant other-events. Fiske (1980) argued that it is beneficial to pay more attention to negative stimuli, which should lead to better recall for negative information. Consistent with this reasoning, Skowronski and Carlston (1987) demonstrated in an impression-formation paradigm that negative information about other people was better recalled than positive information.

These outcomes suggest that the comparison of self-event recall and other-event recall should be particularly informative. If, for example, better recall is found for pleasant self-events but not for pleasant other-events, then the mechanisms driving the effect would appear to be specific to self-relevant events. By comparison, if better recall is found for all pleasant events, then that positivity bias would appear to be produced by mechanisms inherent in the memory system that favor positivity.

As we noted in chapter 4, both Skowronski et al. (1991) and Betz and Skowronski (1995) found that pleasant self-events were recalled better than negative self-events, an outcome that matches the trend in most of the earlier diary studies (see Table 4.1). However, this effect was not present for other-events; in fact, in the Betz and Skowronski data set, unpleasant other-events were significantly better recalled than pleasant other-events. The elimination of positivity effects in other-event recall suggests that nothing about the events themselves may predispose preferential recall of pleasant self-events; instead, the critical causal factor in the affect–recall relation may lie in how the self influences processing of the events.

GENERAL CONCLUSIONS

We believe that the most important point about the self-schema made by our research is that the self-schema cannot be regarded as just another type of organization. Two findings support our view that the self-schema has special characteristics. First, we found that participants remembered their own events better than events they had recorded for other individuals. An initial interpretation of that finding is that participants actually participated in their own events but only heard about the events they recorded for others. However, our data show that even when the recorder is present at an event recorded for another individual, memory for that event is not as good as an equivalent personal event. That outcome is particularly impressive when one considers that the recorder selected the event for recording, knew that it would be tested later, and was forced to rehearse the event when recording it. All these factors (i.e., event selection, intentional encoding, and rehearsal) should facilitate later recall. Obviously, if there is facilitation from those factors, it is not sufficient to overcome the advantage accruing from the self-schema.

Second, we found different effects for self and other events. We found that, in general, events with strong affect (either very pleasant or very unpleasant) were remembered better than neutral events. However, the critical finding was with regard to the Pollyanna effect—the notion that pleasant events are remembered better than unpleasant events. We found that memory ratings correlated with pleasantness ratings only for personal events, provided that those events were neither very typical or very atypical. In short, the Pollyanna effect only held for certain types of personal memories. No such effect held for memory for others' events. This difference between memory for personal events and memory for others' events suggests that the self-schema is not just another organizational strategy. Rather, the self-schema produces an effect not found when using the schema for another person.

In addition to providing evidence that the self-schema cannot be regarded as just another type of organization, our diary studies emphasize the facilitating effects of the self-schema. Personal events are remembered better than other-events or news events. They also are retrieved faster than news events and, although we did not measure retrieval time in our self–other studies, we are fairly confident that we could generalize the results to predict that personal events will be retrieved more rapidly than other-events.

In summary, the self-schema is an efficient and powerful tool for storage and retrieval. Those studying expert performance are well advised to include the study of the self-schema. When it comes to knowledge about ourselves, we are all experts!

Reconstructive Memory for Time

THE TEMPORAL ASPECT OF MEMORIES

To this point we have considered memory for the properties that characterize the content of individual, single episodes. In some ways, our approach is conceptually similar to traditional laboratory research in which words presented to a subject and later used in a memory test make up an experimental episode. However, at least two important differences exist between laboratory and naturalistic memory research. First, personal memories concern natural, meaningful events. Second, memory for these events includes information indicating that the individual who now remembers them was also present to experience them originally. Thus, unlike items in the typical list-learning experiment, personal memories have autobiographical reference (Tulving, 1972) or self-reference (Brewer, 1986; Nelson, 1993).

Memory for the "what" of events is, of course, necessary for anybody to have personal memories. However, early memory researchers commonly emphasized an additional feature of personal memories, namely that the events are "expressly referred to the past, thought of as in the past" (James, 1890/1950, p. 650). Similarly, Höffding (1885/1891, p. 135) emphasized "definite reference of the representation to a definite point in time" as a feature of "memory proper," as opposed to sheer familiarity or recognition. In other words, some awareness of the time of the event, a temporal location that is at least more definite than a feeling of pastness, is required for a genuine personal memory.

The importance of time has re-emerged in recent conceptions of personal memory. Tulving (1972) argued that episodic memory contains "information about temporally dated episodes or events, and temporal-spatial relations among these events" (p. 385). In Brewer's (1986) discussion of the concepts of autobiographical and personal memory, temporal properties were not explicitly mentioned as a defining feature of these types of memory. However, Brewer endorsed Tulving's statement as a precise description of personal memory; he thus seems to take temporal location as a self-evident ingredient of the definition (but see Brewer, 1994). Nelson (1993) explicitly emphasized time when she wrote that autobiographical memory is "a particular form of episodic memory in which specificity of time and place is significant" (p. 357).

In spite of the fundamental importance accorded to the temporal aspect of personal memory, research on memory for time has been a very limited part of the past century's burgeoning psychology of memory (e.g., Jackson, 1990). To some extent, this situation is due to methodological constraints of the laboratory paradigms that have dominated memory research since the work of Ebbinghaus (1885/1964). In such paradigms, time is invariably operationalized as the serial order and serial position of items within lists or among successive lists. This is far removed from the way time is represented in everyday circumstances (i.e., by reference to watches, calendars, etc.). Moreover, a wealth of natural and social information about time is excluded from the laboratory situation: diurnal and seasonal cycles, week cycles, anniversaries and holidays, and so forth. Finally, the scale of time in the to-be-remembered lists of items in an experiment is several orders of magnitude smaller than the time that is typical of a person's temporal horizon. In sum, studying memory for time with classical laboratory paradigms is enormously difficult, if not downright impossible.

Our corpus of real-world diary studies enables us to investigate memory for time in unusual detail. These studies build on and extend the results of other studies that have used a realistic range of time, both for personal events (Baddeley, Lewis, & Nimmo-Smith, 1978; Bruce & van Pelt, 1989; Linton, 1975; Friedman, 1987; Rubin & Baddeley, 1989; Wagenaar, 1986; White, 1982) and public events (Brown, Rips, & Shevell, 1985; Friedman & Wilkins, 1985; Loftus & Marburger, 1983). In this chapter, we discuss results that are relevant to a number of basic conceptual and theoretical issues. This forms the background for the presentation, in the following chapters, of more extensive results on the variables that affect memory for time.

TOPOLOGY OF TIME:
PHYSICAL, ECOLOGICAL, AND COGNITIVE

Time is basic to the conception of the universe in the natural sciences. However, the common expression that time is the fourth dimension glosses over a number of difficult problems concerning the relation between the three spatial dimensions and the temporal one. Some of these questions have occupied philosophers and physicists for centuries (cf. Whitrow, 1975). We briefly note two pertinent issues from the philosophical discussion of the topology of time.

First, is the structure of time linear or cyclic? In the modern philosophical and scientific view, there is no question that time is linear and unidirectional. Cyclic notions of time—for example, that history repeats itself—were entertained among some philosophers in ancient Greece. Such views were opposed by the Christian church with the claim that the world has an absolute beginning (i.e., Creation) and end (i.e., Doomsday) and with the institutionalization of the calendar. Newton's theory of physics and Darwin's theory of evolution finally established the linear view of time in natural science. Cyclic processes in the micro- and macro-physical world are necessary to measure time, but they are held to carry no ontological implications for temporal topology.

A second important philosophical question is whether time is objective or subjective. The answer is both. It is logically necessary to distinguish between objective time (also called static time), which is the time of physics and can be described logically with before–after relations, and subjective time (also called dynamic time), in which the concepts past, present, and future have meaning. The ontological status of subjective or dynamic time is disputed; it is often claimed by physicists to be a purely mental construction, either independent from or only partly constrained by the objective time of the material world.

However, dynamic time may be seen as analogous to Gibson's (1979) concept of ecological optics. That is, dynamic time is objective physical time described with reference to a particular organism at a particular point of observation (which specifies past, present, and future). This *ecological time* is thus fully objective, though it is relative rather than absolute. The *cognitive topology of time* may then be defined as the way that temporal structure is represented mentally, that is, the functional structure of time that can be observed in behavior, thought, language, and memory.

At first glance, a straightforward relation appears between ecological time and the cognitive representation of time as it is reflected in autobiographical memory. Life is a succession of events that are intricately related, causally and intentionally. Nevertheless, however complicated the relations may be, the events occur in a chronological sequence. Many events are repeated with minor variations from day to day, from week to week, or from year to year and therefore merge to become general knowledge. No matter how small the variations are, any two events in a person's life can in principle be distinguished by the unique times when they occurred. Though we may not recall the time of events precisely, autobiographical memories appear to our present consciousness as representing, more or less completely, a chronologically ordered, continuous, past reality. Accordingly, in the art of biography that flourished in the 18th century (Boswell's *Life of Johnson*, 1791/1980, is probably the most famous example), the description of the life of the subject was fastidiously chronological.

The linear view of time is inherent to the common metaphors of the time line and the arrow of time. Generally, the metaphors suggest that time is similar to space, except that time is simpler: It has only one dimension. However, the ecology of time is much richer than this simple linear sequence, including numerous cyclic changes that are likely to be part of cognitive representations. Thus, the cyclic changes of the natural environment—day and night, seasons of the year—impose inescapable constraints on human life. The social environment reinforces and extends these cyclic temporal patterns. The culturally developed technologies for measuring, symbolizing, and communicating about time (e.g., the clock and the calendar) as well as social rules and rituals structure people's activities in a more detailed fashion than demanded by the natural cycles. Clock hours are used to fix the time of work, school, transportation, entertainment, and so on. Calendar months and dates determine the time of semesters and vacations as well as national, religious, and personal events of celebration. The purely cultural pattern of the days of the week extends the range of cyclic temporal structures even further (see Larsen, Thompson, & Hansen, 1995, for a more extensive discussion).

To the extent that such temporal cycles are important in cognitive functioning, an appropriate model of the representation of time—the *cognitive calendar*—may have to be not only more complex than a time line but also quite different from the cognitive maps used to model the representation of space.

THEORIES OF MEMORY FOR TIME

William James (1890/1950) asserted that beyond the immediate past, "*dates are conceived*, not perceived; known symbolically by names, such as 'last week,' '1850'; or thought of by events which happened in them, as the year in which we attended school, or met with such a loss" (p. 650, our emphasis). Psychological research has come around to something quite similar to the view of James. The reconstructive theory that we prefer holds that the time of past events is indeed conceived—reconstructed rather than retrieved, in modern language. The major advance over James' view is that researchers are now able to specify much more fully the essence and ingredients of this conception.

To illustrate why we prefer the reconstructive view, we briefly consider the main theoretical alternatives to reconstruction, namely time tag theories, trace strength theories, and event order theories. Our discussion of the problems with each of these positions is indebted to Friedman's (1993) comprehensive review; we refer interested readers to that paper for a more detailed review of the evidence from laboratory research.

Time Tag Theories

Time tag theories provide the simplest form of theory in which the location of events in time is specified explicitly in memory. The core of time tag theory is the assumption that time information is added on to the memory trace at encoding as a dedicated tag or *temporal trace*. This time tag can then be retrieved later along with the memory trace. Time tag theories have been quite commonly suggested (e.g., Glenberg, 1987; Tulving, 1972; Yntema & Trask, 1963), but because the nature of the time tags and the tagging process has never been spelled out sufficiently, the position is difficult to evaluate (see Friedman, 1993).

Under the conditions of ordinary life in a modern society, conventional calendar and clock labels may seem obvious ways to conceive of time tags, analogous to a date stamp on a photograph. A theoretically more neutral term for such symbolic labels is *temporal symbols*. Studies examining whether people use temporal labels have yielded mixed results. On the one hand, research suggests that calendar time is not explicitly represented in memory because dates are invariably the worst possible cues for recalling events (Barsalou, 1988; Brewer, 1988; Wagenaar, 1986). On the other hand, we have found that subjects who date diary events sometimes indicate that they know the exact date and retrieve it directly from memory. Such answers are commonly given for about 10% of the datings in a 15-week academic term (e.g., Thompson, Skowronski, & Lee, 1988a). This finding suggests that acquisition of the exact date does occur, though we argue that the actual percentage is less than 10. Friedman (1993) noted that occasional representation of dates does not require a general time-tagging model; we only need to assume that dates can be learned and remembered just like any other information if they are attended and processed.

Trace Strength Theories

Trace strength theories suggest that the time since an event occurred is gauged from the strength of its memory trace; because strength is assumed to decline across time, a stronger trace indicates a more recent event. Strength may be assessed by vividness of the memory, ease of retrieving it, confidence in its correctness, or amount of detail recalled. Strength theories were proposed very early (e.g., Höffding, 1885/1891; see also Michon, Pouthas, & Jackson, 1988) and exist in a number of forms. A modest version is the *accessibility principle* proposed by Brown et al. (1985), which states that estimates of time are biased by the ease of retrieving information about the events.

The accessibility principle may have some limited validity for explaining biases in dating nonpersonal events (like the news events employed by Brown et al.), but as a general account of memory for time, strength theory fails seriously. When personal events are studied, high-strength events do not tend to be telescoped forward as the theory predicts but rather are dated more accurately than low-strength events (Rubin & Baddeley, 1989; Thompson et al., 1988a). Moreover, subjects very rarely mention vividness or other supposed aspects of strength when they are asked how they judge the time of events (Thompson, Skowonski, & Betz, 1993).

Event Order Theories

Event order theories propose that each event is somehow associated with its position in the sequence of events experienced by the individual. For example, the succession of events receding into the past, like bags on a moving conveyer belt (Murdock, 1974), may be automatically coded in memory. To the extent that a temporal metric is assumed to be provided by the steady movement of time (the "conveyer belt"), this theory attempts to incorporate duration, not just event order. The theory is consistent with a common tendency to recall events in chronological order (either forwards or backwards) and to be reminded of events close in time to a target event one is trying to put a date to. Furthermore, the perceptual metaphor of judging distance into the past along the moving belt appears to fit with the linear increase of the magnitude of dating errors as retention time increases (e.g., Rubin & Baddeley, 1989; Thompson, 1982). However, no account has been proposed for how the temporal information is represented in memory and how temporal distance may be maintained when the events themselves are forgotten. Moreover, there is strong evidence against the strictly linear view of memory for time that this kind of theory presupposes.

Order code theory represents a more limited version of the event order notion. The occurrence of an event may remind one of an earlier, similar event and thus create a link between the two events that encodes their before–after relation. For instance, hearing of the Chernobyl nuclear power plant disaster may bring the Three Mile Island accident to mind. This order code mechanism has been demonstrated in the laboratory (e.g., Winograd & Soloway, 1985) by showing that the order of two items can be judged with greater success if they are meaningfully related. Similar studies on autobiographical memory are not available, but because order codes do not specify the duration of the interval between the events or their temporal location, they can only be of supplementary value to temporal memory.

Reconstructive Theories

Reconstructive theories propose that memory for time is primarily accomplished by using fragments of information remembered about the event (which we call *temporal cues*) to draw inferences from general knowledge about time patterns (i.e., *temporal schemata*) and thus constrain the likely time of the event. To anchor these relative temporal estimates to the conventional time scale, people may remember the precise calendar time of a few events that are used as reference points (i.e., *landmarks*).

Friedman (1993) showed that reconstructive theories can in principle accommodate all the extant empirical findings. He found no contradictory evidence from either laboratory or naturalistic studies or from personal or public events. Three kinds of evidence speak for a reconstructive theory at the expense of other views. First, the dating accuracy of well-remembered events is generally high. An abundance of cues exist for accessing the temporal schemata, and dating is improved by procedures that increase memory for the event itself. We explore the possible limits of this relation between event memory and dating accuracy in subsequent chapters. Second, subjects' reports of their strategies as well as think-aloud protocols show that regular time patterns and reference events are used extensively to arrive at temporal estimates. We discuss this kind of evidence in the following section. Third, so-called scale effects provide particularly strong support for reconstructive theories. Scale effects refer to the empirical findings that the accuracy of memory can be high on one level of temporal scale (e.g., the hour of an event) while it is low on others (e.g., the month it occurred) and that scale differences are not correlated with the grain of the scales (Bruce & van Pelt, 1989; Friedman, 1987; Friedman & Wilkins, 1985; White, 1982). If a linear view of time held true, memory should by necessity be more accurate at higher and more coarse-grained scale levels. In a reconstructive account, scale effects are readily explained by the use of independent schemata at each level.

The power of reconstructive theories is in large part due to their flexible, almost amorphous nature. Any kind of information that can constrain temporal estimates may be incorporated in the reconstructive process. This is clearly illustrated in the particular version elaborated by Friedman (1993). Though location in a generic, temporal schema is considered the main basis for temporal memory, the use of landmark events with specifically remembered temporal labels (i.e., time tags) is also assumed. In principle, there is no reason to stop here. To the extent that order codes and duration information exist (even though the evidence suggests that their use is limited), they can be incorporated in the theory as auxiliary factors to narrow further the possible time of the event. In this manner, the theory may assimilate elements from all the other views of temporal memory.

TEMPORAL RECONSTRUCTION
AND AUTOBIOGRAPHICAL MEMORY THEORY

Although we believe that Friedman's reconstructive view is correct in general terms, we regard it as rather uneconomical and ad hoc, theoretically as well as empirically. In order to tie memory for time more closely to a general account of autobiographical memory, we briefly suggest how the main claims of the reconstructive view may be framed in the terms of Nelson's (1993) theory, as it was outlined in chapter 1.

Nelson's theory suggests three sources of information to be used in the reconstructive process: generic event memory, autobiographical memory, and episodic memory. *Generic event memory* includes schemata of the activities that have tended to recur during a certain time period, for instance, a day, a week, or a year. These are the cyclic temporal schemata on which Friedman (1993) placed most of the responsibility for reconstructing the time of events. Recurrent particular dates, such as birthdays, anniversaries, and certain national and religious holidays that may be used as landmarks, are also part of generic event memory.

Autobiographical memory includes the events that have been significant in the individual's life and is thus assumed to be a stable knowledge structure. Autobiographical memory is organized in terms of higher order periods or extended event time lines (Barsalou, 1988; Conway & Rubin, 1993). The period structure is schematic, but it is linear rather than cyclic; for this reason, periods make it possible to keep track of consecutive cycles of time, in particular the years, which cyclic schemata cannot. Transition events that mark the boundaries between periods (e.g., first event memories, cf. Robinson, 1992) often seem to be well remembered and may be obvious candidates for use as temporal landmarks, similar to recurrent events in cyclic schemata.

Finally, *episodic memory* concerns individual events that are neither general nor necessarily important to the history of the self. It is rather short-lived but rich in regard to details of events and relations between events. Information from episodic memory may be seen as furnishing an important part of the cues by which generic temporal schemata are accessed as well as the associations that relate individual events to temporal landmarks.

This sketch suggests that a theory of temporal reconstruction needs to consider both linear and cyclic schemata. It may be useful to distinguish recurrent (cyclic) and transition (linear) landmarks, and the dependence of schema and landmark use on episodic event information should be investigated.

The results from our research presented in the following chapters significantly enlarge the empirical evidence on memory for the time of natural events and allow us to address these questions in some detail. In the remainder of this chapter, we discuss two kinds of data that support reconstructive theories. First, we consider subjects' reports of how they determine the time of remembered events. Subjective strategies can reveal the contributors to the reconstructive process and the extent to which these contributors are employed. Second, we analyze the striking periodicities that we have observed in the errors people commit in such temporal estimates; an example of the error pattern from one of our studies was shown in chapter 1, Fig. 1.5. These periodicities can reveal the process and the conditions of using schematic knowledge at particular levels of temporal scale. The chapter ends with a summary of the theoretical account we propose.

SUBJECTIVE REPORTS OF MEMORY STRATEGIES

Although it has been noted for many years that the time of at least some events is determined by a process of conscious reasoning, the first attempt to collect systematic evidence about the nature of this process was not made until the 1970s. In her pioneering diary study of her own memory, Linton (1975) categorized the strategies she used to date and order pairs of events into four major groups: those in which the exact date was known, those for which the period in which the event occurred was known, those for which time was "counted" between the target and a reference event with a known date (including counting backwards from the present), and those that involved pure guessing.

Although Linton's strategy list reflects some of the dating sources we have outlined, it does not include different temporal cycles or different levels of time. Because Linton's study had been running for more than a year at the time her paper was written, it can be presumed that she had found the four categories to be satisfactory for capturing the strategies she actually used. However, Linton never reported any systematic results concerning her use of these memory strategies.

In contrast, Friedman (1987) obtained quite detailed information about subjects' memory strategies at each of five levels of time for a single, common event, an earthquake that occurred 9 months earlier. The 99 subjects were asked for separate estimates of the year, the month, the day of month, the day of week, and the hour of the earthquake. It is worthwhile to examine the strategies mentioned at each temporal level (except for estimates of the year; these are incommensurate with the other levels because less than one full year had passed). In Table 6.1, the 11 categories used by Friedman are simplified to reflect theoretically interesting differences.

It is remarkable that no subject mentioned relating the earthquake to a known period of linear time, a strategy that Linton listed as a separate category (a similar neglect of reference to linear time periods is present in the data provided by Baddeley et al., 1978). On the other hand, Friedman's subjects reported heavy use of cyclic temporal schemata, which Linton did not consider at all. This difference illustrates an important weakness of collecting subjective reports in predefined categories: If alternatives are omitted by the experimenter, subjects may fail to think about them. Though we must regard the magnitude of the percentages in each cell very cautiously, the pattern of data is informative. First, recall of exact time tags does occur, although not commonly (10% of the time or less), and a sense of duration is simply not reported at levels more fine-grained than the month. Second, the use of landmark event references seems to occur at a substantial and rather uniform rate at every temporal level (20%–30%); this category appears more frequently than suggested by Friedman (1993), who claimed that landmark events are a "small minority." Third, the use of schematic knowledge

TABLE 6.1
Percentage of Strategies of Temporal Reconstruction Reported
(Adapted From Friedman, 1987)

Strategy	Temporal Level			
	Month	Day of Month	Day of Week	Hour
Recall of exact time	10	10	5	3
Landmark relation	30	33	17	27
Cyclic schema relation	54	9	59	64
Duration since event	4	0	0	0
Guess	2	41	18	1
Other	1	8	1	3

Note. The cyclic schema category includes daily, weekly, and annual routines, as well as the use of recalled clothing and weather that must be referred to schematic knowledge (e.g., seasons) if it is to contribute to a temporal estimate; the landmark category designates nonroutine events and includes recall of hearing news about the earthquake.

accounts for more than half of the responses at the three levels at which cyclic temporal schemata can be expected to exist: month of the year, day of the week, and hour. When such schemata are not available, as is probably the case for days of the month, subjects apparently resort to pure guessing.

We have collected strategy reports from subjects in several studies. Subjects were asked to indicate from a fixed set of alternatives the strategy they used for dating each event. The first of these studies (Thompson et al., 1988a) had far too many undecodable responses and mainly served to develop a satisfactory set of alternatives. However, two recent studies used identical, improved response categories and produced robust results (Skowronski et al., 1995; Thompson et al., 1993). They are summarized in Table 6.2.

It should be noted that the categories offered in our studies did not distinguish between cyclic periods (e.g., summer, final part of semester) and linear periods (e.g., vacation in Europe, writing a particular project paper). Because only one semester was covered in the diaries, in practice the distinction is often irrelevant. For instance, summer and vacation in Europe may actually identify the same time period. On the other hand, the categories used in our studies distinguished two types of landmark events, recurrent or *cyclic landmarks* (e.g., always bowl on Wednesdays, mother's birthday, Thanksgiving) and specific or *linear landmarks* that do not recur in every temporal cycle (e.g., the day I returned from Europe, the day of xeroxing the project paper).

The results in the first two columns of Table 6.2, where retention times are equivalent, are quite similar. This is reassuring, indicating that our procedure is sufficiently reliable. At middle and long retention intervals, our findings show substantial decreases of exact date recall and use of landmarks, with corresponding increases in the use of schematic period knowledge

TABLE 6.2
Percentage of Strategies of Temporal Reconstruction Reported
(Adapted From Thompson et al., 1993; Skowronski et al., 1995)

Strategy	1993 Study	1995 Study		
		Recent	Middle	Old
Exact date recalled	18	21	7	3
Cyclic landmark	13	9	4	3
Linear landmark	22	19	16	9
Period (cyclic or linear)	29	37	58	56
Clarity of memory	5	8	2	6
No. intervening events	4	0	0	1
Guess	10	5	12	21
Other	–	2	1	2

Note. Retention time in the 1993 study ranged from 2 days to 10–15 weeks (70–105 days). In the 1995 study, the recent events were 1–100 days into the past, the middle events covered a period from 100 days to 1 year, and the old events happened more than 1 year ago.

(already observed at the middle interval) and pure guessing (at the longest interval). This shift as time passes from an emphasis on strategies that may be presumed to depend heavily on memory of specific event information to strategies that rely more on generic knowledge is reassuring for the validity of the procedure.

Concerning the usage of particular strategies, the data in Table 6.2 suggest that exact date recall for recent events is more frequent than indicated by Friedman's earthquake study. However, in the middling part of our 1994 study, in which retention time is roughly comparable to Friedman's 9 months, the exact dating rate of 7% is similar to Friedman's findings.

Landmark events seem to be used at a rate of about 30% for recent memories when cyclic and linear landmarks are combined; cyclic landmarks are used less often than linear ones. The combined frequency of the two kinds of landmarks is close to the level suggested by Friedman, although the rate of 20% for landmarks in our middling period may be slightly less than he found.

The use of schematic knowledge accounts for the largest share of the reports in our two studies, even at the most recent retention interval. At the longer intervals, reports of schema use reach a level close to 60%—nearly identical to Friedman's results for estimating month, day of week, and hour, although we asked for only one strategy (the major one) to cover all levels of the temporal estimate.

Use of memory clarity and estimating the number of intervening events are infrequently mentioned in both studies—less than 10% taken together—and across the entire retention period, extending to more than two years. Friedman's duration category is perhaps comparable to our number of intervening events, and the percentages are again similar: close to zero.

Considering the differences between the events being dated and the categories used, as well as the suspicion that subjective reports on mental processes may be highly susceptible to demand characteristics, this convergence of results is remarkable. To address further the possibility that demand characteristics may be at work, we calculated measures of dating accuracy for each strategy in the long-term study (Skowronski et al., 1995). The findings conformed nicely to one's intuitions about the accuracy of the strategies. For example, at the longest retention time (i.e., above 1 year), the proportion of events dated exactly when subjects said that they had recalled the exact date was 72%; this dropped to 25% when the use of a linear landmark was reported and to 32% when cyclic landmarks were used. Use of a schematic period resulted in only 10% exact dates, and memory clarity and guessing were clearly the lowest at 2–3% exact dates.

Given these data, we feel confident that our findings validly reflect the relative weight of these different strategies of estimating the dates of everyday, autobiographical events. It is clear that the choice of strategies depends on retention time, presumably in response to the decreasing amount of information available about the events. It may also be expected that the use of strategies depends on the content of events and the availability of appropriate schematic knowledge in particular domains of the person's life. We return to this issue in chapter 9 where the relation of events to the self-schema is discussed.

With these provisos, the reports from subjects suggest the following conclusions about the process of date estimation. Recall of exact dates drops off quickly with the passage of time and is quite rare after a year, but even then, it does occur occasionally. Landmark use also drops sharply with time but is still relatively frequent after a year. Specific (linear) landmarks are used more often than recurrent (cyclic) ones. Schematic knowledge that identifies the period (i.e., linear or cyclic) in which the event took place accounts for one-third of the strategies that are applied when recent events are dated, and its use increases with time, dominating more than half the datings before a year has passed. The use of memory clarity and duration information is negligible under the circumstances studied so far. Finally, for recent events, subjects are occasionally completely lacking information that can be used to estimate the date and therefore resort to guessing. When a year has passed, every fifth event has too little information to provide a basis for any reconstructive effort.

DATING ACCURACY AND ERRORS: THE USE OF GENERIC SCHEMATA

The strategies reported by subjects suggest that generic knowledge of the year, the week, and the day—temporal schemata—are the major sources of information for attempts to date events that occurred up to a year in the past. The use of temporal schemata does not require that any temporal information is stored and remembered with the particular event. No temporal traces are needed. As long as the content of memory for an event can provide cues that are relevant for determining a more or less precise location in the schema, an approximate time for the event can be reconstructed. Thus, a schema-based account does not imply that memory for specific details of the events is immaterial to memory for time. On the contrary, the more details that are remembered, the greater the chance that schema-invoking cues will be present.

However, are people really right when they report that they most often do not retrieve even the approximate time of events from memory, but rather rely on temporal schemata? To what extent can schema use account for the dating attempts that are actually made, without invoking underlying, nonconscious registration and retrieval of temporal information—temporal traces that people cannot report? A schema-based account does not exclude the notion that temporal memory traces exist and are employed alongside inferences from schemata.

As we discussed in chapter 1, subjects' use of the week schema can be observed in the pattern of errors they make. Subjects hit the correct day of the week far more often than chance, even when their estimates were several weeks in error. Results showed a characteristic, jagged distribution of errors instead of the smooth distribution one may expect if no day-of-week information is available. Analogously, periodicities are expected for estimates of the month and the hour of events. Hour memory studies have not been published (see Larsen, Thompson, & Hansen, 1995, for some preliminary results). However, for memory of the month of moving to a new home, Auriat (1992) found a periodic pattern closely similar to Fig. 1.5, with peaks every 12 months. Even for the less remarkable events in our long-term diary study, a 12-month peak was evident (see Fig. 1.7). Nevertheless, memory for the day of the week remains the most well-researched instance of temporal schema use. We examine the findings in some detail and present a simple model showing that reconstructive processes account nicely for the particulars of the observed error pattern.

The Week Schema Model

The Basic Model. In the examples of week schema use, the event could be placed on a single day (e.g., Monday "because bowling league always meets on Mondays"). That is indistinguishable from using a symbolic tag indicating "Monday" attached to the memory of the event. However, such single-day responses cannot result in the smooth curves between the 7-day peaks shown in Fig. 1.5 and again reflected in the averaged day-of-week (DOW) error distributions in Fig. 1.6 and Fig. 1.8. We should instead obtain isolated peaks at the right day, perhaps superimposed on an even spread of random errors. Thus, if single-day tags were used, there should be no difference among errors of 1, 2, and 3 days in either direction (when we first observed the pattern of 7-day peaks in Skowronski et al., 1991, we fell prey to interpreting it as resulting from time tags).

However, reference to a week schema need not point to a single day. Quite likely, a group of days may often be indicated, as in "that dinner was in the weekend" or "I met her on my way to work so it must have been on a workday." Using data from a replication study (Thompson et al., 1993), we showed that such approximate temporal information could account very closely for the error pattern, provided a few reasonable assumptions were made. When two days are indicated—as when the subject knows that an event was in the weekend but cannot decide whether it was Saturday or Sunday— selection of one of those days has a 50% chance of hitting the right day whereas the remaining choices are split evenly (25% each) between being one day too long and one day too short. Analogous arguments can easily be developed for larger subcategories of the week, such as the five workdays.

For the purpose of illustrating this model of how the week schema is used, Thompson et al. (1993) assumed that reference to the week schema would equally often point to a single day, to the 2-day weekend group, to a 3-day midweek group (i.e., Tuesday, Wednesday, Thursday), and to the 5 typical work days (i.e., Monday through Friday). The calculation of predicted error probabilities is shown in Table 6.3. It is also depicted by the cumulative bars in Fig. 6.1, in which the observed error distribution is shown by the overlaid line graph. For a model this simple, the fit seems encouraging.

The Use of Approximate Temporal Information

Thompson et al. (1993) discussed two problems with this model. The first is the simplifying assumption that the four categories of approximate information in the model occur equally often. Another set of categories may be

TABLE 6.3
Predicted Error Probabilities Used by Thompson et al.
(1993, Table 2) for Illustration of Week Schema Model

Partial Information	Day-of-week Error						
	−3	−2	−1	0	1	2	3
Single day	0	0	0	100	0	0	0
Weekend (2 days)	0	0	25	50	25	0	0
Midweek (3 days)	0	11	22	33	22	11	0
Workday (5 days)	12	12	16	20	16	12	12
Mean errors	3	6	16	51	16	6	3

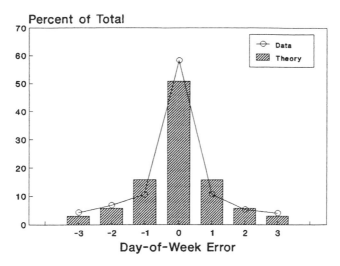

FIG. 6.1. Probabilities from Thompson et al. (1993, Table 2) presented as a bar graph with the observed data overlaid as a line graph.

more appropriate, and the relative frequency of using them is most likely not equal. The second problem is whether these categories of approximate information actually exist. An even simpler model may hold that there only are single-day estimates (whether derived from a schema or from time tags), but they are compromised by errors that are distributed exponentially: Errors of one day are more likely than errors of two days, and so forth. A much elaborated variant of this model was put forward by Huttenlocher et al. (1992), and we discuss that model later in this chapter.

Evidence that addresses these two problems was collected by Hansen (1993) as part of an experiment reported fully by Larsen and Thompson (in press, Exp. 1). In Hansen's study, subjects were interrogated about events they had recorded in a diary 10–14 months earlier. They did not have a calendar at hand, and instead of picking a single day for each event, they selected any group of days of the week within which they believed the event had occurred. Their success was also recorded, that is, whether the chosen group of possible days included the actual day of the week. The choices for 280 events are shown in the first two columns of Table 6.4 (the last two columns are discussed in chapter 10). All multi-day choices were contiguous days.

The frequencies in Table 6.4 show that for 99% of events subjects summoned information to constrain the possible days of the week. In the majority of cases (more than 60%), they chose just a single day; in other words, they felt fairly certain of the day and they were right in more than two-thirds of the cases. When subjects indicated only approximate information, they most commonly selected groups of 2 or 5 days. This suggests that a major dis-

TABLE 6.4
Groups of Days of the Week Chosen by Subjects and
Associated Success Rate (From Larsen & Thompson, in press).

Number of Days in Group	Personal Events		Public News	
	Pct Choices	Success	Pct Choices	Success
1	61	.68	44	.52
2	15	.72	16	.58
3	4	.80	6	.64
4	5	.92	4	.67
5	14	.95	18	.88
6	0	–	1	.67
7	1	1.00	11	1.00

Note. Day groups of 7 are pure guesses.

tinction in the week schema may correspond to the usual linguistic labels of work days and weekend and that the schema is a hierarchical structure of 5 + 2 days (as asserted by Huttenlocher et al., 1992). All the 5-day groups indeed consisted of the five usual work days, Monday through Friday. However, the 2-day groups were not exclusively Saturday + Sunday; other pairs were actually chosen equally or more often, namely, Thursday + Friday, Wednesday + Thursday, and even Friday + Saturday, which crosses the weekend–work day distinction.

To summarize, people always had knowledge of when in the week an event took place. Though this knowledge was sometimes approximate, it was quite reliable. The week schema suggested by the approximate information people indicated has the five usual work days as the most prominent subcategory, but it is otherwise too flexible or idiosyncratic to fit a neat hierarchical structure like the 5 + 2 formula.

The Improved Model. We used these findings to improve the model of week schema use shown in Table 6.3 and Fig. 6.1. We assumed that when the choice of a day group was unsuccessful, the final response of the subject was a pure guess (which had a 14% chance of hitting the right day). That is, the erroneous choices were pooled with the few cases in which the subjects acknowledged that they were just guessing. Furthermore, to avoid reliance on minor details that might easily change under different conditions, the few 3-day groups were pooled with the 2-day groups, and the few 4-day groups were pooled with the 5-day ones. In the calculation of average probabilities, the effects of these two simplifications cancel each other. Similarly, we rounded the frequencies to the nearest 5%. The resulting relative frequencies indicate how often the different categories of day-of-week knowledge can validly be derived from the week schema, given the conditions in this study.

TABLE 6.5
Weights Derived by Larsen and Thompson (in press, Exp. 1) from
Subjects' Choices of Day Groups and Resulting Error Probabilities (in %)

Number of Days in Group	Weight	Day-of-Week Error						
		−3	−2	−1	0	1	2	3
1	.40	0	0	0	100	0	0	0
2	.15	0	0	25	50	25	0	0
5	.20	12	12	16	20	16	12	12
7	.25	14	14	14	14	14	14	14
Weighted mean		6	6	10	55	10	6	6

These frequencies were entered as weights in calculating the expected probabilities of DOW hits and errors, as shown in Table 6.5. To test these predictions, we compared them with dating estimates observed in two different studies (Larsen & Thompson, in press). The first set of datings came from the same Danish subjects who provided the day group choices, but the datings were collected 5 months earlier using events not included in their original 14-week diary period (11 subjects, 773 responses, average retention time about 5 months). The second set of datings were collected from 25 American subjects, based on 12-week diaries (2217 responses, average retention time 1.5 months). The two observed distributions are graphed in Fig. 6.2 (Danish) and Fig. 6.3 (American) along with the predictions derived in Table 6.5.

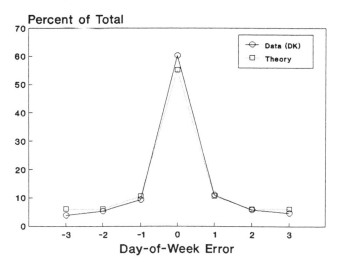

FIG. 6.2. The Danish empirical day-of-week curve compared to the day-of-week curve generated by our theoretical model.

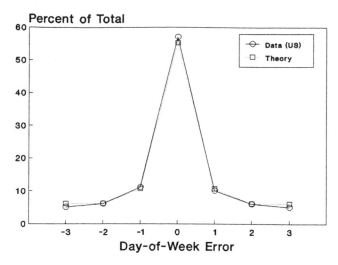

FIG. 6.3. The American empirical day-of-week curve compared to the day-of-week curve generated by our theoretical model.

It is seen that the model provides a very close fit to both sets of data— closer to the American data, which are the more distant in terms of subject population and retention time from the findings on which the model was based. The agreement between model and data was evaluated by chi-square statistics on the observed response frequencies pooled across all subjects. This is a very conservative test because the observations are far from being statistically independent; with more than 700 observations and only 6 degrees of freedom, almost any deviation will be significant. Still, the difference between model and data was just barely significant for the Danish study ($\chi^2(6) = 14.05$, N = 773, $.05 > p > .02$) and was not significant for the American study ($\chi^2(6) = 9.41$, N = 2217, $p > .10$). Taken together with the day-group choices, we consider this fit of the improved schema model to be strong evidence that memory for the time of events at the particular level of day of the week examined here can be accounted for without assuming an underlying temporal trace or time tag.

Huttenlocher et al. (1992) developed an alternative model that assumes that temporal judgments are based on sampling from the uncertainty distribution of an underlying memory trace that is basically accurate, though inexact. A week schema is also assumed, but its function is secondary; it works only to modify the temporal judgment through boundary effects that impose limits on the sampling process. Huttenlocher et al. (1992) formulated these ideas in a complex mathematical model with 22 parameters. The parameters were estimated by empirical data from a study of the confusions among days of the week that people made when they judged how long ago they were visited by a survey interviewer (which happened within the last 10 weeks). This method is quite different from our diary method and calendar date task. Nevertheless, Huttenlocher et al. (1992) arrived at a week schema structure similar to the one we have described, a work days category plus two separate weekend days.

Are there grounds to choose between these two models? Empirically, the models have complementary strengths. They converge on the overall structure of the week schema. The Huttenlocher et al. model goes into more detail, providing separate parameters for each of the 7 days of the week. Our model accounts for a broader variety of data, including the average errors in the Huttenlocher et al. study (i.e., we confirmed the fit of our model to these data by a chi-square test, $\chi^2(6) = 11.48$, N = 814, $p > .05$). Theoretically, however, our model is more parsimonious. It avoids a number of dubious assumptions made by the model of Huttenlocher et al. (1992), most importantly, the postulate of a dedicated day-of-the-week memory trace that is located on an underlying cognitive dimension for the week scale and that has a particular uncertainty distribution. These problems become particularly evident because a comprehensive theory of memory for time along these lines demands assumptions of separate traces and underlying cognitive dimensions at each level of temporal scale, in addition to separate schemata.

Looking at the fit of our model in Figs. 6.2 and 6.3, two more points are noteworthy. First, the fit of the model does not seem to be affected by the difference in retention time between the data sets. Second, the model slightly underestimates the frequency of correct-day judgments in both studies. We examine these two points next.

The Week Schema is Immune to Forgetting

Average retention time for the events in the American study (shown in Fig. 6.3) was about 1.5 months, and in the Danish study (shown in Fig. 6.2) it was 5 months. The theoretical model was based on data collected 10 months after the events had happened. Despite these differences in the duration of the studies, the fit between model and data was not affected. The pattern of DOW judgments therefore appears to be immune to forgetting, at least over an interval of a year. To test this finding further, we compared the DOW error distributions obtained in two phases of the Danish study (Larsen & Thompson, in press, Exp. 1). Test 1 was conducted a couple of days after the diary period (average retention time 2 months); test 2 took place 5 months later, using a different sample of diary events (average retention time 7 months). A within-subjects ANOVA showed that this substantial difference in retention interval did not change the DOW distribution (the interaction between time and DOW errors was not significant, $F < 1$).

This robustness of the DOW pattern is an important finding for a reconstructive theory because a schema for the regular pattern of weekly activities must be expected to be fairly stable across time. For instance, the division into work days and weekend that is common in a certain country may remain valid for decades. The week schema account would be hard to uphold if day-of-the-week memory were only noticeable during the first few months following an event. On the other hand, if the information pointing to the day of the week had been separately stored and retained as a temporal code or a symbolic time tag, a clear effect of degradation of the memory trace over time would be expected.

However, the stability observed in the relatively short time window of these experiments would hardly last indefinitely. Over intervals of years, the weekly activities of individuals are likely to change, leading to corresponding changes (i.e., updating) of the week schema. This is likely to be the reason for the difference between the DOW patterns for events below and above one year that we observed in chapter 1 (Fig. 1.8). Nevertheless, that difference was not great, and a noticeable DOW effect was still present for events between 1 and 2.5 years old. Modification of the week schema indeed appears to be a slow process.

It might be suspected that, because our subjects were provided with the text of their original diary record before dating each event, the resistance of DOW errors to forgetting is a methodological artifact. A diary may have contained such an abundance of cues for access to the week schema that it masked any possible effect of forgetting. However, recall that the pattern of errors we obtained is very close to that reported by Huttenlocher et al. (1992), who gave minimal cues to their subjects. Moreover, as we demonstrate in the following section, another aspect of temporal memory, exact datings, proved sensitive to forgetting.

Exact Datings are Partly Schema-Independent

In the two studies depicted in Figs. 6.2 and 6.3, our model of reconstructing the day of the week slightly underestimated the frequency (by 2–5%) of correct-day judgments. The reason may be that some hits on the right day are not reconstructed from the week schema. Thus, if the subject can retrieve or infer the exact date (e.g., November 22), the day of the week (e.g., Wednesday) will be correct by necessity. The exact date was mentioned in subjects' strategy reports at a surprisingly high frequency (10–20%; see Tables 6.1 and 6.2), but this stategy may have included converging schematic reconstructions that the subject could not disentangle. Even so, to the extent that exact datings are made without support from the week schema, there should be a surplus of DOW hits in the correct week of the event.

We calculated the proportion of such excess DOW hits for each subject at increasing retention times in the two studies of Larsen and Thompson (in press); because this calculation requires a substantial number of responses to yield reliable proportions, we could not achieve as fine a resolution in

TABLE 6.6
Estimated Percentage of Exact Datings in Excess of
Week Schema Reconstruction (From Larsen & Thompson, 1995)

	Average Retention Time (Weeks)				
	2	6	8	10	29
90AU (Exp. 1)	–	–	17.9	–	6.0
91KS (Exp. 2)	18.4	3.2	–	4.1	–

time for the Danish data as for the American study. The average percentages are shown in Table 6.6. It is clear that the level of schema-independent exact datings is initially higher in the Danish study, perhaps because this was a nonstudent population; family and work may provide a greater variety of distinctive everyday events. However, in both groups the rate of these exact datings drops sharply with time and ends at a level close to 5%. The decrease over time was highly significant in both groups ($p < .005$). Thus, forgetting of event information seems to strongly affect this component of event dating. This is in stark opposition to the DOW error pattern, which was minimally affected by retention time.

Most exact datings are probably due to knowledge of *recurrent dates* in the annual schema (e.g., a birthday or national holiday); exact datings may also rely on such recurrent dates as landmarks (e.g., "the excursion was the day before Mother's birthday"). Other exact datings may be *retrieved dates* from events that are so recent (e.g., within the last 1–2 weeks) that specific, episodic memory leaves little room for uncertainty about the date; an exact date may also occasionally be stored in memory as a temporal label (e.g., "I wrecked my car on October 3"). Retrieved dates presumably depend on the amount of detailed information retained about the event and its specific relations to other events; retrieved exact dates should therefore be strongly affected by forgetting.

In our view, the 5% exact datings in excess of the week schema at long delays are mostly to be ascribed to recurrent dates in the year schema—that is, reconstruction from a temporal schema at a higher level than the week. However, the use of unique, nonrecurrent temporal landmarks (e.g., transition events) must be included in this small minority of exact datings. The frequency of such entirely schema-independent datings is likely to be very limited when only periods of a few months are considered.

Higher-Level Schemata

One more component is needed to account for the distribution of dating errors, in addition to week schema reconstructions and supernumerary exact datings. This component is concerned with hitting (or missing) the right week. The accuracy of dating at this level of week errors can be observed in Fig. 1.5 in the diminishing height of the 7-day peaks as the error magnitude increases. When the extra exact datings are removed and the week schema effect is smoothed, we get a smooth distribution with no sign of periodicity. Thompson et al. (1993) showed that this pattern can be described very well by a monotonically decreasing function (more precisely, a negative exponential function). Reanalyses of several earlier studies yielded analogous mathematical functions.

This monotonic error distribution suggests that there is no temporal schema at the level of weeks of the month, which would predict a periodicity of about 4 weeks. As mentioned in an earlier section, Auriat (1992) reported a striking 12-month periodicity in people's dating of home moves several years ago. Figure 1.7 shows a similar annual periodicity in our long-term diary study. Thus, cyclic schemata seem to exist at the level of months of the year, perhaps described in terms of seasons or semesters (see Robinson, 1986). However, periodicities at higher levels than the month cannot be detected unless a larger time window into the past is used, with the possible exception of the annually recurring dates that contribute to exact datings. Furthermore, as the time window is expanded, we expect that linear temporal structures life periods and transition event landmarks become increasingly important for temporal memory.

SCHEMATIC AND EPISODIC ASPECTS
OF MEMORY FOR TIME

We suggested that all three memory systems in Nelson's (1993) theory of event memory may contribute to people's reconstruction of the date and time of past events in their lives. Generic event memory provides cyclic temporal schemata at different levels as well as recurrent particular dates that can be used as landmarks. Episodic memory of individual event details and relations between events provides cues for accessing the generic schemata as well as associations to relate individual events to each other and to temporal landmarks (e.g., order and duration information). Autobiographical memory, which Nelson distinguishes by its significance to the self, provides information about the temporal structure of the individual's life periods as well as the temporal location of singular events that are significant for delimiting and defining these periods.

In the analyses of the datings collected in a number of our diary studies, we identified three components that represent different mixtures of generic event memory and episodic memory information. First is a *day-of-the-week periodicity*, which is the most well understood and simple component. It seems to reflect application of a generic week schema and to depend only minimally on the availability of details from episodic event memory. Second, the overall, absolute *dating error magnitude* is observed in the width and slope of the error distribution when the weekly peaks are disregarded. The error magnitude probably reflects the use of generic schemata above the week level as well as episodic order and duration information that relate the target event to landmarks in such higher order schemata. Finally, most of the surprisingly high number of *exact datings* observed in the studies seem to arise from the convergent use of several schemata (including the week schema) and landmark events. This conclusion presupposes that sufficient episodic detail is available about the dated event and its relations to other events. However, a minor part of the exact datings exceeds what would be expected on the basis of the two previous components; these exact datings seem to reflect generic knowledge of recurrent dates and occasional retrieval of temporal labels, or tags, stored in episodic memory.

To summarize, we interpret these three components as measures of date reconstruction that depend increasingly on episodic event memory, whereas dependence on generic event memory decreases from the first to the last in the list. In the relatively brief time ranges with which we have worked—compared to the life span of an individual—the utility of information about higher order autobiographical periods and transition events is bound to be limited.

Reconstructing Event Dates:
The Effects of Retention Interval,
Event Characteristics, and
Person Characteristics

In chapter 6, we vigorously advocated the notion that people routinely engage in temporal reconstruction (as opposed to some form of temporal recall), and we attempted to bolster this notion by documenting some of the specific sources of information that people apparently use in those reconstructions. We return to the theme of temporal reconstruction at several points in this chapter and present more evidence supporting this idea. However, another purpose of this chapter is to provide a more general view of patterns of accuracy and error in event dating and also to discuss several variables that may be related to those patterns.

In many ways, the issues that we address in this chapter parallel those addressed for event memory in chapter 3. You may recall that in chapter 3 we were concerned with the relation between retention interval and memory, the relations between various event characteristics (e.g., event content, frequency, person-typicality) and memory, people's ability to predict their memory for events, and some of the variables that are related to these memory predictions. In the present chapter, the same issues are addressed with a focus on event dating. That is, we present data assessing the relations between retention interval and various measures of dating error and accuracy, various event characteristics (e.g., event content, frequency, person-typicality) and dating error and dating accuracy, and people's accuracy predictions and their actual dating accuracy. We also discuss whether these predictions are related both to the characteristics of events and to the different information sources that we discussed in chapter 6. One final topic that we touch on in this chapter is gender: Several of our studies suggest that females tend to be more accurate daters than males. We present data documenting this gender difference, note the limitations on this difference, and discuss why this difference may occur.

A full understanding of our temporal judgment data requires that they be examined in several different ways. In chapter 6, we presented data from one such examination, assessing the frequency with which subjects made errors of various magnitudes and relating those data to issues of date reconstruction and temporal schema use. In the analyses presented in this chapter, we frequently examine three additional key dependent measures: raw error magnitude, which is the difference (in number of days) between the actual date and the estimated date, with the sign of the difference retained; absolute error magnitude, which is simply the absolute value of the raw error; and an exact hit rate measure, which reflects the number of times that an exact date was provided. Variations on these measures (e.g., exact hit rate, deleting hits due to retrieval of a date from memory) are also occasionally reported, often to clarify the processes that appear to be causing particular patterns of results on the main dependent measures.

Where appropriate and informative, both descriptive and inferential statistics are provided for each of these dating measures. The analytic technique that we employed for these inferential analyses was almost always the pooled within-subject multiple regression analysis that we described in detail in chapter 2. The variables used in the regression models were generally the same as used in the analyses described in chapter 3. These include retention interval (both linear and quadratic effects), event memory, and several rated characteristics of the events (e.g., person-typicality). However, in the discussion of gender differences in this chapter, we occasionally revert back to more basic analyses of variance.

RETENTION INTERVAL, DATING ACCURACY, AND DATING ERROR

One of the important issues in event dating is the extent to which dating performance is affected by retention interval. It is logically obvious that dating performance should decrease with retention interval. However, the exact form of that decrease may be affected by several factors. First, the form of the decrease may depend on the exact measure of dating performance used. As we discussed in chapter 3, the form of the relation between retention interval and event memory depended on how one treated the memory measure. When the full memory scale was used, the apparent decrease in memory with retention interval, though curvilinear, was relatively gradual. By comparison, conversion of the memory data to the perfect memory measure (i.e., a binary score in which memory ratings of 6 and 7 were scored as 1 and other ratings were scored as 0) produced a forgetting function that was much more Ebbinghausian, in the sense that it was characterized by a steep drop in recall in short retention intervals. Because we suspect that event dates are sometimes reconstructed from event memory, we thought that similar patterns might be observed in the event dating data. This possibility suggested that we examine the dating data in at least two ways: in terms of the exact dating measure and in terms of the absolute error magnitude measure.

A second factor that may affect the form of the decrease in dating accuracy with lengthening retention interval relates to the idea of anchoring processes. We saw such processes at work in the memory data presented in chapters 1 and 3: The long-term study appeared to produce a much more gradual decrease in memory with lengthening retention interval than our shorter-term studies. We wondered if similar anchoring processes affect the event dates that subjects provide. In particular, we were interested in the possibility that subjects' event dates are systematically biased by their knowledge of the start and end dates of the diary study. The most reasonable possibility is that the erroneous dates provided by subjects would tend to gravitate toward the center of the interval bounded by a study's start and end dates. Assessment of this possibility required examination of the raw dating error, which provides both the direction of the error and the magnitude of the error.

Retention Interval and Exact Dating

As we noted in the previous paragraphs, one way in which we examined dating error was to score each date provided by subjects as either exactly correct or incorrect. These binary exact dating scores were then analyzed using within-subject regression. A dummy vector for subjects, a linear term for retention interval, and a quadratic term for retention interval were the predictors in each regression model. The results were straightforward. Each of the 11 self-event data sets that we examined, all with 10-week to 15-week retention intervals, exhibited both significant linear and quadratic retention interval effects (smallest $F = 12.17$, all $ps < .001$).

The basic form of these effects is illustrated in Fig. 7.1 (in this figure, means for every other day are plotted). Figure 7.1 depicts the exact dating data for six data sets: Three of these data sets had retention intervals of about 15 weeks, and the remaining three had retention intervals of about 10 weeks. (Throughout this chapter, for comparability to other studies, the 88OH and 91OH data presented are for self-events only. To assist comparison between 10-week and 15-week studies, the visual confusion in this figure and other figures containing these data sets is reduced by assigning one common symbol to the shorter term studies and another common symbol to the longer term studies.) The high degree of consistency (with, as always, a few outliers) suggests that the data tell a consistent story. In the most

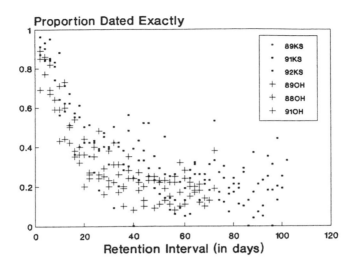

FIG. 7.1. Scatterplot of exact dating data (daily means plotted every second day) for three data sets with 15-week retention intervals and three data sets with 10-week retention intervals.

recent 40 days (approximately), as retention interval lengthens the proportion of exact dates provided decreases relatively rapidly. When the retention interval is longer than 40 days, the exact dating rate is relatively low and decreases relatively slowly with lengthening retention interval.

The general impression left by these data is that people's ability to date events exactly is relatively poor. Even in the most recent week of the diary study, when one might expect subjects to get all the dates correct, dating accuracy was not perfect—instead, subjects tended to be exactly correct only about 85 to 90% of the time. At retention intervals of 3 months (i.e., about 60 to 90 days), subjects were exactly correct only 15 to 20% of the time. In concrete terms, for events that happened in the third month of the retention interval, subjects averaged only five or six exactly dated events. This deficiency in exact dating is all the more surprising given the advantages that our diary procedure should provide to event dating (e.g., opportunity to associate dates with events by writing in the diary, possibility of reviewing event-date relations, possible enhanced sense of event orderings because there were seven consecutive events listed on a common diary sheet).

However, as is always the case in these types of studies, considerable between-subjects variability appeared in dating performance. A sense of these individual differences can be conveyed in two ways. The first comes from the regression analyses done on 11 data sets.[1] The dummy-coded term

---

[1]Many of the analyses that follow were performed on the six data sets shown in Fig. 1.1 plus 79KS, 80KS, 83KS, 86KS, and 87KS.

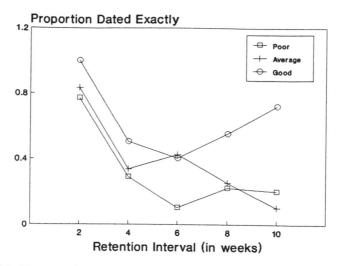

FIG. 7.2. Exact dating data across retention interval for the best dater, the worst dater, and an average dater from the 89OH data set.

for subjects was significant in all 11 data sets (smallest $F(24, 1630) = 4.26$, all $ps < .0001$). Because this term in the model essentially reflects between-subjects differences, these results confirm significant individual differences in terms of overall exact dating accuracy, but simply to say that people were different is neither very informative nor surprising.

A second, potentially more informative way in which between-subjects differences can be conveyed is to plot individual subject means across retention intervals. Such a plot, using the best dater, the worst dater, and an average dater from the 89OH data set, is presented in Fig. 7.2. For purposes of presentational clarity and for stability of the means, the exact dating measure has been collapsed into 2-week blocks. Despite such collapsing, because the means are typically based only 9 or 10 data points, the means depicted in the figure are highly unstable. Nonetheless, as these data indicate, all the subjects showed evidence of a decrease in accuracy across retention interval. Furthermore, although the curvilinearity exhibited is certainly not equivalent across subjects, the response functions for all three subjects tend toward curvilinearity. These data suggest that the general trends that are reflected in the overall data sets are reflective of processes occurring at the level of the individual subjects and are not a consequence of aggregation of data across subjects.

As reflected by the data from two of our subjects, exact dating performance is very poor, especially at long retention intervals. This generally poor dating performance converges quite well with subjects' reports of the cognitive sources of their event dates. As noted in Table 6.2, subjects reported remembering the exact date of an event relatively infrequently. Furthermore, the frequency with which subjects reported being able to recall the exact dates of events decreased with lengthening retention interval.

That subjects cannot often recall the exact date of events, of course, implies that they often have to estimate the date. A sense of the relative importance of date estimation and date retrieval processes across retention intervals can be gained by examining those data sets in which we asked subjects to report on the sources of information used to date their events. More specifically, we can delete from the data those exactly dated events that subjects also reported as directly retrieved from memory (i.e., *recalled-exact* dates). The remainder of the exactly dated events should reflect those cases in which subjects accurately reconstructed the dates of the events. One reasonable expectation, especially given the self-report data shown in Table 6.2, is that the majority of recalled-exact dates will occur for relatively recent events. Hence, removing events for which the date was recalled from the data set should generally have the effect of flattening the relation between exact dating and retention interval. The percentage of events that are exactly correct should decrease substantially relative to unadjusted values in recent retention intervals but should be less affected in later intervals.

In Fig. 7.3 we present a comparison of the exactly correct data and the adjusted exact data (i.e., recalled-exact dates removed) as a function of retention interval (by week) for two data sets, 89KS and 89OH. As the data illustrate, deleting the recalled-exact events from the data set does not alter the form of the relation between the proportion of events exactly dated and retention interval: The basic Ebbinghaus-like curvilinearity was still present.

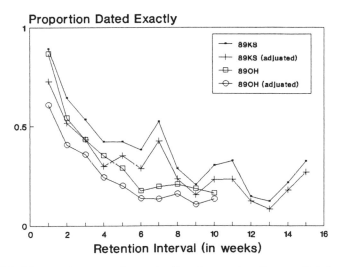

FIG. 7.3. Exactly correct data and adjusted exact data (i.e., recalled dates removed) as a function of retention interval (by week) for two data sets, 89KS and 88OH.

Given that we found similar curvilinearity in event memory and that event memory is one of the prime sources of event date reconstruction, this outcome is not surprising.

Although it may not be readily apparent at first glance, the expected flattening of the response function also occurred. The deletion of events for which the date was recalled had a greater impact at early retention intervals than at later intervals. To illustrate this effect, in Fig. 7.4 we present the calculated difference between the raw proportion of events exactly dated and the proportion of events exactly dated after the recalled-exact deletions were made. As that figure illustrates, when events were a week old, deletion of the recalled-exact events produced a decrease of about 25 percentage points in the proportion of events dated exactly. By the time events were about 4 weeks old, the decrease due to recalled-exact date deletion was reduced to about 10 percentage points, and it remained at or below that level as the retention interval further lengthened.

In many ways, the consistency of the relation between exact dating and retention interval across subjects and across studies is quite comforting. This might lead one to suspect that this response function is relatively invariant. That is, it reflects a basic pattern of degradation in exact dating accuracy that would not be affected by such factors as alterations in the length of the diary study. Unfortunately, appealing as that notion might be, it appears that it is not correct. In fact, there are several hints in our data that the length of the diary study affects the relation between retention interval and exact dating. For example, Fig. 7.1 suggests that the diary studies with a shorter

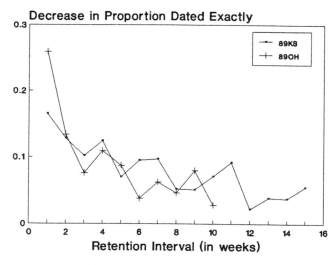

FIG. 7.4. Calculated difference between the raw proportion of events exactly dated and the proportion of events exactly dated after the date-recalled deletions were made for the 89KS and 89OH data sets, by retention interval.

retention interval (i.e., 10 weeks) have a steeper decline in exact dating in the early retention intervals than the studies with a longer retention interval.

A minor confound in this short versus long comparison, is that the shorter term studies were done at Ohio State (on a 10-week academic term) and the longer term studies were done at Kansas State (on a 15-week term). Although the methods used at both institutions were highly similar, minor differences in the procedures or materials could somehow be responsible for these effects. However, we have another reason to believe that a methodological or procedural artifact is not responsible for the effect. Figure 1.3 shows a plot of the proportion of events dated exactly calculated from our long-term study and reveals that the asymptote of the accuracy function is at about 6 months—by that point, subjects were dating only 10% of events exactly. In our shorter term studies, subjects reached that low point in only 40 to 60 days. This seems to be relatively strong evidence that the relation between exact dating and retention interval is affected by the length of the retention interval. However, these data are not yet definitive. It appears that one of the tasks before us in future research is to explore whether the length of the diary study does indeed alter the relation between the proportion of events dated exactly and retention interval and to discover why such an effect may occur.

An immediate explanation for these effects is not readily apparent. However, they may be a consequence of influence of the length of the retention interval on the magnitude and direction of subjects' errors. It is to this phenomenon that we next turn our attention.

Retention Interval and the Direction of Dating Errors

When people estimate the date of events, one source of information potentially available for their estimates is a bounded period. For example, one might know that an event happened while one was on sabbatical, and the start and stop dates of the sabbatical can serve as upper and lower boundaries for the date of the event. As noted by Thompson et al. (1988b; also see Betz & Skowronski, 1995; Huttenlocher et al., 1990; Rubin & Baddeley, 1989; Thompson et al., 1993), event date estimations are systematically distorted by such boundaries. Events near the older boundary tend to exhibit *telescoping*: They are dated as being more recent than their actual date of occurrence. Events near the more recent boundary exhibit *time expansion*: They are dated as occurring before their actual date of occurrence.

Although different psychological explanations such as memory accessibility (Bradburn, Rips, & Shevell, 1987) and assessment of the number of events that intervene between the boundary and the estimated event (Thompson et al., 1988b) have been proffered for these effects. The best explanation probably lies in the simple fact that the boundaries constrain the direction of the errors that are made (Rubin & Baddeley, 1989). For events near the older boundary (assuming the boundary is known), the magnitude of time expansion errors is highly restricted by the boundary, whereas the magnitude of telescoping errors is not. Hence, near the older boundary, dating errors tend to be pushed toward the center of the boundary period, so that overall evidence of telescoping occurs near that boundary. Similarly, at the more recent boundary, the magnitude of telescoping errors is highly restricted, whereas the magnitude of time expansion errors is not. Hence, near the more recent boundary, dating errors again tend to be pushed toward the center of the bounded period, so that evidence of time expansion appears near that boundary. Errors toward the middle of the dating period show no directional preference. Finally, because (as we show in the next section) the tendency toward dating error is greater for events that are older, the telescoping error at the older boundary tends to be somewhat greater than the time expansion error at the recent boundary.

The start and stop dates of our diary studies provide a natural set of boundaries that our subjects can use when dating events. Figure 7.5 presents scatterplots of the mean signed dating error (i.e., the difference in days between the actual date and the estimated date) plotted against retention interval (i.e., means calculated and presented every 2 days) for three 15-week studies and three 10-week studies. As the figure reveals, time expansion near the recent boundary and telescoping near the older boundary were quite pervasive. Regression analyses indicated that all 11 data sets exhibited

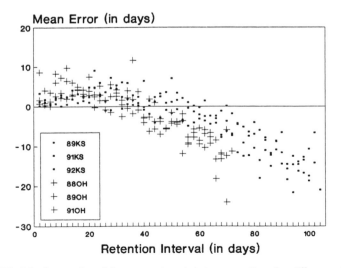

FIG. 7.5. Scatterplot of the mean signed dating error (i.e., the difference in days between the actual date and the estimated date) plotted against retention interval (i.e., daily means calculated and presented every 2 days) for three 15-week studies and three 10-week studies.

significant linear as well as curvilinear relations between retention interval and signed dating error (smallest $F = 11.39$, all $ps < .0001$).

As we noted in the exact error data, one natural question that arises is whether the effects depicted in Fig. 7.5 reflect the response tendencies of individual subjects or whether such effects are somehow a consequence of collapsing the data across all subjects in a study. This question is addressed by the data shown in Fig. 7.6, which presents the signed error data from the same three subjects whose exact dating performance was described earlier: the best dater, the worst dater, and an average dater from the 89OH data set. Considerable variability in dating performance occurred among the subjects. Although the individual means in this figure are highly unstable because of the relatively few observations that go into the calculation of each mean, the general tendency is for individual subjects to show the same kinds of response patterns that are depicted in the overall data. All three subjects show evidence of telescoping due to the date set by the oldest boundary. The good dater shows little evidence of consistent time expansion at the upper bound, but the other two subjects show time expansion effects.

The consistency of the error function produced across studies and subjects is quite impressive. However, this consistency is likely a partial consequence of the relatively short retention interval used in many of the studies. Indeed, the boundary hypothesis implicitly suggests that the nature of the relation between signed error magnitude and the retention interval is affected by the length of the retention interval: Compressing the interval should "squeeze" the error function, whereas stretching the interval should "stretch" the function.

Some evidence of these effects can be seen in Fig. 7.5, which presents data from both the 10-week and the 15-week studies. Because Fig. 7.5 assigns one

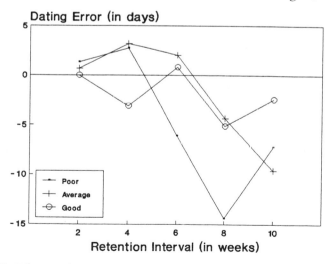

FIG. 7.6. Signed error data from the best dater, the worst dater, and an average dater from the 89OH data set.

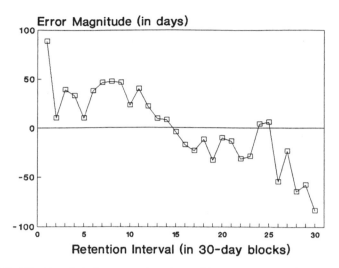

FIG. 7.7. Signed dating error plotted monthly over a 30-month retention interval for the long-term study.

common symbol to the 15-week studies and a second symbol to the 10-week studies, it is easy to see that both time expansion and telescoping effects occur earlier in the 10-week than in the 15-week studies. This conclusion is more than an "eyeball" analysis. In a prior paper (Thompson et al., 1993), we used an ANOVA to directly compare the response functions produced by the 89KS and 89OH data sets in the first 8 weeks of each study and found a significant Boundary Condition × Retention Interval interaction, $F(7, 427) = 4.67, p < .001$.

Of course, the difference in retention interval between the 10-week and 15-week studies is relatively small, so the consequent difference in the signed error-retention interval relation between studies is also small. However, because of its 2-year retention interval, the long-term study should have a more stretched response function. This is exactly what the data show. In Fig. 7.7, the signed dating error is plotted monthly over approximately a 30-month retention interval. In the short-term studies, subjects showed evidence of time expansion for retention intervals of about 30 to 40 days; in the long-term study, time expansion effects occurred for an interval of about 13 months. At a 3-month retention interval, subjects in the short-term studies showed significant telescoping; in the long-term study, they continued to show time expansion.

The signed dating error measure is useful for conveying information about the general direction of the biases exhibited by subjects in their dating attempts. However, it is not very useful for conveying information about the nature of the relation between the absolute magnitude of subjects' dating errors and retention interval. We investigate this measure of dating error in the next section.

Retention Interval and the Absolute Magnitude of Dating Error

The exact dating data presented earlier in this chapter suggested that dating performance declines sharply in recent retention intervals, then more slowly in later intervals. This pattern may lead one to suspect that an error magnitude measure (i.e., the absolute value of the dating error) may evince a similar pattern. However, our experience with the memory measures discussed in the first half of this book suggests that something a bit different will emerge. That is, the relation between error magnitude and retention interval may, indeed, show more of an increase in early than in later retention intervals, but the effect will be relatively gradual, not exhibiting the sharp shift that is present in the binary exact dating data.

The form of the relation between retention interval and the magnitude of subjects' dating errors is depicted in Fig. 7.8, which presents the data from three 15-week studies and from three 10-week studies. The figure displays a consistent linear increase in error magnitude with increasing retention interval, a perception that is confirmed by our regression analyses of the 11 data sets (smallest $F = 125.97$, all $ps < .0001$). As illustrated by the data presented in Fig. 7.9, the data from individual subjects (i.e., the same three subjects whose data have been presented in earlier sections in this chapter) suggest that this effect occurs at the level of individual subjects and is not an artifact of pooling across subjects.

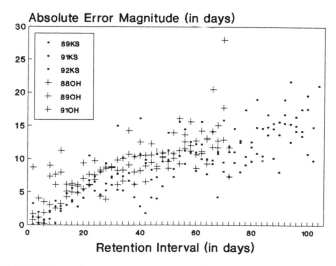

FIG. 7.8. Relation between retention interval and the magnitude of subjects' dating errors (means for every second day plotted) for three 15-week studies and from three 10-week studies.

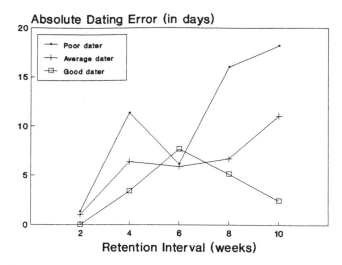

FIG. 7.9. Error magnitude data from the best dater, the worst dater, and an average dater from the 89OH data set.

In contrast to this robust linear effect, the curvilinearity in the data was relatively weak. The expected negatively accelerating response function (i.e., larger error increases in early intervals, smaller error increases in later intervals) emerged in 11 of the 12 data sets. This effect was statistically reliable in only 6 of the data sets, and it approached significance in two others. Because of the modest curvilinearity in the absolute error data, this measure leads to a somewhat different conclusion about the relation between retention interval and dating accuracy than the exact dating measure. More specifically, the error magnitude measure suggests that dating performance decreases relatively uniformly with increasing retention interval. In the recent retention intervals, no sharp decrease in accuracy (which here would be reflected by a sharp increase in error) of the kind reflected in the exact dating measure occurs. Moreover, there is relatively little evidence of the leveling off error at long retention intervals that is exhibited by the exact dating measure. One gets the sense that dating error would continue to increase further with even longer retention intervals.

This expectation is confirmed by the results of the long-term memory study. The relation between absolute error magnitude and dating error in that study is depicted in Fig. 7.10, which clearly indicates that the magnitude of dating error continues to increase linearly with lengthening retention interval ($F(1, 3501) = 229.12$). The curvilinear effect did not approach statistical reliability in the long-term data.

A comparison of the data in Fig. 7.10 with the data in Fig. 7.8 also indicates that the length of the retention interval does not appear to have much of an impact on the shape of the error magnitude function. In the short-term studies,

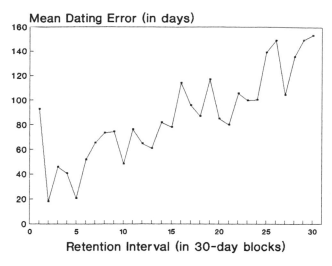

FIG. 7.10. Relation between absolute error magnitude and dating error in the long-term study.

the rate of increase in error magnitude with lengthening retention interval is roughly 5 days of error for every month (i.e., approximately 30 days) of retention interval. This is quite similar to the rate of increase observed in the long-term study. This result contrasts strongly with the data from the exact dating and raw signed error magnitude measures, both of which exhibited some degree of sensitivity to the length of the retention interval.

THE CONTENT OF EVENTS AND DATING ACCURACY

Another issue of interest is in this chapter is whether a consistent relation exists between the content of events and the dating accuracy or error magnitude associated with the event. We approach this problem in two ways. First, we present samples of individual events from the diaries and examine the content of the events in relation to the dating error magnitude associated with each event. Second, for a more general view, we apply the content analysis categories described in chapter 3, searching for general event content factors that may be related to dating accuracy and error magnitude.

Event Samples

To provide a general feeling for the relation between events and event dating, we present some of the events that were listed in subjects' diaries and report the error magnitudes associated with those events. All the examples listed here are events that subjects attempted to date 10 to 15 weeks after they were listed in the diaries. This first group of events were dated well: In fact, subjects reported the date exactly.

> Received a phone call about my dad's death.
> We had our first cross country meet at Iowa State. It was on a golf course and golfers played through!
> I had surgery on my foot at Memorial Hospital.

This second group of events were dated moderately well: They had error magnitudes from 2 to 7 days.

> Anne and I watched Frank compete in the Little Apple triathalon.
> Went to an all-campus party at Phi Delta.
> First chemistry lab of the semester. I didn't get everything done.

This third group of events were poorly dated: They had error magnitudes greater than 10 days.

> Highlighted Linda's hair while she talked on the phone.
> Went over to Tim and Brian's to see their new couch.
> While talking on the phone to the cable company, the cable came back on the air. I was so embarrassed!

Obviously, these event listings cannot provide a complete picture of the relation between event content and event dating error magnitude. However, perusal of these events yields some preliminary ideas about the relation between event content and dating accuracy. For example, the exactly dated events are such that they are likely to promote storage of the exact date in memory or are likely to be strongly associated with a schedule or temporal schema such as the death of a parent, the first cross-country meet, or foot surgery. The moderately well-dated events seem to be somewhat unusual but not enough to warrant an exact date, and they are not strongly tied enough to a temporal schema to be exactly reconstructed. Finally, the poorly dated events seem to be drawn from the events in a person's life that are not likely to be at all tied to ideas about time. We explore some of these themes in our subsequent analyses.

Content Analyses

Obviously, although event sampling can be useful for getting a feel for the data, a different method should be used to convey the relations between event content and the dependent measures of dating accuracy and error magnitude. After all, if we were unscrupulous, we could intentionally select events that could mislead about the relations between content and the dependent measures. Thus, in an attempt to investigate content-exact dating and content-error magnitude relations more systematically, as in chapter 3 we conducted a content analysis of two data sets (88OH and 91OH, self-events only). The results of these analyses are presented in Table 7.1. In our content analysis we categorized the data in several different ways—by type of person(s) involved in the event, by location, by activity type, and so on. Because each event can be placed into several categories, we report only the results of descriptive analyses—the mean error magnitude for events in each category and the percentage of events in each category that were exactly dated.

The content analysis did not significantly aid in the understanding of the memory data that we reported in chapter 3, and because event memory is one of the primary sources used in the reconstruction of event dates, one might expect a similar outcome to emerge for the dating measures. However, an examination of the data reported in Table 7.1 suggests that the content analysis is somewhat useful in understanding event dating. Unlike the memory data, the event data show differences in dating accuracy across the content categories, and at least some of these differences seem to hold up across both studies.

Other Person(s) Involved in the Event. One of the ways that we classified events was by the other person(s) involved in the event. This classification yielded several interesting outcomes. For example, events in the category of family group were associated with low error magnitude and were frequently dated exactly. Because gatherings involving family groups often occur on holidays and special occasions, it is not surprising that such events were dated well. The dating accuracy and error for the holidays and special events category (listed in the activities superordinate category) showed similar results: low error magnitude and a high proportion of exactly dated events. Although the event memory data presented in Table 3.2 suggest that these family gatherings are generally associated with somewhat heightened memory ratings, the high proportion of exactly dated events in this category suggests that event memory may play only a small role in people's ability to provide dates for family gathering events. Instead, exact dates may be remembered, or the dates may be reconstructed from temporal schemata or from real-world knowledge.

Other potentially sensible relations between person categories and dating also emerged. For example, for numerous reasons (e.g., richer, more detailed knowledge structures), event dates for events involving family members may be more accurate than events involving unrelated others. The data in Table 7.1 hint at such an effect. For example, in both data sets, family members are associated with the lowest error magnitudes ($Ms = 7.33$ and 7.60), friends with average error magnitudes ($Ms = 8.78$ and 7.99) and acquaintances and strangers (data combined) with the highest error magnitudes ($Ms = 9.96$ and 8.23).

Two findings are notable regarding the data in the love-related category. First, dating error magnitude is lower and exact dating rates higher for the

TABLE 7.1
Mean Absolute Dating Error Magnitude and Percentage of Events
Dated Exactly by Content Categories, 88OS and 91OS Self-Event Data

		88OS			91OS	
Content	N	Mean Error	% Exact	N	Mean Error	% Exact
I. Others in event						
A. Family						
mother	81	7.09	.370	88	7.78	.352
father	56	10.07	.232	46	6.41	.391
sister	28	10.46	.285	31	10.12	.322
brother	30	6.27	.433	13	10.61	.231
husband	24	6.16	.291	45	7.28	.267
wife	–	–	–	16	4.18	.375
son	25	4.56	.360	73	10.23	.178
daughter	30	7.50	.267	37	7.78	.270
nonimmediate family	123	7.29	.358	47	8.45	.425
family group	27	3.96	.629	97	4.96	.484
B. Friends						
same sex	155	7.29	.354	117	9.68	.214
opposite sex	23	9.86	.260	67	6.56	.313
old	40	9.85	.325	8	12.37	.000
new	2	10.00	.000	0	–	–
unspecified	35	12.05	.228	36	9.41	.416
group of friends	111	9.21	.333	133	6.60	.421
C. Love related						
boyfriend	133	6.39	.368	141	7.17	.382
girlfriend	44	10.34	.181	1	0.00	1.000
ex-boyfriend	15	11.47	.267	19	14.89	.210
ex-girlfriend	6	10.67	.167	0	–	–
unspecified	73	9.00	.328	38	10.15	.236
D. Acquaintance						
same sex	4	12.00	.250	21	4.47	.428
opposite sex	1	9.00	.000	32	7.37	.218
old	–	–	–	1	5.00	.000
new	1	0.00	1.00	0	–	–
unspecified	8	14.37	.125	23	11.26	.097
group	2	6.50	.500	18	10.44	.222
E. Strangers						
same sex	2	3.00	.500	10	4.60	.200
opposite sex	4	7.25	.250	15	10.40	.000
unspecified	1	11.00	.000	11	17.36	.091
group	4	9.50	.250	10	11.50	.000
II. Activities						
sports related	148	8.21	.243	124	7.75	.331
party activities	101	8.06	.405	73	8.48	.383
music related	39	8.23	.435	15	8.80	.333
food related	284	7.62	.387	226	8.60	.336
media	127	9.00	.331	108	8.90	.315

(Continued)

140

TABLE 7.1
(Continued)

Content	N	88OS Mean Error	88OS % Exact	N	91OS Mean Error	91OS % Exact
sexual	6	7.00	.333	2	0.00	1.000
rest/relaxation	74	9.32	.324	74	12.81	.189
socializing/commun.	92	8.51	.293	226	10.40	.203
holiday/special occasions	202	3.31	.698	108	3.03	.620
holidays/entertainment	8	6.50	.250	127	7.69	.314
health related	51	9.07	.274	54	7.57	.314
law	19	4.68	.421	11	8.82	.272
shopping/purchasing	178	7.88	.286	167	7.16	.233
home improvements/chores	105	9.57	.285	79	10.34	.304
car/vehicle related	68	9.75	.220	99	9.17	.212
school related	463	9.22	.302	477	9.15	.293
work related	167	9.22	.263	154	9.70	.305
family related	15	10.13	.200	80	8.60	.312
personal appearance/fitness	66	9.27	.288	44	10.09	.250
volunteer/civic work	14	6.78	.428	9	6.44	.444
pet related	35	8.05	.229	27	13.74	.259
financial	35	6.20	.342	41	10.92	.195
personal favors	83	8.57	.253	60	7.27	.412
church	47	7.70	.468	20	5.40	.450
other	51	6.98	.313	91	9.89	.318
III. Unforeseen						
health	124	9.60	.306	64	8.37	.250
car/vehicle	80	11.56	.212	38	8.13	.078
conflicts	38	8.00	.210	39	8.49	.231
birth/death	11	8.54	.272	15	6.80	.333
home	12	6.92	.333	12	8.83	.250
emotional	34	7.85	.382	64	8.28	.266
weather	32	4.50	.375	41	10.78	.146
school	142	8.39	.147	57	10.56	.175
sports	16	12.62	.187	6	5.00	.167
love related	33	4.54	.272	21	6.09	.428
work	167	8.49	.281	41	10.80	.122
other	48	9.58	.229	32	7.25	.281
IV. Location						
home	50	9.80	.280	272	11.77	.242
school	31	10.41	.258	130	8.66	.246
work	13	7.46	.307	40	13.00	.225
church	2	3.50	.500	11	7.81	.454
public	309	8.99	.288	305	7.82	.324
other	123	6.57	.414	115	10.13	.313

category of boyfriend than for the category of girlfriend. Because our subjects' sexual orientations seemed to be predominantly heterosexual, we interpret this outcome in terms of the gender of the rater: Females were more accurate daters for events involving their boyfriends than males were for their girl-friends. Although distastefully stereotypic, this interpretation is consistent with data that we present later suggesting that females are more often exactly correct than males in their dating efforts.

The second outcome of note in the love interest data is that events involving current love interests are dated more accurately than events involving ex-love interests. This is interesting because the memory ratings for the events involving ex-love interests tend to be quite high compared to memory ratings for current love interests (see Table 3.2). Thus, although one can have good memory for events, it is not automatically true that event dating will also be accurate for well-recalled events. Instead, the ability of event recall to facilitate dating estimates will depend on the date cues that are involved in recall for the event. Apparently our two data sets included relatively few useful event dating cues in the otherwise strong memories surrounding encounters with ex-love interests.

Activities. The data within the activities category demonstrated some differences among events in terms of error magnitude and exact dating. Events that are relatively routine or a part of everyday life seem to be associated with heightened error magnitude. For example, categories such as rest and relaxa-tion, socializing and communication, home improvements and chores, car-related events, school events, work events, and fitness activities were not dated very accurately. By comparison, relatively unusual events, perhaps also associated with specific dates, were dated relatively accurately. As we have already noted, the category of holidays and special occasions contained such items. Other events that were, relatively speaking, dated accurately in both data sets were in the categories of volunteer and civic work, holidays and entertainment, shopping and purchasing, and church.

One category that exhibits somewhat unusual characteristics is the category of party activities. People exhibited a relatively high exact dating rate for events in this category, but the magnitude of dating error is only average. This finding suggests a split in the kinds of parties that subjects were involved in. Some parties were probably strongly associated with calendar dates and so were dated exactly. Other parties were probably impromptu or informal. Recon-struction of the dates of such informal parties, especially when they occur as frequently as they seem to in the lives of many students, is probably difficult (the reader is left to speculate on the various causes of such difficulties).

Unforeseen Events. In our content analysis, we included a superordi-nate category for events that were unexpected or unforeseen, and we looked at event dating accuracy for individual event types within the broad class of unforeseen events. Unfortunately, little consistency in dating accuracy appeared across specific event types. The only category that seemed to exhibit consistent facilitation across both data sets was that including unexpected love-related events. Results for other content categories were inconsistent across the two data sets or did not show either substantial facilitation or degradation in dating performance. In fact, contrary to what one might expect, unforeseen events did not seem to increase the frequency of exact dating (as might be expected from Thompson's Red Letter Day hypothesis; see Thompson, 1985a), nor did they reduce error magnitude.

Event Location. Like unforeseen events, the location categories that we used in the content analysis were not powerfully related to dating accuracy and error magnitude, but some small effects appeared. For example, these data suggest that the routine, everyday events in our lives are not dated well. For example, events that occur at home are dated relatively poorly, as are events at school. By comparison (and consistent with the data presented previously), events that occurred at church were dated relatively well.

THE RATED CHARACTERISTICS OF EVENTS AND EVENT DATING

Predicting Dating Accuracy and Error

The results of the content analysis provide one quantitative demonstration that the characteristics of events are related to dating accuracy and error. Another approach is to investigate this relation using subjects' ratings for each event. We adopted this approach, and we report the results of some of our investigations in this section. However, because we have a longstanding interest in the variables of event affective intensity and event valence and because we have those two predictors in most of our studies, we delay discussion of those predictors until chapter 8. In this section, we explore the relations between the dating accuracy and error dependent measures and subjects' ratings of event frequency, event person typicality, event rehearsal, event emotionality, and the initial mental involvement prompted by an event.

Because of the nature of regression analysis, we were confronted with several difficult choices about how to proceed with our analyses. By comparison, our memory analyses were relatively straightforward: In memory analyses, we were most interested in which of the event ratings uniquely predicted memory. This interest was prompted by past research and by theoretical issues, such as Banaji and Hardin's (1994) claim that valence effects in memory are a consequence of the differential extremity of events. In the memory analyses, then, our general strategy was to employ regression models with multiple simultaneous predictors and to employ nonsimultaneous models (e.g., one variable at a time) in subsidiary analyses only when they were necessary to understand the data better.

By comparison, we did not have the results of prior research and theory to guide our choices of analyses for event dating accuracy and error. After considerable thought, we settled on the following strategy. In general, we segregated our predictors into two classes: variables describing external characteristics of events (e.g., frequency, person-typicality) and variables describing an individual's internal responses to events (e.g., emotionality, rehearsal, initial mental involvement). We then ran initial regression models, entering all the predictors of interest in a given class into any given model. If one or more of the predictors was not statistically reliable, we conducted a follow-up analysis with the nonsignificant measure entered into the model (along with our other usual entries) to see if the predictor was at all related to the dependent measure. Thus, these analyses allow us to examine both whether a variable significantly predicts event dating and whether it predicts event dating uniquely (e.g., in the context of other predictors within the same class).

Our interest in the extent to which dating is aided by event memory prompted a set of additional analyses. In these analyses, we examined whether each predictor was related to the dependent measure, even when event memory was accounted for in the regression models. Memory certainly needs to be accounted for: In all the data sets, event memory significantly predicts both error magnitude (smallest $F(1, 2569) = 17.85$, $p < .0001$) and exact dating (smallest $F(1, 1628) = 28.06$, $p < .0001$). If predictor–dating relations persist with event memory in the regression models, then it would appear that the predictor is effective because it is related to factors that are independent of event memory (such as temporal schemata or date recall). If the relation between a predictor and a dating measure dissipates with memory entered into the model, then the relation between a predictor and dating would seem to be mediated largely by reconstructions from event memory.

Event Frequency. In three data sets (89KS, 91KS, and 92KS) we asked subjects to provide a rating of the base rate frequency for each event. This is essentially a rating of how often the type of event depicted in the description occurs (the measure was scaled so that higher ratings indicate greater infrequency). In all three data sets, the data indicated that infrequent events were associated with lower error magnitude (89KS $F(1, 2851) = 21.13$, $p < .0001$, $\beta = -.086$; 91KS $F(1, 1629) = 5.96$, $p < .02$, $\beta = -.061$; 92KS $F(1, 3255) = 13.94$, $p < .001$, $\beta = -.064$). However, in two of the data sets, this effect dissipated when the predictive relation between event frequency and error magnitude controlled for the memory ratings (89KS $F(1, 2850) = 4.87$, $p < .03$, $\beta = -.042$; 91KS $F(1, 1628) = 1.58$, $p > .21$, $\beta = -.032$; 92KS $F(1,$

3254) = .77, $p > .40$, β = −.015). Thus, these data suggest that event frequency primarily contributes to exact dating by prompting event memory, although infrequency may also be somewhat related to the recall of other cues (e.g., date recall) that contribute to event dating.

The same conclusion can be derived from analyses of the exact dating variable. In all three data sets, events that were infrequent were associated with significantly higher exact dating rates than were frequent events (89KS $F(1, 2851) = 10.65$, $p < .01$, β = .060; 91KS $F(1, 1629) = 4.31$, $p < .04$, β = .049; 92KS $F(1, 3255) = 33.35$, $p < .0001$, β = .094). Again, in two of the three cases, entering the memory variable into the model eliminated the predictive relation between event frequency and exact dating (89KS $F(1, 2850) = .23$, $p > .63$, β = .008; 91KS $F(1, 1628) = .16$, $p > .70$, β = .009; 92KS $F(1, 3254) = 5.32$, $p < .03$, β = .037).

Event Person-Typicality. The data suggest that the person typicality of an event is related to event dating. For both data sets that included person-typicality as a predictor, person-typical events were significantly associated with greater error magnitude than person-atypical events (88OH $F(1, 3224) = 19.31$, $p < .0001$, β = .078; 91OH $F(1, 2265) = 8.28$, $p < .01$, β = .065). However, in one data set (88OH), there was an indication that substantially lower error magnitude was associated with both extremely typical events ($M = 6.58$) and extremely atypical events ($M = 7.66$). Both of these means were substantially lower than the error for the five other possible ratings on the response scale (lowest $M = 8.45$). This lowering of error for both extreme person-typical and person-atypical events produced a significant quadratic typicality effect, $F(1, 3223) = 19.61$, $p < .0001$. This curvilinear effect did not emerge in the 91OH data set.

The data sets are also not consistent regarding whether these person-typicality effects are due to event memory. Entering the memory ratings into the regression model rendered the relation between person-typicality and error magnitude nonsignificant in the 91OH data set, $F(1, 2264) = 1.34$, $p > .25$, β = .025. However, it did not eliminate the linear or quadratic relation between person-typicality and error magnitude in the 88OH data set (linear $F(1, 3223) = 7.99$, $p < .01$, β = .050; quadratic $F(1, 3222) = 8.44$, $p < .01$).

The results for the exact dating variable were similar to those reported previously. In both data sets, events that were person-typical were associated with lower exact dating rates than person-atypical events, but this effect was statistically reliable in only one data set (88OH $F(1, 3224) = 6.52$, $p < .02$, β = −.043; 91OH $F(1, 2265) = 1.91$, $p < .17$, β = −.029). Like the error magnitude data, the exact dating data for the 88OH data revealed a significant curvilinear effect, $F(1, 3223) = 20.85$, $p < .0001$. Inspection of the means indicated that this curvilinear effect was largely due to increased exact dating for extremely person-typical events ($M − .37$) relative to other ratings (largest

$M = .33$, smallest $M = .29$). In contrast to the finding from the error magnitude data, the linear person-typicality effect in the 88OH data set was eliminated by the addition of the memory ratings to the regression model, $F(1, 3223) = .28$, $p > .60$, $\beta = -.008$, but the quadratic effect remained significant, $F(1, 3222) = 8.44$, $p < .01$.

In combination, these data suggest that the relation between person-typicality and error magnitude may be substantially mediated by event memory. However, the data also hint at the possibility that the attributes of highly person-typical and highly person-atypical events may invoke factors such as temporal schemata that aid event dating independent of event memory.

Emotionality. The data suggest that the emotionality prompted by an event is associated with dating error. For all three data sets that included emotionality as a predictor, higher emotionality was significantly associated with lowered error (89KS $F(1, 2851) = 10.74$, $p < .01$, $\beta = -.065$; 91KS $F(1, 1629) = 4.92$, $p < .05$, $\beta = -.065$; 92KS $F(1, 3255) = 14.89$, $p < .001$, $\beta = -.071$). However, in the single data set obtaining measures of both rehearsal and emotionality, the addition of rehearsal to the regression model eliminated the predictive relation between emotionality and error magnitude, 91KS $F(1, 1628) = 1.15$, $p > .30$, $\beta = -.033$. Moreover, regression models examining the predictive relation between emotionality and error magnitude with the memory ratings in the model indicated no such relation in all three data sets (89KS $F(1, 2850) = .87$, $p > .35$, $\beta = -.019$; 91KS $F(1, 1628) = 1.43$, $p > .23$, $\beta = -.035$; 92KS $F(1, 3254) = .36$, $p > .54$, $\beta = -.011$). Thus, these results suggest that the relation between emotionality and error may be mediated almost entirely by event memory.

A similar conclusion emerges from the data examining the relation between event emotionality and exact dating. The results of the regression analyses indicated that emotionality significantly predicted exact dating: Higher emotionality was associated with higher exact dating rates (89KS $F(1, 2851) = 12.30$, $p < .001$, $\beta = .068$; 91KS $F(1, 1628) = 4.77$, $p < .05$, $\beta = .064$; 92KS $F(1, 3255) = 27.62$, $p < .0001$, $\beta = .093$). The 91KS data set contained measures of both rehearsal and emotionality, so the regression results indicate that rehearsal does not eliminate the predictive relation between event emotionality and exact dating.

However, event memory has a substantial impact on that relation. Regression models examining whether emotionality predicts exact dating in the context of event memory indicated that the memory measure eliminated the predictive relation between emotionality and exact dating in two data sets (89KS $F(1, 2850) = .72$, $p > .40$, $\beta = .017$; 91KS $F(1, 1628) = 3.91$, $p < .05$, $\beta = .055$; 92KS $F(1, 3254) = 1.54$, $p > .22$, $\beta = .022$). These data suggest that event emotionality primarily contributes to exact dating by prompting event memory.

Rehearsal. The data suggest that the mental rehearsal prompted by an event is associated with dating error. The results of the regression analyses indicated that, in all five data sets containing the rehearsal measure, higher rehearsal rates were associated with significantly lower error magnitude (79KS $F(1, 2570) = 18.61$, $p < .0001$, $\beta = -.084$; 80KS $F(1, 2408) = 79.36$, $p < .0001$, $\beta = -.187$; 83KS $F(1, 1606) = 26.21$, $p < .0001$, $\beta = -.142$; 91KS $F(1, 1628) = 10.12$, $p < .01$, $\beta = -.087$; 91OH $F(1, 2264) = 9.37$, $p < .01$, $\beta = -.065$). Furthermore, the relation between rehearsal and error magnitude is apparently independent of other psychological factors: The result reported for the 91KS data set included emotionality in the regression model, and the result reported above for the 91OH data set included initial mental involvement in the model. The same independence is sometimes observed when event memory is entered into the regression models. With the memory ratings in the models, the rehearsal–exact dating relation was significant in two data sets, approached significance in a third data set, and was not significant in the other two (79KS $F(1, 2569) = 4.32$, $p < .05$, $\beta = -.045$; 80KS $F(1, 2407) = 14.22$, $p < .001$, $\beta = -.097$; 83KS $F(1, 1605) = .46$, $p > .50$, $\beta = -.022$; 91KS $F(1, 1628) = 3.76$, $p < .06$, $\beta = -.052$; 91OH $F(1, 2264) = 1.04$, $p > .31$, $\beta = .022$). These data thus suggest that event memory is strongly involved in the relation between rehearsal and error magnitude, but not exclusively so. Other factors also appear to contribute to this relation.

A similar conclusion comes from examination of the exact dating data. For all five data sets that included rehearsal as a predictor, the results of the regression analyses indicated that higher rehearsal rates were significantly associated with higher accuracy rates (79KS $F(1, 2570) = 16.12$, $p < .0001$, $\beta = .078$; 80KS $F(1, 2408) = 106.24$, $p < .0001$, $\beta = .206$; 83KS $F(1, 1606) = 51.55$, $p < .0001$, $\beta = .190$; 91KS $F(1, 1628) = 9.88$, $p < .01$, $\beta = .081$; 91OH $F(1, 2264) = 15.77$, $p < .001$, $\beta = .080$). The relation between rehearsal and exact dating is apparently independent of some other psychological factors: The result reported for the 91KS data set included emotionality in the regression model, and the result reported for the 91OH data set included initial mental involvement in the model. However, regression models examining the relation between rehearsal and exact dating in the context of the memory ratings showed that the relation was significant in one data set, approached significance in two data sets, and was not significant in the other two (79KS $F(1, 2569) = .27$, $p > .61$, $\beta = -.011$; 80KS $F(1, 2407) = 8.67$, $p < .01$, $\beta = .071$; 83KS $F(1, 1605) = 2.46$, $p < .12$, $\beta = .049$; 91KS $F(1, 1628) = 2.29$, $p < .14$, $\beta = .039$; 91OH $F(1, 2264) = .17$, $p > .69$, $\beta = .008$). These data thus suggest that event memory also is strongly involved in the relation between rehearsal and exact dating, but perhaps not exclusively so. Other factors (e.g., temporal schemata, date recall) may also contribute to this relation.

Initial Mental Involvement. Only one data set (91OH) explored whether initial mental involvement was related to event dating. The data suggest that higher initial mental involvement is related to lower dating error magnitude and that this relation is independent of rehearsal, $F(1, 2264) = 7.96$, $p < .01$, $\beta = -.061$. However, when the data were entered into a model in which the memory ratings were also being used to predict dating error magnitude, the relation between initial mental involvement and dating error magnitude was nonsignificant, $F(1, 2264) = .07$, $p > .80$, $\beta = -.005$. The same results characterize the exact dating measure. Initial mental involvement significantly predicts the exact dating rate, even when event rehearsal is controlled, $F(1, 2264) = 5.77$, $p < .02$, $\beta = .050$, but not when event memory is controlled, $F(1, 2264) = .01$, $p > .90$, $\beta = .002$. Although the relative lack of data on this measure should lead to caution, these results suggest that event memory mediates the relation between initial mental involvement and event dating.

Reports of Information Source Use and Dating Accuracy

Another way to approach the relation between the characteristics of events and dating accuracy is to examine subjects' self-reports of the sources of information that they used to construct event dates and how those sources relate to dating accuracy. In chapter 6, we noted that we sometimes asked subjects to tell us the information sources that they used to derive the dates that they provided. Subjects often could not recall an event date but instead estimated the date from one or more alternative sources of information (e.g., event memory, temporal schemata, etc.). In this section, we address the question of whether some of those sources provide better fodder than others for the reconstruction of event dates.

We analyzed the absolute magnitude of the dating error associated with each of seven information sources reported by subjects: (1) remembered date, (2) estimated date relative to another event, (3) dated relative to a general time period, (4) estimated the number of events that have occurred since the event to be dated, (5) used the clarity of memory for an event to construct an estimate, (6) used prototypic information from the event to construct an estimate, and (7) guessed. Statistical analysis was accomplished by means of pooled within-subject regression, with absolute magnitude of dating error as the dependent measure and linear retention interval, quadratic retention interval, information source, and a dummy vector representing subjects as predictors.

We present the data from the three data sets that contain assessments of information sources (i.e., 89KS, 89OH and 91OH). The data from these studies all converge on a common conclusion: The sources of information that people report using to provide dates are related to the magnitude of the dating error (smallest $F(6, 1578) = 22.96$, all $ps < .0001$). The mean error magnitude for each information source, presented by study, is presented in Table 7.2.

As these data indicate, people were quite accurate (but not perfectly so) when they reported remembering the exact date. They were also somewhat accurate when they used two sources that tie strongly into temporal infor-

TABLE 7.2
Relation Between Subjects' Reports of Information Sources
Used to Provide an Event Date and the Absolute Magnitude
of Error in Dating (in Days)

	Study		
	89KS	*89OH*	*91OH*
Knew exact date	1.08	1.41	1.93
Used reference event	4.00	4.26	7.40
Knew general reference period	9.19	8.62	8.67
Estimated number of intervening events	11.81	10.03	12.14
Used memory clarity to estimate	11.46	10.25	11.46
Used prototypic information	10.00	13.58	13.76
Guessed	15.38	2.43	15.93

mation—the use of a reference event to aid dating (e.g., before or after my test) and the use of a general reference period (e.g., sometime during finals week). The reference event source appears to lead to greater dating precision than the reference period source. Dating performance was moderately poor when subjects were forced to rely on recall of event orders (e.g., intervening events), event memory, or event prototypes (e.g., this is a weekday event). Guessing appears to lead to the worst dating of all. The apparently high level of accuracy for the 89OH data set is based on only seven observations, so it is highly unstable.

SUBJECTS' ESTIMATES OF DATING ACCURACY

In the early diary studies, one of the things that seemed to be quite obvious from our observations of subjects' behaviors during diary testing was that they had some sense of whether they knew or were even close to the exact date of an event. This possibility is bolstered by the fact that subjects' reports of the sources of knowledge used to construct their date estimates are related to actual dating error (see Table 7.2). To pursue more directly the extent to which subjects were aware of the accuracy of the dates that they provided, in several studies we asked subjects to estimate the accuracy in days. We examine these confidence estimates in three ways. First, we examine the extent to which these estimates actually predict absolute error magnitude. Second, we examine the extent to which the error estimates are related to the information sources that subjects report using to construct event dates. Third, we examine whether the various characteristics of events (e.g., valence) and retention interval predict the accuracy estimates.

Predicting Actual Error Magnitude
From Estimated Error

If subjects have some degree of awareness of the accuracy of the event dates that they provide, then their estimates of accuracy should be related to the magnitude of the dating errors that are made. To investigate this possibility, we conducted regression analyses in which the absolute magnitude of the dating error for an event was the dependent measure, and the linear and quadratic effects of retention interval, subjects' error estimates, and a vector representing the effects of subjects were the predictors.

Four data sets contained such error estimates (i.e., 89KS, 92KS, 89OH, and 91OH). The data from these studies converge on a common conclusion: People's error estimates are related to the dating errors that they make. In all four data sets, estimated error was strongly and positively related to actual error (βs = .322, .334, .235, and .253, respectively, smallest $F(1, 1584)$ = 75.39, all ps < .0001). Although not perfect, people have some sense of the accuracy of the event dates that they provide.

Predicting Error Estimates From Information Used
in Event Dating

Earlier in this chapter, we noted that people were able to report the information sources that they used to construct event dates and that these sources were related to actual dating error. If people are aware of the accuracy of their estimates (as the analyses in the previous section of this chapter suggest), then these information sources also should be predictive of the error estimates that people construct. To investigate this possibility, we conducted regression analyses in which the dependent measure was subjects' error estimates for each event and the predictors were the linear and quadratic effects of retention interval, the dating source that subjects reported using, and a vector representing the effects of subjects.

We have three data sets that contain both error range estimates and assessments of information sources (i.e., 89KS, 89OH, and 91OH). Again, the data from these studies converge on a common conclusion: The sources of information that people report using to provide their dates are related to the error range provided for each estimate (smallest $F(6, 1578)$ = 133.19, all ps < .0001). The mean error estimate for each information source, by study, is presented in Table 7.3.

In general, estimated error was low when people reported knowing the exact date of the events and was also relatively low when they reported using reference events for dating. As Table 7.2 shows, the same two dating sources were associated with high actual accuracy. In fact, the means in Table 7.3 indicate estimated error rates that closely approximate the actual

TABLE 7.3
Relation Between Subjects' Reports of Information Sources Used
to Provide Event Date and Subjects' Error Estimates (in Days)

	Study		
	89KS	89OH	91OH
Knew exact date	.13	.26	.06
Used reference event	3.45	3.46	4.18
Knew general reference period	8.46	8.26	8.18
Estimated number of intervening events	8.57	9.65	10.27
Used memory clarity to estimate	9.46	8.18	8.01
Used prototypic information	7.12	13.83	13.92
Guessed	11.59	2.58	10.92

error rates depicted in Table 7.2, even the relatively exceptional data for the guess category in the 89OH data set. However, this comparison also reveals that subjects appear to be a bit optimistic in their assessments of the accuracy of their event dates. In most cases, the actual error associated with an information source was somewhat higher than the estimated error.

Predicting Error Estimates: Retention Interval

Another way to explore subjects' accuracy estimates is to assess other factors that are related to subjects' predictions of dating accuracy. Certainly, one would expect retention interval to relate to subjects' error estimates: Subjects' estimates of error should increase with lengthening retention interval. After all, retention interval is powerfully related to absolute error magnitude. If subjects have some degree of awareness of the accuracy of their event dates (as our earlier analyses suggest they do), then these error estimates should also certainly be related to retention interval.

To examine the relation between retention interval and subjects' error estimates, we entered those estimates into our pooled within-subject regression models with linear retention interval, quadratic retention interval, and a vector representing subjects as predictors. We have error estimates in four data sets (89KS, 92KS, 89OH, and 91OH). As expected, retention interval was linearly related to estimated error in all four (βs = .352, .337, .366, and .298, respectively, smallest $F(1, 2266) = 293.66$, all $ps < .0001$). However, the relation between error estimates and retention interval was not simply linear. The curvilinear relation between retention interval and estimated error was also reliable in all four data sets (smallest $F(1, 2266) = 21.80$, all $ps < .0001$). The form of this curvilinear relation indicated that the rate of increase in the error estimates decreased with increasing retention interval.

In some ways, this curvilinear relation may not seem surprising. After all, our analyses of absolute dating error indicated a similar curvilinear pattern.

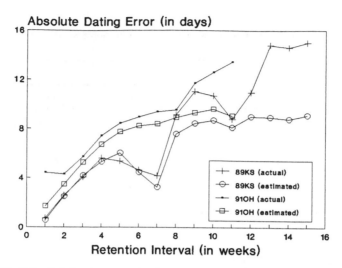

FIG. 7.11. Relation between absolute error magnitude and estimated error across retention interval in the 89KS and 91OH data sets.

Thus, subjects' error estimates may simply be realistic, matching the absolute error data. However, a closer inspection of the data suggests that this is not the case. Of the four data sets for which we have error estimates, only one (92KS) showed significant evidence of curvilinearity in the actual error magnitude data. Results for the curvilinearity effect in a second data set (89OH) merely approached significance, and no significant curvilinearity appeared in the error magnitude data from the other two studies (89KS and 91OH). Hence, it seems that the degree of curvilinearity in the data is greater in the error estimates than in the actual error data. This may be another reflection of the error underestimation pattern that we observed in the information source data, but these data suggest the additional possibility that these underestimations are particularly likely to occur at longer retention intervals. In support of this conclusion, Fig. 7.11 presents both the actual error data and the estimated error data (by week) for the 89KS and the 91OH data sets.

Predicting Error Estimates: Event Characteristics

In the preceding section, we noted that if subjects have insight into their level of dating accuracy, then their dating accuracy estimates may also be sensitive to those factors that are related to dating accuracy. Retention interval is one of those factors. However, by the same logic, it is possible that other event characteristics related to event dating accuracy, such as event valence or event affective intensity, are also related to subjects' error estimates. In a set of pooled within-subject regression analyses, we examined the extent to which subjects' estimates of error could be predicted by the event ratings that subjects provided. The predictors in these analyses were event affective intensity, event valence, event typicality, event emotionality, and event frequency. These predictors were used to determine subjects' dating estimates; as always, linear retention interval, quadratic retention interval, and a vector representing subjects were in these regressions.

Event Affective Intensity. As we document in chapter 8, event affective intensity predicts dating error. Thus, affective intensity may also predict error estimates. All four of the studies that included error estimates assessed event affective intensity, and our initial analyses of the relation between event affective intensity and error estimates yielded apparently inconsistent results. For the 89OH and 91OH data sets, event affective intensity significantly predicted estimated error, with more extreme events associated with lower error ($F(1, 1577) = 19.97$, $p < .0001$, $\beta = -.107$; $F(1, 2263) = 5.66$, $p < .01$, $\beta = -.043$, respectively). For the 89KS and 92KS data sets, event affective intensity did not predict estimated error ($F(1, 2848) = 1.22$, $p > .26$, $\beta = -.023$; $F(1, 3252) = .43$, $\beta = -.012$).

This inconsistency is illusory and is due to the different regression models that we used to analyze the data from each of the studies. That is, one of the peculiarities of regression is that a variable may significantly predict a dependent measure in one study and not in another solely because the set of predictors in the regression models used to analyze the two data sets differ. This is the case for the affective intensity variable—the two analyses that did not show any relation between affective intensity and estimated error also had a frequency rating and an emotionality rating in the regression models. We reasoned that these two variables might share significant amounts of variance with the affective intensity variable, causing affective intensity to drop out as a significant predictor of estimated error when frequency and emotionality were also in the regression model. Reanalyses of the data from the 89KS and the 92KS data sets suggested that this conjecture was correct. When the frequency ratings and the emotionality ratings were removed from the model, affective intensity predicted estimated error in both data sets ($F(1, 2850) = 8.84$, $p > .01$, $\beta = -.050$; $F(1, 3254) = 24.31$, $p < .0001$, $\beta = -.078$). Event affective intensity predicts error estimates, but the predictive effects may not be entirely independent of event frequency and emotionality. These affective intensity effects probably are independent of event valence, which was included in all the models, and event person-typicality, which was included in analyses of the data from the 91OH data.

Event Valence. As we document in chapter 8, event valence predicts dating error. Thus, one might also expect valence to predict error estimates. All four studies that included error estimates assessed event valence, and our analyses of the relation between event affective intensity and error estimates yielded fairly consistent results across studies. In two of the data sets (89OH and 92KS), event valence was significantly related to error estimates, ($F(1, 1577) = 9.49$, $p < .01$, $\beta = -.067$; $F(1, 3252) = 12.64$, $p < .0001$, $\beta = -.054$, respectively): Positive events were associated with lower error estimates than were negative events. In the other two data sets (89KS and 91OH), positive events were again associated with lower error estimates than were negative events, but the results merely approached statistical reliability ($F(1, 2848) = 3.09$, $p < .08$, $\beta = -.029$; $F(1, 2263) = 3.31$, $p < .06$, $\beta = -.033$).

Valence effects were evaluated with numerous other predictors in the regression models, and the relation between event valence and estimates of error appears to be independent of event affective intensity, emotionality, frequency, and person-typicality. This finding differs quite noticeably from the affective intensity–estimated error relation, which was substantially affected by the other factors entered into the regression models. This difference foreshadows the data in chapter 8, where a similar divergence seems to exist in the relations between event valence and actual dating performance and event affective intensity and dating performance.

Frequency Rating. In two studies, 89KS and 92KS, subjects provided a frequency rating for each event in addition to their accuracy estimate. This frequency rating reflects the overall base rate of an event (i.e., higher ratings indicate infrequently-occurring events; lower ratings indicate frequently-occurring events). Analyses of the actual errors indicated that low frequency was predictive of both low error magnitude and high exact dating rates. The same finding appears regarding for accuracy estimates: Low frequency is associated with lower error magnitude estimates. This relation was statistically reliable for both data sets ($F(1, 2848) = 31.45$, $p < .0001$, $\beta = -.099$, $F(1, 3252) = 34.51$, $p < .0001$, $\beta = -.093$). Furthermore, this effect occurred independent of the effects of event valence, event emotionality, and event affective intensity.

Person-Typicality Rating. The person-typicality rating reflects the extent to which an event is typical or atypical for a person (as distinguished from the population). Only one data set, 91OH, included both the person-typicality variable and error estimates. In that data set, neither atypical nor typical events appeared to be associated with heightened accuracy estimates, $F(1, 2265) = 1.63$, $p > .20$. However, a quadratic test of this predictor approached significance, $F(1, 2264) = 3.11$, $p < .08$. Examination of the means for this quadratic effect suggests that highly person-typical events may be associated with lower error estimates (M for a +3 [highly typical] rating = 5.92) than the estimated error for any other rating (lowest $M = 7.22$; highest $M = 7.60$). This pattern is especially noteworthy, given that the analyses of of error magnitude indicated that heightened person-typicality was associated with heightened (not lowered) actual error magnitude. If this divergence holds, it will represent one of the few cases in our data in which the relation between a variable and subjects' error estimates differed substantially from the relation between a variable and actual error magnitude. However, given that these data come from only one study and that the person-typicality effect for the error estimates is not statistically reliable, this divergence should be treated with caution.

Event Emotionality. In two studies, 89KS and 92KS, subjects provided an emotionality rating for each event. This rating reflects the extent to which the event was associated with an emotional response. As indicated earlier, these ratings were inversely related to the magnitude of subjects' dating errors: Higher emotionality was associated with lowered error. Regression analyses indicate that these emotionality ratings are also inversely related to error estimates. This relation was statistically reliable for the 92KS data set ($F(1, 3252) = 24.02$, $p < .0001$, $\beta = -.099$) but was not statistically reliable for the 89KS data set ($F(1, 2848) = 1.20$, $p > .27$, $\beta = -.024$). This discrepancy cannot be entirely explained by differences in the models used to analyze the data. In both cases, event valence, affective intensity, and an initial frequency rating were in the regression models. Nonetheless, it is possible that the shared variance between the predictors diminished the apparent relation between emotionality and estimated error. We verified this by means of simple regression models in which only the dummy-coded subjects term, the linear and quadratic effects of retention interval, and the emotionality rating was used to predict estimated error. In both of these analyses, heightened emotionality was significantly associated with lowered error estimates ($F(1, 3255) = 57.64$, $p < .0001$, $\beta = -.127$; $F(1, 2851) = 11.40$, $p > .001$, $\beta = -.061$). Hence, emotionality is related but, in the context of the other variables we have investigated, perhaps not uniquely related to predictions of dating error.

Summary. The results of our analyses of the relations between event characteristics and estimated error indicate that event affective intensity, event valence, event emotionality, event frequency, and event person-typicality individually predict subjects' estimates of dating error. However, in combination, they do not all uniquely predict that error. The predictive relation between event pleasantness and error estimates and between the frequency ratings and error estimates are robust, in that they continue to show predictive effects despite the entry of the other effects into the regression models.

The data suggest similar patterns of relations between actual dating error and the various item characteristics. It is unclear whether subjects' are actually aware of this when making their error estimations. Such relations may emerge simply because subjects have some general sense of how accurate their dating attempts are or because the various event characteristics that we have measured causally affect actual dating error. This latter state of affairs would lead the event characteristics to predict estimated dating error regardless of whether subjects were aware of the relations.

In addition, although not definitive, these results suggest that the underlying causes of the predictive relations differ. That is, it may be the case that emotionality, affective intensity, and person-typicality tend to predict dating error estimates because of their common relation to event memory. Thus, when all three factors are entered in the regression model, they all tie into a single common underlying factor (i.e., event memory), and this tends to weaken or eliminate the ability of any single factor to predict estimated error. By comparison, the ability of frequency and pleasantness to predict error estimates, regardless of other entries into the model, suggests that the effects of these factors are not mediated by event memory. Instead, the predictive effects of these factors may come from other causes, such as temporal schemata or direct date recall.

It is worth noting that these speculations are congruent with the conclusions that can be drawn from subjects' actual dating performance. For example, the relation between event affective intensity and dating seems to depend on goodness of estimation, whereas the relation between valence and exact dating seems to depend more on exact correctness (for further discussion, see chapter 8). This is consistent with the implication left by these error estimation data.

We explored this line of thinking further by rerunning our regression models. The new models included subjects' final memory rating of each event as one of the predictors. If memory mediates the relation between a predictor or a set of predictors and estimated error, then inclusion of the memory ratings in the model should eliminate those effects. If memory does not mediate the effect of a predictor, then the relation between that predictor and the dependent measure should remain significant.

In these regressions, memory was always strongly related to subjects' error estimates (smallest $F(1, 3252) = 34.51$, $p < .0001$, $\beta = -.296$). The better the event memory, the smaller the estimated error. This makes sense: The better one is able to remember an event, the more accurately one should be able to date the event. Subjects apparently perceive this heightened accuracy. However, the more important question involves the impact of the memory rating on the predictive relations between the other effects in the regression models and estimated error. We speculated that event frequency and event valence should be relatively robust to event recall, and this prediction was largely confirmed. Despite the entry of the memory term into the model, frequency predicted estimated error in both data sets containing the frequency measure ($F(1, 2847) = 6.30$, $p < .02$, $\beta = -.043$; $F(1, 3251) =$

5.73, $p < .02$, $\beta = -.036$). Valence significantly predicted estimated error in the same two data sets (89OH and 92KS) in which the valence-estimated error relation was originally significant ($F(1, 1576) = 11.89$, $p < .001$, $\beta = -.070$; $F(1, 3251) = 7.84$, $p < .01$, $\beta = -.040$, respectively). The results for the other two data sets containing event valence, which originally approached significance, no longer did so.

In comparison, with one exception, none of the other predictors in any of the models was statistically reliable. That exception was in the 92KS data set, where emotionality continued to predict error estimates, despite the entry of the memory term into the regression model $F(1, 3251) = 5.43$, $p < .02$, $\beta = -.045$. With memory in the models, affective intensity and person typicality never significantly predicted error estimates. Thus, these results again suggest that event dates are constructed from different sources and that the characteristics of events differentially tap into these sources.

GENDER DIFFERENCES IN DATING ACCURACY AND ERROR

The road through the research domain is often filled with unexpected twists. As we noted in the preface of this book, one of the outcomes that we fortuitously stumbled on was a possible gender difference in event dating. Because we know that the preface is not often read, let us briefly reiterate that story. Two of the authors of this book (Drs. Thompson & Skowronski) were using an old TRS-80 personal computer to analyze data from the diaries. During one session, they were manually sorting some printouts. On these printouts were preliminary tabulations of the average dating error for each subject. As the printouts were being sorted (using a median split) into "good dater" and "poor dater" piles, it was noticed that females were predominantly being classified as good daters, and males as poor daters.

The Early Results: Females Are More Accurate Than Males

This serendipitous outcome induced reanalyses of four data sets that were available at the time (86KS, 80KS, 83KS, and 79KS). The intent of these analyses was to examine the possibility that females were better daters than males. The results of these analyses, presented in Table 7.4, revealed that this female superiority in event dating was relatively consistent across studies (see Skowronski & Thompson, 1990). Three analyses yielded results that were consistent with female superiority in dating. Two of these three were statistically reliable, and the third approached significance.

TABLE 7.4
Mean Dating Error Magnitude (in Days) in Four Diary Studies by Subject
Gender, With t-Test Results (One-Directional) and Gender Frequencies
(in Parentheses) for Each Study

Study	Male Mean	Female Mean	t	p	SEM
86KS	7.58 (19)	4.31 (16)	3.27	.01	1.13
83KS	6.22 (9)	4.07 (14)	1.29	.11	1.67
80KS	4.50 (10)	4.75 (20) ,	−.24	.70	1.01
79KS	10.56 (17)	6.40 (15)	4.16	.01	1.70

The Recent Qualification: Females Are More Often Accurate Than Males

We have also pursued this gender effect in more recent studies. For example, we looked for evidence of enhanced dating by females relative to males in the 88OH data set, which includes event dates for both self-events and other-events (e.g., the events of a friend or relative). Analysis of the data suggested that females ($M = 8.43$) made errors of lower magnitude than males ($M = 9.65$), $F(1, 60) = 3.53$, $p < .05$ (one-tailed). However, this effect does not always appear to be reliable: A replication of the self–other study (i.e., the 91OH data set) found little overall gender difference in error magnitude (female $M = 9.25$, male $M = 9.28$, $F(1, 49) = .12$).

In these studies we pushed our data further and attempted to examine more closely why females made smaller errors than males. There are two obvious possibilities. Females simply may be exactly correct more often than males, which would reduce the overall error magnitude for females relative to males. Alternatively, even when estimates are incorrect, females may still provide more accurate estimates of event dates than males. This would occur if females had better information available for use in the construction of date estimates (e.g., more well-developed temporal schemata, better event memory).

The data seem to fall on the side of exact dating, not estimation accuracy. Analyses of the exact dating data in the 88OH data set indicate that females ($M = .312$) were more often exactly correct about the dates of events than males ($M = .240$), $F(1, 60) = 5.23$, $p < .05$. Furthermore, our analyses of these data also showed a Rater Gender × Diary Target interaction, $F(1, 60) = 4.14$, $p < .05$, indicating that the superiority for females was much stronger for self-events (female $M = .349$, male $M = .252$) than for other-events (female $M = .280$, male $M = .249$). The second self–other study (91OH) found a similar self–other accuracy pattern (self-events: female $M = .300$, male $M = .251$; other-events: female $M = .220$, male $M = .200$), although the interaction only approached statistical significance, $F(1, 4264) = 2.05$, $p < .12$. (The shift in the magnitude of the error term across studies appears because of differences in our statistical procedures. Earlier analyses in this series were conducted using ANOVA methods; this last study was analyzed using regression methods, with the residual error used as the error term.)

In the 88OH data, we also examined whether the incorrect date estimates of females were more accurate than the incorrect date estimates of males. To do this, we removed the exactly dated events from the data set. With these exact events removed, the error magnitudes of the date estimates of males and females were equally poor (female $M = 12.47$, male $M = 12.55$, $F(1, 60) = .01$).

In short, then, it appears that the proper characterization of the gender difference is not that females make smaller errors than males but rather that they are more often exactly accurate. Furthermore, this superiority in exact dating is limited, in that it appears to apply only to self-events, not to other-events.

Assessing Explanations: Artifact or Real?

Collectively, these outcomes suggest that the speculations of Skowronski and Thompson (1990) about the causes of the gender difference in event dating accuracy are substantially correct. In that paper the authors argued that the heightened dating performance by females reflects the role that females tend to occupy in society—they are the date keepers, the ones responsible for remembering the dates on which events occur. Indeed, one of the authors of this book readily admits that his wife always takes responsibility for writing important dates on the social calendar. Obviously, if this example is representative of the population in general, such activity has the potential for enhancing women's ability to remember or reconstruct exact dates. However, we should point out that if the critical variable is event dating experience or practice, then nothing inherent in being a female leads to dating accuracy. Thus, males who occupy roles requiring heightened dating activity should date events better than females who do not occupy such a role—a potential direction for future research.

Although the role-based explanation for the gender effects that we observed seems sensible, it is always possible that these effects are caused by one of two (or both) methodological artifacts. The first of these is an event selection issue. Females may tend to record events that are more personally revealing than males and, hence, can better use their diary entries to reconstruct the dates of events than do males. To investigate this explanation, we asked a separate group of subjects to rate a sample of females' and males' entries taken from the 79KS diaries on a scale from *not at all revealing* (1) to *very revealing* (7). As expected, females' entries were seen as more personally revealing ($M = 3.19$) than males' ($M = 2.98$), $F(1, 142) = 56.40$, $p < .001$. A second possible explanation lies in the event records themselves. For example, females may tend to write longer entries than males, and these longer entries may provide additional memory cues that are useful in estimating or recalling an event date. Examination of a sample of the diary entries from the 79KS data set suggested that this was also true: Females' entries tended to employ about 50% more words ($M = 12.80$) than males' entries ($M = 8.28$), $F(1, 30) = 17.29$, $p < .01$.

However, at least three reasons lead us to believe that the gender effect in dating does not reflect such artifacts. First, it seems reasonable to hypothesize that heightened revealingness and longer entry length are related to event memory; hence, females should remember events better than males. In our data, this does not occur. For example, in the 88OH data set, despite the significant event dating effect for gender, no significant gender difference appeared in rated event memory, $F(1, 60) = 1.82$, $p > .24$. Second, both of the confound explanations imply that females should be both better date estimators and better exact daters than males. That is, there is no reason to expect the effects of these artifacts to be limited to exact dating accuracy, but our data suggest that this limitation exists. Finally, the entry length and revealingness effects should apply to both self-diaries and other-diaries; this implies that female dating superiority should be observed for both diary types. Instead, the effect seems to be limited to the self-diaries.

The bottom line is that within our diary paradigm, there is relatively consistent evidence indicating that females are better daters than males. More precisely, females are more often exactly correct about the dates of autobiographical events than males. Whether this effect is due to our paradigm or to more theoretically interesting sources remains an open question. We believe that the data suggest that the difference is a real one, and we propose that the effect is due to the differing roles that males and females tend to occupy. Additional research needs to establish the gender difference more definitively, and to explore more thoroughly the potential causes of this difference.

CHAPTER RETROSPECTIVE

This chapter dealt with a number of factors related to dating accuracy and dating error and also with factors related to subjects' predictions of the error associated with the event dates that they provided. Despite the complexity of the analyses and the wealth of data that we present, the overall story told by this chapter is a relatively simple one.

We first presented data showing the effects of retention interval on dating performance. In general, subjects' dating performance decreases rather rapidly with lengthening retention interval. This rapid degradation seems to be due to at least two factors: forgetting of the event dates and forgetting of information (e.g., event content) that can be used to reconstruct the event dates. These decreases in accuracy across retention interval do not seem to be due to artifacts introduced by pooling the data across subjects: Examination of the error patterns of individual subjects indicates that their individual response functions match the group functions, despite fairly large individual differences.

The exact form of the decrease in dating performance depends on the dating measure that one prefers. The exact dating measure shows strong Ebbinghaus-like tendencies with lengthening retention intervals. Exact dating rapidly decreases in recent retention intervals and slowly decreases at longer intervals. The error magnitude data show much more continuity, with error magnitude increasing in a relatively linear fashion with lengthening retention interval. Finally, the raw (i.e., signed) error measure indicated that dating error is affected by bounded periods. We observed significant evidence of time expansion for events that occurred near the end of the diary study (i.e., recent events) and significant telescoping for events near the start of the study (i.e., oldest events). These telescoping and time expansion effects were obviously dependent on the boundaries set by length of the dating study, and evidence suggested that the exact dating data may have been similarly affected. By comparison, the rate of increase in the absolute magnitude measure seemed to have been relatively unaffected by the length of the retention interval in the diary studies.

We also presented data documenting how the characteristics of the events were systematically related to dating error and accuracy. We did this in three ways. First, we listed event samples and noted the dating error associated with those samples. Second, we conducted a content analysis of the data. The results of this analysis revealed that certain content categories were consistently associated with better event dating than were other categories. Finally, we used subjects' event ratings to explore event dating performance and found that events that were infrequent, person-atypical, emotional, frequently rehearsed, and mentally involving were related to low error magnitude and high exact dating.

The results of our mediational analyses suggested that these relations occurred largely because of event memory. That is, infrequent, person-atypical, emotional, frequently rehearsed, and mentally involving events are well-remembered events; these variables often are related to dating because of their effects on memory. However, throughout our analyses there were continuing hints of other factors at work—these variables would occasionally continue to predict event dating even when event memory was accounted for. By extension, then, one can assume that these variables are also associated with other factors, such as temporal schemata or direct date recall, that can serve to enhance event dating independent of event memory.

We also explored the extent to which subjects' reported information sources were related to event dating. We found that the sources that subjects reported using to produce event dates were reliably related to error magnitude, with date recall producing the most accurate dates (although even here, subjects' dates were not always correct). The category of relational sources (e.g., dating relative to another event) also was associated with good accuracy.

That subjects can report on the information sources that they use to construct dates and that these sources are, indeed, associated with error magnitude suggests that subjects have some general sense of the accuracy of their event dates. Our analyses of subjects' accuracy estimates indicated that this was, indeed, the case. Furthermore, the same factors that predict actual dating accuracy were also significantly related to error estimates. Whether subjects overtly used these factors (e.g., pleasantness) to construct event dates is uncertain; most likely, these factors are related to error estimates because they affect the sources of information that subjects use to construct event dates.

Finally, we presented evidence suggesting that females are more accurate daters than males. More specifically, these data suggest that females more often are able to recall or reconstruct exact dates than males are. When the event dates are inexact, females do not seem to have an advantage over males. We suggested that this gender difference relates to the different roles that males and females occupy in society.

In the next chapter, we continue with the themes established in this chapter. We again investigate the relation between two predictors, event affective intensity and event valence, and dating performance. In looking at these relations, we again look for evidence of the extent to which dating performance is tied to underlying cognitive mechanisms involved in date estimation and recall.

...antness
...ting

...ween the valence (i.e., pleasant-
...e's recall for that event and the
...of an event and one's recall for
...evaluative intensity are also of
...s, a reasonable question concerns
...uative intensity of an event are
...te provided for the event.
...l literature exists pertaining either
...d event dating or to the relation
...nt dating. To our knowledge, the
...ossibility of such relations was a
...ose data are difficult to evaluate
because they were from a questionnaire focusing on people's opinions about
memory for events. In more recent times, researchers (e.g., Thomson, 1930)
have used diary procedures which allow them to establish the initial pleasantness or unpleasantness of the events. In our first attempt to look at the
effect of intensity and valence (Thompson, 1985b), our data suggested that
pleasant events were dated more accurately than unpleasant events, particularly when those events were extreme. In addition, the data reported in
that paper did not indicate a consistent relation between event evaluative
intensity and event dating accuracy. Whereas extremely pleasant events were
dated with the greatest accuracy, extremely unpleasant events were dated
with the least accuracy.

Given that the current zeitgeist in the dating literature is that event dates are reconstructed rather than directly recalled (see Friedman, 1993), this intensity outcome is a bit surprising. One reason for the surprise is that a primary source of material for use in the process of date reconstruction should be one's memory for the event itself (i.e., *event memory-based reconstruction*). As we noted in chapter 4, our event recall data suggest that event memory ratings tend to be substantially greater for affectively extreme events than for less extreme events and slightly greater for pleasant events than for unpleasant events. Hence, to the extent that event memory is involved in the reconstruction of event dates, one would expect dating accuracy measures to evince similar evaluative intensity and valence effects. The Thompson (1985b) data are clearly consistent with this valence prediction but are not consistent with this evaluative intensity prediction.

Thompson (1985b) proposed an explanation that revolves around an asymmetry in the tendency for dates to be consciously associated with different types of events. That is, Thompson suggested that event dates are more often consciously associated with events that are pleasant than with events that are unpleasant. For example, birthdays, anniversaries, graduations, holidays, and the like are events that are generally perceived to be pleasant and that often have dates associated with them.

It should be noted that recalled calendar dates (we use the term *date availability* in this chapter) for events may come from at least two memory sources. One of these sources reflects unique personal history and corresponds to a circumstance in which an event date is associated with an event. Examples of such events are the date on which the car was wrecked or the date on which one's sister died. However, as we argued in chapter 6, other event dates associated with an event can be recalled from schematic or general world knowledge. Examples of these types of occasions in the United States are Christmas, New Year's Day, and Independence Day.

From our current perspective (10 years later), we believe that Thompson's original proposal has some merit, especially as an explanation for valence effects in event dating. The most likely competing explanation for the valence effect in dating is that the better memory associated with pleasant events allows those events to be dated more accurately than unpleasant events. However, the small magnitude of the valence effect in memory (see chapter 4) suggests that this explanation may not be correct. One of the goals of this chapter is to attempt to discriminate between date availability and memory-based reconstruction as possible explanations for pleasantness.

A second goal of the chapter is to examine more closely the relation between evaluative intensity and dating accuracy and the possible causes of that relation. Because intense events are associated with strong memories, a reconstructive explanation of event dating in which event memory is used to reconstruct event dates is plausible. Such an explanation suggests that intense events, both pleasant and unpleasant, will be more accurately dated than less intense events. By comparison, Thompson's (1985b) data and his date availability explanation for those data suggest that enhanced dating accuracy will only be associated with extremely pleasant events.

The extensive data on event dating that we have collected in the last 15 years allow us to examine the possible predictive relations between event valence and dating accuracy and between event evaluative intensity and dating accuracy. With these data we can also examine some of the possible cognitive causes that underlie these relations. In the remainder of this chapter, we report the results of numerous analyses examining these relations.

The intent of our initial analyses was to examine whether event valence and event evaluative intensity were predictive of various measures of event dating error and dating accuracy and to determine the nature of those predictive relations. In subsequent analyses, we attempted to explore in more detail the possible cognitive mechanisms of date availability and event memory-based reconstruction in event dating. We gave special attention to whether these mechanisms could account for the relations that emerged in our initial analyses between event valence and dating error (and accuracy), and between event evaluative intensity and dating error (and accuracy).

In our search for evidence of these two cognitive mechanisms, we analyzed several different measures of dating accuracy and error. In some of our analyses, we used an error magnitude measure, which was the absolute value of the difference (in number of days) between the exact date and the estimated date of the event. In other analyses, we used a measure of exact dating accuracy, essentially transforming all the data into a binary measure (i.e., exactly correct or not exactly correct). We also examined the error magnitude measure with the exactly dated events deleted from the data set. In a subset of those analyses, we deleted only those exactly dated events for which the date was recalled rather than reconstructed. Finally, we compared the characteristics of the events for which subjects reported recalling the date to the characteristics of the events whose dates were reconstructed.

The analytic technique that we employed for these analyses was the pooled within-subject multiple regression analysis described in detail in chapter 2, and the variables used in the regression models were the same ones used in the event memory analyses described in chapter 4. As we discussed in chapter 4, the results of the regression models looking at the relations between event valence and the event memory ratings and between event evaluative intensity and the event memory ratings were straightforward. Event valence and event evaluative intensity generally predicted the memory ratings, and these effects generally did not dissipate when additional predictors were added to the regression models. In contrast to those outcomes, the results of the regression models looking at the relation between event valence and dating accuracy (or error) measures and between event evaluative intensity and dating accuracy (or error) measures were not as straightforward. To discuss these relations fully, we present the results of several different regression models involving several different dependent measures.

ERROR MAGNITUDE

Basic Regression Analyses

The first set of analyses that we present examines whether event valence and event evaluative intensity predict the magnitude of dating error. The results of the regression analyses across studies are presented in Table 8.1. The analyses described in this table report the results for the same regression model across the studies. This model included as predictors only the dummy vector for each subject, linear event retention interval, quadratic event retention interval, event valence, and event evaluative intensity. Hence, the effects of event valence that we report in Table 8.1 control for the effects of event evaluative intensity (as well as for the other terms in the model), and the effects of event evaluative intensity that we report control for the effects of event valence (again, as well as for the other terms in the model).

The results for the evaluative intensity measure indicate that as event intensity increases, error magnitude decreases. The direction of the relation was negative in all 12 data sets that are included in Table 8.1, although it was significantly negative for only 8 data sets. It is interesting to note that this effect appeared not only in the standard 10- to 15-week self-diary studies that we conducted but also in the studies that deviated from this basic paradigm. That is, the effect emerged in the study that asked subjects to keep diaries for an exceptionally long period of time (the 90KS data set had diaries that included events up to 2½ years of age) and in one of the studies that asked subjects to keep diaries of events in someone else's life (i.e., the 91OH data set).

By comparison, the results of the analyses examining the relation between event valence and error magnitude are not as consistent across studies. The valence variable was coded so that a negative beta reflects lower error magnitudes for pleasant events than for unpleasant events. Pleasant events were generally associated with lower error magnitudes than were unpleasant events: This outcome occurred in 10 of the 12 data sets. However, this pleasantness effect was significant in only 3 of those data sets (although the results for 3 others approached statistical significance). The relation between event valence and dating error magnitude was not significant in either of the studies in which unpleasant events were associated with error magnitudes lower than those for pleasant events.

TABLE 8.1
Regression Betas, F-Test Results, and p Values Describing the Relation
between Event Evaluative Intensity and Event Valence and the Magnitude
of the Dating Error (Simple Model Only)

Data Source & Year		Valence of Event Affect	Derived Evaluative Intensity of Affect
Self-Events			
80KS	β	−.031	−.044
$F(1, 2407)$	F	2.28	4.19
	p	.1310	.0409
86KS	β	−.007	−.053
$F(1, 2564)$	F	.14	7.19
	p	.7083	.0074
87KS	β	−.017	−.117
$F(1, 3293)$	F	.99	.40
	p	.3191	.5270
88OH	β	−.042	−.030
$F(1, 3231)$	F	6.34	2.98
	p	.0119	.0844
89KS	β	−.029	−.062
$F(1, 2850)$	F	2.64	11.19
	p	.1044	.0008
89OH	β	−.049	−.049
$F(1, 1577)$	F	4.88	3.95
	p	.0274	.0470
90KS(long-term)	β	.009	−.050
$F(1, 3508)$	F	.47	13.23
	p	.4952	.0003
91OH	β	−.020	−.045
$F(1, 2264)$	F	.96	4.46
	p	.3275	.0347
91KS	β	.003	−.034
$F(1, 1628)$	F	.02	2.01
	p	.8908	.1568
92KS	β	−.011	−.061
$F(1, 3252)$	F	.42	12.33
	p	.5189	.0005
Other-Events			
88OH	β	−.045	−.009
$F(1, 2726)$	F	6.06	.23
	p	.0139	.6326
91OH	β	−.038	−.059
$F(1, 1951)$	F	3.09	6.28
	p	.0787	.0123

The relations observed in these error magnitude data, then, are similar to the relations obtained for the memory ratings described in chapter 4: better memory (or in this case, less error) for affectively extreme events than for less extreme events and better memory (or in this case, less error) for pleasant events than for unpleasant events. As indicated earlier, there are at least two possible mechanisms that may underlie these effects.

As we argued in chapter 4, pleasant and extreme events appear to be better recalled than unpleasant and moderate events, and this enhanced recall may allow subjects to reconstruct a more accurate estimate of the dates on which these pleasant and affectively extreme events occurred. In essence, this position assumes that recall of the details of events contributes to dating estimation accuracy (e.g., in the climate of the north-central United States, recalling snow on the ground will likely mean that the event occurred between late fall and early spring). In theory, the more detail available (e.g., the better the memory), the lower the error accompanying the estimated date. A second mechanism that may be responsible for the accuracy enhancement observed for pleasant and extreme events may be a function of the event either explicitly being assigned a date tag (e.g., The Thompson "red letter day" argument—I wrecked my car on June 28th) or having a date tag already attached because of some form of schematic knowledge (e.g., it was on my birthday, which is on August 29th).

We conducted several additional regression analyses designed to garner evidence for both of these ideas and to investigate the roles that these mechanisms play in the valence and evaluative intensity effects that we observed in our initial analyses of the error magnitude data. In one series of analyses, we entered subjects' memory rating for each event (as described in the Appendix) as an additional predictor in the regression models. If this memory term is significant, event memory is likely used in the process of date reconstruction, and the details of an event aid reconstruction accuracy. This mechanism would be further implicated if the addition of the event memory term to the model rendered the event valence and event evaluative intensity terms nonsignificant. Alternatively, if the evaluative intensity and event valence terms are significant even with a significant event memory term in the models, some other factor, such as date tagging, is partially responsible for the relations between those variables and error magnitude.

Regression Analyses Including Event Memory as a Predictor

The results of these analyses are presented in Table 8.2. As indicated by the data presented in the far right column, subjects' memory ratings were always highly predictive of dating accuracy. A significant negative relation between memory ratings and error magnitude emerged in all 12 data sets (i.e., higher

TABLE 8.2

Regression Betas, F-Test Results, and p Values Describing the Relation
Between Event Evaluative Intensity and Event Valence and the Magnitude
of Dating Error (Controlling for Rated Memory for Events)

Data Source & Year		Valence of Event Affect	Derived Evaluative Intensity of Affect	Event Memory Rating
Self-Events				
80KS	β	−.030	.005	−.238
$F(1, 2406)$	F	2.26	.06	93.14
	p	.1326	.8140	.0001
86KS	β	−.009	−.000	−.213
$F(1, 2563)$	F	.22	.00	96.56
	p	.6398	.9824	.0001
87KS	β	−.010	.026	−.239
$F(1, 3292)$	F	.36	2.04	147.08
	p	.5510	.1534	.0001
88OH	β	−.032	.008	−.232
$F(1, 3230)$	F	3.78	.21	153.23
	p	.0518	.6474	.0001
89KS	β	−.025	−.028	−.215
$F(1, 2850)$	F	1.92	2.30	91.29
	p	.1655	.1296	.0001
89OH	β	−.051	−.010	−.257
$F(1, 1577)$	F	5.43	.17	65.05
	p	.0199	.6831	.0001
90KS(long-term)	β	.010	−.028	−.082
$F(1, 3506)$	F	.66	4.00	36.03
	p	.4149	.0455	.0001
91OH	β	−.016	.0196	−.304
$F(1, 2263)$	F	.66	.86	172.73
	p	.4164	.3552	.0001
91KS	β	.011	−.014	−.158
$F(1, 1627)$	F	.23	.32	30.97
	p	.6295	.5715	.0001
92KS	β	−.007	−.012	−.252
$F(1, 3253)$	F	.18	.50	168.84
	p	.6697	.4795	.0001
Other-Events				
88OH	β	−.049	.023	−.250
$F(1, 2725)$	F	7.60	2.10	139.12
	p	.0059	.1479	.0001
91OH	β	−.053	−.033	−.185
$F(1, 1950)$	F	6.12	1.92	59.37
	p	.0134	.1662	.0001

memory ratings were associated with lowered dating error). This result directly supports the idea that at least some event dates are reconstructed from memory.

This outcome provides converging evidence verifying the utility of the memory rating procedure as a technique of memory assessment. After all, if the memory ratings did not reflect the actual contents of event memory, then one would not expect these ratings to be predictive of error magnitude in event dating. Belying this idea, the evidence suggests that these memory ratings are, indeed, highly predictive of error in event dating. Hence, the data suggest that the memory ratings reflect the contents of subjects' memories.

More important to the purposes of this chapter, however, is whether the event valence and event evaluative intensity terms continued to predict the magnitude of dating error with event memory accounted for. The results for the event valence variable seem to provide relatively solid evidence for both of these effects. In evaluating the impact of the event memory term on the event valence effect, it is useful to recall that in the results presented in Table 8.1; pleasant events were associated with lower error magnitudes than unpleasant events in 10 data sets and that this relation was statistically reliable in 3 data sets. As illustrated by the data presented in Table 8.2, with event memory accounted for, pleasant events were associated with lower error magnitudes than unpleasant events in 10 of the 12 data sets. Although this relation was statistically reliable only for 3 data sets, the event valence variable approached statistical significance for 3 others. Given these results, the conclusion that seems most appropriate is that although the predictive relation between event valence and error magnitude is relatively weak, it is not much affected by the entry of the event memory term into the regression models. By implication, then, the lower error magnitude for pleasant events relative to unpleasant events may be due to the tendency for pleasant events to be more frequently associated with dates, either from date tags or from schematic sources, than are unpleasant events.

Two data sets in which the relation between event valence and error magnitude was maintained most strongly were those in which people kept a diary of others' events. This may be a sensible outcome. It seems to be intuitively reasonable that event-memory based reconstructive processes would likely have a proportionally greater impact on the dating of self-events than of other-events, especially if many of the event dates that we have available are schema-based (e.g., existing as a result of cultural factors such as Christmas Day, New Year's Day, Independence Day). The tendency of people to have these dates available should not much depend on whether the event is a self-event or an other-event. By comparison, a very large difference likely exists in the amount of detail available in memory about events pertaining to the self and events pertaining to others. The self-event store is likely to be much richer in detail and thus more useful in reconstruction. This reasoning implies that the models controlling for the contents of event memory have a greater impact in the self-event data than in the other-event data. At least with respect to the event valence variable, this is what appears to occur.

The results for the event evaluative intensity variable reveal that the relation between evaluative intensity and error magnitude is substantially affected by inclusion of the memory term in the regression models. In evaluating this impact, it is useful to recall that the results shown in Table 8.1 indicated that affectively extreme events were associated with lower error magnitudes in all 12 data sets and that this relation was statistically reliable in 8 of those data sets. As indicated in Table 8.2, when event memory was entered into the regression models, event evaluative intensity was associated with lower error magnitudes in only 7 data sets, and this relation was statistically reliable in only 1 of those 7. Not one of the reversals was statistically reliable, although two approached statistical significance. The implication left by these results is that reconstruction from memory is substantially responsible for the relations that we observed between event evaluative intensity and error magnitude.

In summary, then, both availability of date information, either from memory tags or schemata, and event memory-based date reconstruction appear to be involved in event dating, although these two mechanisms appear to be differentially important to the relations between event valence and dating error magnitude and between event evaluative intensity and dating error magnitude. The evaluative intensity effect seems to be primarily driven by event memory-based reconstruction: When event memory is controlled for, the evaluative intensity–error magnitude relation substantially dissipates. The valence effect seems to be primarily driven by the availability of date information: When event memory is accounted for, the event valence–error magnitude relation is minimally affected.

EXACT DATING ACCURACY

We attempted to explore our data and these theoretical mechanisms further by examining an alternative dependent measure. In this set of analyses, we transformed our dating estimates into a binary measure (i.e., date exactly correct or date incorrect). We were interested in the possibilities that pleasant events were more often exactly dated than unpleasant events and that affectively extreme events were more often exactly dated than affectively moderate events. This prediction can be obtained most directly from the mechanisms (e.g., tagging or schematic knowledge) focusing on date availability. If pleasant and affectively extreme events are associated with temporal tags, then they should be dated exactly at a higher rate than unpleasant and moderate events.

Such outcomes are not inconsistent with event memory-based reconstructive processes. It is reasonable to assume that even when event dates are reconstructed from memory, the better memories associated with pleasant and extreme events may occasionally lead to a higher frequency of exactly dated events than memories associated with unpleasant and moderate events do. However, because the enhanced exact accuracy associated with the reconstruction process is a side effect of generalized enhanced estimation accuracy (i.e., some reconstructed dates for events just happen to be exactly correct) rather than the sole reason for enhanced accuracy (as with the date availability mechanisms), we thought that we would gain some insight into the use of these two dating processes by examining the binary dependent measure.

Basic Regression Analyses

The results of the regression analyses of the binary correctness frequency data are presented in Table 8.3. For ease of comparison with the data presented in Table 8.1 and later in Table 8.5, we have included in Table 8.3 only the results from the basic regression models (i.e., no other terms in the regression models except those terms included in all our models).

In Table 8.3, the positive betas for the derived event evaluative intensity variable indicate that, as the events became more affectively extreme, the exact accuracy hit rate increased. The positive betas for the event valence variable indicate that the exact accuracy hit rate was greater for pleasant than for unpleasant events. In both cases, these relations were highly consistent across studies. The betas were positive for both the evaluative intensity and valence variables in all 12 data sets. The relation between event valence and exact dating accuracy was statistically significant in 9 data sets, and it approached significance in the other 3. The relation between event evaluative intensity and exact dating accuracy was statistically significant in 11 data sets and approached significance in the remaining one.

These results provide support for the two mechanisms promoting date availability, but that support is not unambiguous. Although it is possible that the enhanced exact accuracy for pleasant and extreme events is due to date availability, it is also possible that this accuracy is due to enhanced estimation accuracy that is produced by heightened event memory for pleasant and extreme events. However, if this were the case, then one might expect the effects shown in Table 8.3 to dissipate when event memory is added to the regression model. That is, if the heightened enhanced exact accuracy rates for pleasant and extreme events were due to better event memory for those events, then adding a memory term to the model should eliminate the predictive relations between valence and exact accuracy and intensity and exact accuracy. To the extent that those relations remain, the data suggest

TABLE 8.3
Regression Betas, *F*-Test Results and *p* Values Describing the Relation
Between Event Evaluative Intensity and Event Valence
and Exact Dating Accuracy (Simple Model Only)

Data Source & Year		Valence of Event Affect	Derived Evaluative Intensity of Affect
Self-Events			
80KS	β	.055	.087
$F(1, 2406)$	F	7.90	18.44
	p	.0050	.0001
86KS	β	.033	.061
$F(1, 2564)$	F	3.27	10.12
	p	.0707	.0015
87KS	β	.035	.046
$F(1, 3293)$	F	4.88	6.99
	p	.0272	.0083
88OH	β	.036	.053
$F(1, 3231)$	F	5.23	9.91
	p	.0222	.0017
89KS	β	.051	.043
$F(1, 2850)$	F	8.32	5.56
	p	.0394	.0185
89OH	β	.068	.080
$F(1, 1577)$	F	9.00	10.10
	p	.0027	.0015
90KS(long-term)	β	.083	.140
$F(1, 3508)$	F	21.21	51.99
	p	.0001	.0001
91OH	β	.037	.039
$F(1, 2264)$	F	3.52	4.01
	p	.0607	.0454
91KS	β	.045	.039
$F(1, 1628)$	F	4.14	2.87
	p	.0421	.0903
92KS	β	.034	.068
$F(1, 3252)$	F	4.67	16.24
	p	.0308	.0001
Other-Events			
88OH	β	.029	.063
$F(1, 2726)$	F	2.73	11.18
	p	.0988	.0008
91OH	β	.056	.057
$F(1, 1951)$	F	6.88	6.70
	p	.0088	.0097

that they are due to another factor, likely the availability of date information from tagging or from schemata.

Regression Analyses Including Event Memory as a Predictor

To explore this possibility, we again examined the exact accuracy data but added subjects' memory rating for each event to the regression model used to analyze each data set. The results of these analyses are presented in Table 8.4. As those data indicate, the memory rating variable always significantly predicted exact dating accuracy, and as expected, the higher the memory rating, the higher the accuracy rate. More important, addition of the memory rating variable to the regression model had relatively little impact on the predictive relation between event valence and exact dating accuracy (i.e., the positive betas for the event valence variable indicate that event dates for pleasant events were more often correct than event dates for unpleasant events). The valence variable significantly predicted accuracy in six data sets (as opposed to nine in the analyses that did not include memory ratings) and approached significance in the other six. The conclusion that is suggested by these data is that event memory does not substantially mediate the relation between event affect and exact dating accuracy. By extension, the results of this analysis are consistent with the hypothesis that date information is more often available for positive than for negative events.

Dates do not appear to be as important to the event evaluative intensity effect. The positive betas that appear for the evaluative intensity variable in 11 data sets indicate that exact accuracy increased as intensity rating increased. However, in only one data set was the relation statistically reliable. Given that this relation was statistically significant in 11 of the 12 data sets reported in Table 8.3, the conclusion seems to be a straightforward one. The heightened exact dating accuracy for affectively intense events seems to be primarily a function of event memory: When event memory is accounted for in the regression model, the relation between exact accuracy and event evaluative intensity is weak (at best).

ERROR MAGNITUDE
WITHOUT EXACTLY DATED EVENTS

Although the implications of the results that we have reported seem to be fairly clear, we decided to conduct two additional series of analyses. In the first series, we examined the relations between error magnitude and event valence and between error magnitude and event evaluative intensity when the exactly dated events were discarded from the data sets. We reasoned

TABLE 8.4
Regression Betas, F-Test Results, and p Values Describing the Relation
Between Event Evaluative Intensity and Event Valence and Exact Dating
Accuracy (Model Controlling for Self-Reported Event Memory)

Data Source & Year		Valence of Event Affect	Derived Evaluative Intensity of Affect	Event Memory Rating
Self-Events				
80KS	β	.054	.027	.298
$F(1, 2405)$	F	8.26	1.72	165.20
	p	.0041	.1903	.0001
86KS	β	.035	.010	.208
$F(1, 2563)$	F	3.72	.26	96.48
	p	.0539	.6078	.0001
87KS	β	.029	.013	.204
$F(1, 3292)$	F	3.48	.59	122.28
	p	.0623	.4418	.0001
88OH	β	.025	.008	.273
$F(1, 3230)$	F	2.51	.22	238.91
	p	.1132	.6398	.0001
89KS	β	.046	.005	.243
$F(1, 2849)$	F	6.97	.07	122.56
	p	.0083	.7986	.0001
89OH	β	.070	.024	.362
$F(1, 1576)$	F	10.45	.97	133.27
	p	.0013	.3259	.0001
90KS	β	.080	.093	.179
$F(1, 3506)$	F	19.91	21.89	86.09
	p	.0001	.0001	.0001
91OH	β	.036	−.017	.259
$F(1, 2263)$	F	3.54	.71	136.72
	p	.0602	.4010	.0001
91KS	β	.035	.012	.205
$F(1, 1627)$	F	2.53	.29	59.00
	p	.1118	.5923	.0001
92KS	β	.030	.009	.303
$F(1, 3253)$	F	3.81	.30	269.55
	p	.0511	.5858	.0001
Other-Events				
88OH	β	.034	.021	.283
$F(1, 2725)$	F	3.94	1.27	195.20
	p	.0472	.2601	.0001
91OH	β	.075	.025	.229
$F(1, 1950)$	F	12.83	1.33	100.05
	p	.0003	.2481	.0001

that there is no reason to expect from the reconstruction hypothesis that the estimation advantage for pleasant and extreme events is limited to exactly dated events. That is, if the lower error magnitude for pleasant or extreme events were due to better date reconstruction from memory for those events, then even when the event dates are incorrect the error magnitude for those events will be lower than the error magnitudes for unpleasant and moderate events. From this perspective, if the smaller error magnitudes associated with pleasant and affectively extreme events are due to reconstructive processes, then discarding the exactly dated events will not eliminate the significant effects observed for these variables.

By comparison, the date availability idea suggests that pleasant and extreme events will be dated exactly with a greater frequency than unpleasant and moderate events. This approach implies that when date estimates are not exactly correct, no error magnitude differences will emerge between pleasant and unpleasant events and between affectively extreme and less extreme events. Thus, if the lower error magnitudes associated with pleasant and affectively extreme events are due to their heightened probability of yielding an exactly dated event, then eliminating the exactly dated events from the data set will eliminate the predictive relations between these variables and error magnitude.

Regression Analyses Without Exactly Dated Events

The results of the analyses on the revised error magnitude variable (discarding exacts) are presented in Table 8.5. We have reason to suspect (from the analyses reported in Tables 8.2 and 8.4) that processes enhancing date availability may be more important in the event valence effect and less important in the evaluative intensity effect. The results reported in Table 8.5 seem to be highly congruent with these conclusions. After the exactly dated events are discarded, there is only a slight tendency for pleasant events to have lower error magnitudes than unpleasant events. Pleasant events are associated with lower error magnitudes than unpleasant events in 8 of the 12 data sets, but the effect is statistically significant in only one data set.

These results suggest that memory-based date reconstructive processes are not as important as date availability to the superior event dating associated with pleasant events. These results converge nicely with the results of the analyses that we reported earlier in this chapter. Recall that the results of the error magnitude analyses also indicated a significant event valence–error magnitude relation in three data sets (with three others approaching statistical reliability). Also, entry of an event memory term into the regression models did not reduce the number of data sets in which a significant relation occurred (see Tables 8.1 and 8.2). Similarly, the analyses of the exact accuracy data suggested that pleasant events were more often dated accurately than

TABLE 8.5
Regression Betas, F-Test Results and p Values Describing the Relation
Between Event Evaluative Intensity and Event Valence and the Magnitude
of the Dating Error (Exactly Dated Events Discarded, Simple Model Only)

Data Source & Year		Valence of Event Affect	Derived Evaluative Intensity of Affect
Self-Events			
80KS	β	−.002	−.000
$F(1, 1476)$	F	.01	.00
	p	.9301	.9918
86KS	β	.013	−.027
$F(1, 1727)$	F	.32	1.21
	p	.5744	.2725
87KS	β	−.002	.007
$F(1, 2374)$	F	.01	.10
	p	.9261	.7476
88OH	β	−.034	−.001
$F(1, 2219)$	F	2.61	0.00
	p	.1016	.9634
89KS	β	−.008	−.067
$F(1, 1728)$	F	.12	7.20
	p	.7338	.0073
89OH	β	−.026	−.012
$F(1, 1016)$	F	.87	.14
	p	.3525	.7093
90KS	β	.022	−.038
$F(1, 2917)$	F	2.43	6.68
	p	.1191	.0098
91OH	β	−.006	−.039
$F(1, 1591)$	F	.05	2.24
	p	.8220	.1348
91KS	β	.043	−.017
$F(1, 1090)$	F	2.14	.30
	p	.1439	.5862
92KS	β	.010	−.047
$F(1, 2164)$	F	.23	4.413
	p	.6325	.0359
Other-Events			
88OH	β	−.050	.027
$F(1, 2027)$	F	5.03	1.42
	p	.0251	.2343
91OH	β	−.018	−.047
$F(1, 1516)$	F	.51	2.97
	p	.4747	.0849

unpleasant events and that this effect was not a function of memory (see Tables 8.3 and 8.4). Hence, taken together, the analyses that we have reported in this chapter suggest that pleasant events are dated more accurately (or with less error) than unpleasant events, primarily because pleasant events are more likely to be associated with exact dates than are unpleasant events.

The implications of the results reported in Table 8.5 for the evaluative intensity data do not converge exactly with implications of the results reported earlier in this chapter. The data in Table 8.5 indicate a continuing tendency for extreme events to have lower error magnitudes than less extreme events, even when the exactly dated events were discarded. Extreme events were associated with lower error magnitudes than less extreme events in 10 of the 12 data sets. However, this effect was significant in only 3 of those data sets (as compared to 8 that showed a significant relation in Table 8.1), with the results from two other data sets approaching statistical significance.

These results suggest that the negative relation between event evaluative intensity and error magnitude is a function of both reconstructive processes (which lead to heightened estimation accuracy) and date availability (which leads to an enhancement of exact dating frequency). By comparison, the data reported earlier in this chapter (in Tables 8.2 and 8.4) suggested that reconstructive processes may play the dominant role in the relation between event intensity and dating accuracy.

The data reported in Table 8.4 may help to explain the somewhat divergent conclusions that emerge from the different analyses. Those data suggested that event memory was a mediator of the relation between event evaluative intensity and exact dating accuracy. If this is indeed the case, then the exact event discarding procedure we used for the analyses reported in Table 8.5 may have worked against the event memory-based reconstructive hypothesis. More specifically, the data reported in Table 8.4 suggest that some of the exact dates associated with extreme events may have been reconstructed with no personal or schematic event dates available. If reconstruction produced higher exact accuracy rates for extreme events then for less extreme events (as implied by the results reported in Table 8.4), then discarding the exact events may produce an outcome that is unduly conservative with respect to the relation between event evaluative intensity and nonexact error magnitude. In fact, by the same logic, it is also possible that the impact of estimation processes, as manifested through the relations between event valence and error magnitude and between event evaluative intensity and error magnitude, are also somewhat stronger than indicated by the results of these analyses.

This possibility could be examined if an independent assessment of the source of the dates were provided. That is, this interpretation of the data would be clearer if we could assess whether a given date was known (in the sense that it was stored in a retrievable location in memory, either as a tag or from a schema) or whether it was reconstructed. This independent assessment was available in five of the studies. In these studies, after providing an event date, subjects examined a list of possible date retrieval and date reconstruction strategies and reported how they came to provide the event date. One of the options given to subjects was "I remembered the date"; other options were various reconstructive strategies (see Thompson, Skowronski, & Lee, 1988, for more information on these reconstructive strategies).

Analyses Discarding Exactly Dated Events With Date Remembered

We used the strategy data in analyses of the error magnitude data from the five data sets that included this measure. For these analyses, we discarded dates for which subjects reported remembering the date and were correct. The results of these analyses indicated that the intensity of event affect was significantly associated with lower dating error in three of the data sets and the effect was marginally significant in a fourth: 89OH $F(1, 1322) = .67$, $p < .4129$, $\beta = -.023$; 89KS $F(1, 2426) = 7.83$, $p < .0052$, $\beta = -.0570$; 91OH-self $F(1, 1916) = 2.67$, $p < .1026$, $\beta = -.038$; 91OH-other $F(1, 1765) = 4.21$, $p < .0403$, $\beta = -.052$; 90KS $F(1, 3329) = 9.18$, $p < .0025$, $\beta = -.042$. Thus, these results suggest that the lower error magnitude for events that were affectively extreme is substantially due to heightened memory for those events.

The data also suggest that the lowered error magnitude observed for pleasant events was primarily due to the enhanced exact accuracy associated with pleasant events. In these five data sets for which we discarded exactly dated events whose dates were remembered, pleasant events were not significantly associated with heightened dating accuracy, although the relation did approach significance in one study: 89OH $F(1, 1322) = 3.56$, $p < .0595$, $\beta = -.047$; 89KS $F(1, 2426) = .86$, $p < .3538$, $\beta = -.018$; 91OH-self $F(1, 1916) = .25$, $p < .6148$, $\beta = -.011$; 91OH-other $F(1, 1765) = 1.68$, $p < .1956$, $\beta = -.052$; 90KS $F(1, 3329) = 1.33$, $p < .2493$, $\beta = .015$.

CHARACTERISTICS OF EVENTS FOR WHICH EXACT DATES WERE REMEMBERED

In a final set of analyses, we looked at whether subjects' reports of the dating strategies that they used to produce event dates were related to the evaluative intensity and the valence of events. To examine these possibilities, we coded the dating strategy data so that the value of 1 was assigned to an event date that was reported to be recalled and the value of 0 was assigned to an event date that was reported to be produced by reconstructive strategies. These data were then analyzed using our standard regression model.

Regression analyses indicated relations between event affect and recall of an event date and between event evaluative intensity and recall of an exact date. In all five data sets, subjects more often reported knowing the dates of events when those events were pleasant than when they were unpleasant. This relation was statistically reliable in two data sets and approached statistical reliability in the other three: 89OH $F(1, 1577) = 2.90$, $p < .0890$, $\beta = .039$; 89KS $F(1, 2850) = 7.85$, $p < .0051$, $\beta = .050$; 91OH-self $F(1, 2264) = 3.31$, $p < .0690$, $\beta = .034$; 91OH-other $F(1, 1951) = 3.12$, $p < .0777$, $\beta = .037$; 90KS $F(1, 3508) = 25.76$, $p < .0001$, $\beta = .094$. However, in all five data sets, subjects also reported knowing the dates of events when the events were affectively extreme more often than when the events were affectively moderate. This relation was statistically significant in four data sets and approached statistical significance in the fifth: 89OH $F(1, 1577) = 29.40$, $p < .0001$, $\beta = .138$; 89KS $F(1, 2850) = 17.27$, $p < .0001$, $\beta = .076$; 91OH-self $F(1, 2264) = 3.31$, $p < .0690$, $\beta = .034$; 91OH-other $F(1, 1951) = 6.69$, $p < .0098$, $\beta = .057$; 90KS $F(1, 3508) = 74.77$, $p < .0001$, $\beta = .076$.

SUMMARY AND IMPLICATIONS

The data reported in this chapter suggest that pleasant events are dated more accurately than unpleasant events and that this effect occurs because date information is more often available for pleasant events than for unpleasant events. Although enhanced accuracy from reconstruction may play some role in this valence effect, it is a minor one. The fact that reconstruction plays only a minor role in the relation between dating and event valence is all the more sensible given that pleasant self-events are only marginally better recalled than unpleasant self-events (see chapter 4).

By comparison, the data presented in this chapter implicate both date availability and event memory-based reconstruction in the relation between event evaluative intensity and dating accuracy, although reconstruction seems to be the cognitive process that more strongly mediates this evaluative intensity effect. Again, this result is sensible given relatively substantial memory differences between affectively extreme and affectively moderate events (see chapter 4).

One of the interesting findings in this chapter is that the patterns of outcomes that characterize the dating of self-events and other-events seem to be very similar. However, that does not imply that other-event dating produces the same level of accuracy as self-event dating. Far from it. Direct self-other comparisons have been made in at least two studies (Skowronski et al., 1991; Betz & Skowronski, 1995), and both have indicated that self-event dating is much more accurate than other-event dating. Given that event dating is thought to be highly reconstructive, this outcome makes sense.

After all, there is likely to be much more fodder available for the reconstruction of the dates for self-events than for other-events. In the next chapter, we more explicitly take up the issue of self-event and other-event dating (and related topics) and examine more closely the theoretical mechanism and empirical effects that seem to characterize the event dating patterns for these two types of events.

CHAPTER NINE

The Role of the Self-Schema
in the Reconstruction of Time

SELF-EVENTS, OTHER-EVENTS, AND PUBLIC EVENTS

The relatively limited time range of our studies compared to the human life span has prevented us from investigating the role of higher order autobiographical memory structures in event dating. Life periods, however they are defined, span intervals on the order of years, that is, too long to be useful for people's datings in a study spanning a couple of years at the most. Moreover, events that are clearly "significant to the self-system" (p. 8), as Nelson (1993) defined autobiographical memory, do not occur every day or every week.

We have explored a different approach to studying the memory impact of higher order autobiographical knowledge. As outlined in chapter 5, our reasoning is that several degrees of significance to the self-system can be distinguished in naturally occurring kinds of events. *Self-events* that are about the person himself or herself, in the sense that they were experienced directly and concerned the experiencing person. We assume that self-events are high in self relevance, even if they are not deeply significant. *Other-events* are about some other person who is well known to the first person. We assume that other-events are generally lower in self-relevance than self-events, whether the first person was present to experience them or only heard about them from the other person. We also assumed that *public news events* would be even lower in self-relevance because they are generally about neither the first person nor anybody he or she knows or is personally related to.

When the difference between the three kinds of events is phrased in terms of self-relevance, it invites the prediction that memory is much better

182

for self-events than for other-events and public events. This was argued at length by Larsen (1988), and it was confirmed in chapter 5 of this volume. Correspondingly, we may expect that datings are more accurate for self-events than for nonself-events.

This is not a foregone conclusion, however. Public events have been commonly used in neuropsychological instruments for assessing the time course of amnesia (Squire & Slater, 1975; Warrington & Silberstein, 1970), on the assumption that the results obtained with public events are equivalent to the memory loss existing for autobiographical events. Furthermore, and directly opposed to the prediction from self-relevance, some social psychologists (e.g., Halbwachs and Blondel in the 1920s and 1930s; see Lieury, Richer, & Weeger, 1978) have claimed that public events form the backbone of people's individual personal history and in particular of the sense of time in that history. This *collective memory view* may seem even more reasonable because public events are usually more dramatic than one's personal experiences and certainly get more dramatic publicity. Public events may be especially germane to temporal judgments because their dates are frequently repeated in the media, and they often appear to serve as a kind of common currency to determine location in calendar time: "You know, it was just before the Berlin Wall came down, right? . . . which means 1989." In the collective-memory view, dating of public events should be more straightforward and perhaps also more accurate than dating of self-events.

The reconstructive theory of memory for time that we advanced in previous chapters might be called a *personal schema view*. This view carries different and somewhat more complicated implications for dating. The temporal schemata and recurrent landmarks on which reconstruction relies are assumed to derive primarily from the regularities of personal life. Two predictions follow. First, nonself-events should be harder to relate to generic knowledge that enables reconstruction of time than are self-events. Second, the reconstructive process for nonself-events should typically be mediated by reference to autobiographical schemata and landmarks. Moreover, because episodic memory of the content of nonself-events is relatively poor (see chapter 5), access cues and associations to other events should often be scarce, and this is an additional disadvantage for reconstructing the time of nonself-events.

Certain other factors may modify these predictions of the personal schema view. To some extent, people are likely to share generic knowledge with friends, relatives, and university roommates because their conditions of everyday life are similar. Such similarities may facilitate temporal reconstruction for events that occur to familiar other persons. The dating of public events, on the other hand, may be assisted by generic knowledge that reflects regularities and landmarks of a public nature, like presidential periods, elections, and major changes in world affairs (cf. Brown, 1990). Furthermore, people receive information about public events from mass media reports or from other people. The situation in which this information is received, how-ever, is a personally experienced event; that is, public events have a personal "reception context" (Brown et al., 1985; Larsen, 1988). If a public event remains associated with this personal context in memory, contextual infor-mation may provide a venue of access to generic temporal knowledge when the time of a self-event is reconstructed. The extent to which such factors can offset the expected disadvantage of nonself-events is explored in the following sections.

SUBJECTIVE REPORTS OF RECONSTRUCTIVE STRATEGIES FOR NONSELF-EVENTS

The evidence available regarding the strategies people apply to judge the time of nonself-events is scarce, and it is not directly comparable to the evidence for self-events. The main interest of this research has been the extent to which references to personal memories are used when the time of public events is determined. The findings in three studies of major news events are summa-rized in Table 9.1.

To explore the collective memory view, Lieury, Aiello, Lepreux, and Mellet (1980, Exp. 2) asked subjects for written reports on the reference information they used when dating public events 1–16 years into the past. The use of any reference information was reported in just 22% of the datings; in only

TABLE 9.1
Percentage Reported Use of Various Categories of Information
for Reconstructing the Time of Major, Public News Events

Category of information	Temporal Level						
	Month, year[a]	Year[b]	Month[b]	Day of Month[b]	Day of Week[b]	Hour[b]	Month, year[c]
Personal events	20	25	23	9	14	18	33
Public events	2	14	9	3	1	4	23
Schematic knowledge	–	12	19	2	6	22	17
Other (incl. guess)	–	9	3	2	6	3	5
No report	78	40	45	83	74	53	22

[a]Lieury et al. (1980) obtained from free written responses.

[b]Friedman & Wilkins (1985) obtained from free written responses. Their categories "Some aspect of event itself" and "Logical constraint" are combined into "Schematic knowledge" based on the examples given in the paper; similarly, their category "Interval before or after another event" apparently includes all references to particular "Public events."

[c]Brown (1990) obtained from think-aloud protocols. Because Brown allowed scoring of more than one category per event, his proportions are recalculated to show overall frequency of use. His categories "Same-narrative event" and "Non-narrative event" are combined into "Public events"; his "Specific temporal facts" are classified as "Other" responses.

one-tenth of these cases was there reference to other public events. The vast majority of datings were explicitly mediated by personal memory landmarks. Friedman and Wilkins (1985) employed a similar written procedure but asked for separate reports for the year, the month, the day of the month, the day of the week, and the hour of each public event (up to 20 years old). For day of month and day of week, the results were very close to those of Lieury et al.—about 80% omissions, with personal-memory landmarks accounting for the majority of the positive reports (10–15%). However, Friedman and Wilkins obtained lower omission rates for year, month, and hour (40–50%), but the rate of reference to personal events remained similar to the French study at 20–25%. In addition, subjects reported a fair rate of using schematic knowledge for year, month, and hour (12–22% of the datings), and judging from the examples provided by the authors, the schemata used were personal. Year and month estimates gave rise to the largest share of references to other public news events, some 15%.

A close view of temporal reconstruction for public events through the prism of subjective reports is provided by Brown (1990). He collected concurrent think-aloud protocols from subjects while they tried to determine the year and month of public events that occurred 2–5 years ago. The think-aloud procedure may better reflect the process of reconstruction than reports obtained after dating of the event has been completed (Ericsson & Simon, 1984). Using this procedure, less than 25% of the datings were left unjustified. Because some inferential steps are likely to escape verbalization even in the think-aloud procedure, this proportion may be regarded as the upper limit on the rate of unaided guesses for major news events. Among the justified datings, reference to the personal context associated with getting news of the event was made in almost half of the events, reference to other news events for one third, and reference to schematic knowledge for one fourth. The schema used most commonly in this study of US subjects was not a personal schema but instead was knowledge of presidential periods. This knowledge was successfully applied also to foreign news, like the assassination of Egyptian President Anwar Sadat and the Falkland Islands war.

These studies clearly indicate that the collective memory view of time is not tenable. Although some use of collective memories as landmarks for time estimation is reported at the scale of years and months, public events are much more often located in time through the mediation of personal time markers. Note that the eruption of Mount St. Helens, which Loftus and Marburger (1983) showed to be an effective temporal landmark for people in the Seattle area, was most likely a personal event, as well as a public one, for these subjects.

Furthermore, when compared to the strategy reports for self-events shown in Tables 6.1 and 6.2, the findings for public events suggest that the use of temporal schemata is much less frequent, and guessing (i.e., no justification for the temporal estimate) is correspondingly more common. In particular, the week schema, which figured so prominently in the dating of self-events, is almost never reported upon for these public events. When reference to self-events is not possible, guessing, unaided by generic temporal knowledge, may be the best people can do.

What about events that are more closely related to the self? We obtained strategy reports for the dating of self-events and events of a familiar other person (selected by the subject). Thompson et al. (1988b) asked subjects to record events during 10 weeks prior to the memory test. Following each dating, subjects were given a forced choice among a few strategies. The results for these relatively recent events serve to reinforce the finding that public events are infrequently used as landmarks, accounting for only 2% of the 33% landmark references that were indicated for the nonself-events. The strategies from which subjects could choose unfortunately did not include schematic reconstruction.

In a second experiment (i.e., the 91OH data set), the reported strategies for self- and other-events were compared in more detail. Subjects were offered the same choices as shown in Table 6.2, and the detailed results are given in Table 9.2.

Pure guessing was very rarely reported for either event category. For other-events, the rate of guessing, as opposed to reconstruction, may therefore not be as high as suggested by the great number of omissions in studies of public events. The patterns of strategy use were generally very similar for self- and other-events. However, recall of the exact date was somewhat lower for other-events, and reference to cyclic landmarks (i.e., prototypic information) was correspondingly higher (i.e., both differences of about 10%). Thus, when events concern a familiar other person whom the subject has selected, it may be possible to apply the same schemata and temporal landmarks to the dating of those events as to self-events.

In conclusion, the subjective reports in the literature suggest that reconstruction of the time of public events is strongly mediated by associations to self-events, in particular to memory of the personal context in which one learned about the public event. To a lesser extent, public landmarks and generic public knowledge can be exploited. Thus, the sense of time among events that are essentially unrelated to the self seems to rely significantly on the temporal structure occurring in the autobiographical, self-related sphere. However, these indirect sources of temporal information apparently do not suffice to prevent a high level of guessing when the date of public events is judged. We therefore expect temporal judgments for public events to be considerably less accurate than for self-events. Friedman and Wilkins' (1985) findings suggest, furthermore, that use of the week schema may particularly suffer, which could lead to a different pattern of dating errors for public events than the one we documented in chapter 6.

TABLE 9.2
Subjects' Reports of Information Use in Event Dating by Dating Strategy
and Diary Target: Percentage Used, Error Magnitude, and
Exact Dating Accuracy (From Betz & Skowronski, 1995)

		Diary Event Target	
		Self	Other
	% Used	19.02	11.80
Knew exact date	Error Magnitude	1.93	2.70
	% Exactly Correct	79.63	79.15
	% Used	9.83	10.79
Used reference event	Error Magnitude	7.40	6.72
	% Exactly Correct	31.86	33.95
	% Used	45.87	40.76
Knew general reference period	Error Magnitude	8.66	9.25
	% Exactly Correct	18.03	14.16
	% Used	4.74	5.17
Estimated # intervening events	Error Magnitude	12.14	11.76
	% Exactly Correct	7.34	7.77
	% Used	4.44	4.62
Used memory clarity to estimate	Error Magnitude	11.46	13.94
	% Exactly Correct	24.51	18.48
	% Used	15.49	25.60
Used prototypic information	Error Magnitude	13.76	14.13
	% Exactly Correct	7.30	5.69
	% Used	.61	1.20
Guessed	Error Magnitude	15.93	8.54
	% Exactly Correct	14.29	25.00
	% Used	.00	.05
Other	Error Magnitude	—	6.00
	% Exactly Correct	—	0.00

In contrast to news, the strategies reported for dating the events of other persons who are closely familiar to the self suggest that the error pattern is similar to that for self-events. However, due to the comparatively poor memory of the content of other-events (as discussed in chapter 5), the accuracy of dating other-events may still be substantially lower than self-events.

DATING ACCURACY FOR SELF- AND NONSELF-EVENTS

The possible importance of self-relevance is one of the issues that makes generalizations from the laboratory to naturalistic research on temporal memory questionable (see Friedman, 1993). Nevertheless, to our knowledge the only research that has directly compared temporal memory for events varying in self-relevance is that described in this book. These studies used the double-diary method in which subjects kept parallel diaries of self- and non-self-events. In the sections to follow, we review the results and present some new and more powerful analyses that reflect upon the reconstructive account of temporal memory outlined in previous chapters.

We first examined the global accuracy of temporal judgments for self- and nonself-events, as measured by the magnitude of subjects' dating errors. Figures 9.1a and 9.1b show the overall distributions from two of our studies in which the retention times were similar (i.e., up to 10–15 weeks). The nonself-events are events of familiar others and news events, respectively.

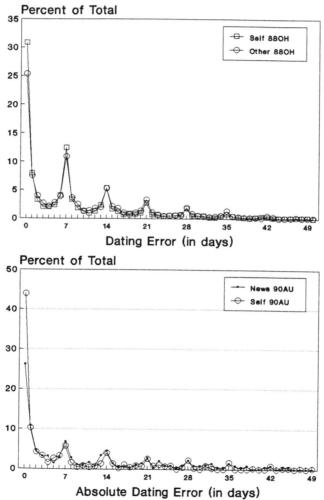

FIG. 9.1. Distribution of absolute dating errors for self-events and other-events (panel A, data from 88OH) and for self-events and news events (panel B, data from 90AU, Test 1).

The three components of the reconstructive process identified in chapter 6 are apparent for both self- and nonself-events: high frequency of exact datings, negatively accelerated decline at larger error magnitudes, and day-of-week (DOW) periodicity. However, exact datings are somewhat lower for the nonself-events, and the rate of large errors appears a little higher. Are these differences reliable, and, if so, can their origins be traced?

To separate the three components of the distribution, we analyzed the proportion of exact datings, then considered the average error magnitude of the remaining, inexact, datings, and finally we examined the DOW periodicity in terms of the rate of hitting the correct day of the week (i.e., DOW hit proportion). As we argued in chapter 6, this ordering of the three measures is supposed to represent a movement from high to low memory dependence and, conversely, from low to high schema dependence.

Whereas the first two measures are logically and mathematically independent, the DOW measure poses some problems. All exact datings are of course DOW hits, but if exact datings are included in the computation of DOW hit proportions, the two measures will not be independent. On the other hand, if the exact datings are excluded from the calculation of DOW hit rates, the proportions will be depressed by the high rate of errors close to the central peak. The frequency of such close errors depends on the dispersion of errors, and thus the DOW hit proportion is confounded with the second measure, the average error magnitude of inexact datings. We therefore decided to exclude from the computation of DOW hits all date estimates falling within a full week of the correct date, that is, −3 through +3 days of error (i.e., week error equals zero). This procedure is supported by our earlier finding that the proportion of DOW hits is elevated when week error equals zero but is stable at week errors larger than zero (Larsen & Thompson, in press).

Table 9.3 shows averages of these three measures for self- and nonself-events obtained in four studies. Subjects were asked to enter one self-event and one nonself-event in their diaries every day of the diary period. In the 83KS, 88OH, and 91OH data sets, the subjects' nonself diary consisted of events occurring to a familiar person—somebody they saw every day. In the study by Larsen and Thompson (1995, Exp.1, which is the 90AU data set), the nonself-events were public news events; news events of a personal nature (e.g., news heard about a friend or relative) that occurred despite our instruction to focus on public news events were excluded from analysis. The data of 1 of the 12 subjects were discarded entirely because more than half of her news events were personal.

As we expected, the pairwise differences between self- and nonself-events indicate generally lower dating accuracy for nonself-events. All these differences were significant at $p < .01$ or better, except the error magnitude measure in the 83KS data set, in which the short diary period limited the

TABLE 9.3

Average Measures of Dating Accuracy for Self-Events and Nonself-Events

Nonself-Events and Study	Diary Period (wks)	Max. Reten. Time (wks)	Exact Datings (Proportion)		Inexact Dates (Days Error)		DOW Hits[a] (Proportion)	
			Self	Non	Self	Non	Self	Non
Other-Events								
83KS	3	7	.25	.16	9.9	10.7	.50	.39
88OH	10	10	.31	.25	12.2	12.8	.42	.38
91OH	10	10	.29	.22	12.2	12.7	.40	.33
News Events								
90AU	14	15[b]	.44	.26	11.2	16.5	.37	.31
	14	37[c]	.31	.15	20.1	25.1	.49	.35

[a]The DOW hit proportions are calculated after deleting all responses that were within 3 days of the correct date, that is, in the correct week.
[b]Test 1.
[c]Test 2, using a different random sample of diary events.

opportunity for errors and the number of observations. We consider the three components of dating in turn.

Exact Datings

As we discussed in chapter 6, only a minority of exact datings seem to be based on explicit temporal tags. Another small subset of exact datings is entirely deduced from generic knowledge of recurrent dates. Usually, however, exact datings result from convergent use of several schemata and landmarks. This process requires memory of event details (i.e., temporal cues) as well as associations to landmarks or other mediating events; we may say that exact date reconstruction is highly memory intensive. The existence of appropriate schematic knowledge is also presupposed. Consequently, the richness of event memory and the availability of temporal schemata are expected to favor strongly self-events over all nonself-events, but especially news events.

The pioneering 83KS study used a diary period of only 3 weeks but the retention interval was comparable to other semester studies (cf. Table 9.3). In the 83KS study, dating of self-events clearly surpassed dating of the events of familiar others ($p < .001$). The two more extensive Ohio State studies produced higher but similar exact dating proportions, with a difference of 6–7% in favor of self-events (for both studies, $p < .001$). Though it is highly reliable, this small difference does not suggest a qualitative distinction between the reconstructive processes applied to self-events and other-events. The difference may be caused by people knowing a greater number of recurrent landmarks pertaining to their personal lives (e.g., birthdays) than to the lives of others.

The 90AU data showed a substantially larger disparity of exact datings between self and news events ($p < .0001$, see the bottom panel of Table 9.3. Test 1 of this study is shown separately because dairy period and retention time is comparable to the other-events studies). The level of exact datings was somewhat higher in this study than in the studies of other-events. This is probably due to a difference in procedure; that is, subjects were given more cues in the news study before judging the date—up to six diary lines, as opposed to three lines in the other-events studies. It is therefore reasonable that the level of exact datings in this study is generally inflated.

To investigate how the variables that relate to memory for the three kinds of events affect the rate of exact datings, the data from the 83KS, 88OH, and 90AU studies were analyzed using a series of repeated-measures multiple regressions. As we discussed in previous chapters, retention interval, quadratic retention interval, and memory clarity ratings were included as predictors, along with the self–nonself variable (coded as 0 and 1, respectively). For the news event study, two ratings of memory clarity were available for each event: clarity of the event itself—the core event, and clarity of the personal context. Both memory measures were entered into the analyses.

The memory ratings assess the clarity of the event plus context viewed in isolation from other events, that is, *intraevent memory*. The memory ratings decline with retention interval, as we showed in chapter 3. If the variables of retention interval and quadratic retention interval remain significant when the effect of memory rating is controlled for in the regression, these variables carry the influence of *interevent memory*, that is, associations between the target event and a network of other events that may aid temporal reconstruction. The intricate web of episodic associations among events—their narrative embedding (cf. Brown, 1990)—is likely to be highly vulnerable to the forgetting indicated by an independent contribution of retention interval. This distinction between intraevent and interevent memory is reminiscent of Mandler's (1980) analysis of recognition as involving two components, intraevent integration (i.e., familiarity) and interevent elaboration (i.e., retrieval).

The results of the regressions are shown in Table 9.4. Strong, independent effects of both retention interval and memory clarity on the rate of exact datings emerge in all three studies. The joint effect of linear and quadratic retention time—a negative, Ebbinghausian, acceleration—also appeared in the exact datings of our other diary studies (see chapter 7). In combination with the equally impressive effects of memory ratings, this finding supports for the contention that exact datings depend critically on rich and accurate memory, intraevent as well as interevent.

Table 9.4 also shows a difference between other-events and news events. When intraevent and interevent memory are partialled out, exact datings of

TABLE 9.4
Exact Dating Proportions for Self- and Nonself-Events: Results
of Repeated-Measures Multiple Regression Analyses

Nonself-Events	Regr. Parameter	Independent Variables			
		Self vs. Nonself	Retention Time	Retention Time 2	Memory Clarity
88OH					
Other-events	β	−.210	−.284	.162	.281
df=(1, 6049)	F	3.52	602.59	168.23	463.42
	p	>.05	<.0001	<.0001	<.0001
91OH					
Other-events	β	−.044	−.238	.181	.235
df=(1, 4267)	F	10.08	282.81	141.46	228.39
	p	<.002	<.0001	<.0001	<.0001
90AU					
News events[a]	β	−.136	−.441	.307	.178
df=(1, 1445)	F	26.64	16.60	8.19	42.14
	p	<.0001	<.0001	<.01	<.0001

[a]Only results for memory clarity of the personal context are shown; the effect of memory clarity of the event core was nonsignificant, $F < 1$.

other-events were only marginally more frequent than self-events. In one study, the difference was just below the 5% level of significance; in the other it was just above the 5% level. In other words, controlling for memory and forgetting differences between the two event types substantially reduces the exact dating disadvantage of other-events. In contrast, the lower frequency of exact datings for news events cannot be explained by inferior memory for these events. It therefore seems likely that differences between personal events and news events in relevant, generic knowledge must be invoked to account for the findings.

Whereas clarity of memory for the personal context was a highly reliable predictor of exact datings for both news and self-events, memory clarity for the core of the events was irrelevant to dating ($F < 1$). The typically poor memory for the context of news events does not fully explain the dating disadvantage. However, the similarity of news and self-events in this respect suggests a fundamental difference between the process of dating the two kinds of events: News events have to be referred to schematic knowledge, which is concerned with personal circumstances and is not inherently connected with the content of the news events. This may be part of the explanation for why news is less often dated exactly: Functionally, it is not the news event but rather the reception of the news (or the response to the news) that is dated.

Error Magnitude of Inexact Datings

The average error magnitude of inexact datings is an indication of the dispersion of the total error distribution, independent of exact datings and DOW periodicity. It is suggestive of constraints on the temporal estimation process that exert their effect at a level above the week schema.

The dating error magnitude of self- and other-events did not differ significantly in the brief 83KS double-diary study (cf. Table 9.3). However, the 88OH and 91OH data sets yielded reliable though rather small differences in error magnitude between events from the two kinds of diary, with self-events being dated more accurately. The differences were significant when retention time was controlled for ($ps < .05$). As shown in Table 9.5, however, the self–other difference was eliminated in both studies when variations in the memory ratings accorded to the events were also partialled out. It therefore seems that the lower error magnitude for other-events can exhaustively be ascribed to the fact that less information is remembered about other-events than self-events. There is no need to suppose that the dating process and the knowledge structures that constrain dating errors are any different for these event categories (as also suggested by the subjective reports reviewed earlier in this chapter).

Memory clarity (i.e., intraevent memory) was by far the strongest predictor of dating error magnitude in the two Ohio State studies. However, the two

TABLE 9.5
Error Magnitude of Inexact Datings for Self- and Nonself-Events:
Results of Repeated-Measures Multiple Regression Analyses

Nonself-Events	Regr. Parameter	Independent Variables			
		Self vs. Nonself	Retention Time	Retention Time 2	Memory Clarity
88OH					
Other-events	β	.014	.205	.008	−.144
df=(1, 4328)	F	<1	190.32	<1	72.18
	p	>.05	<.0001	NA	<.0001
91OH					
Other-events	β	.000	.136	.127	−.179
df=(1, 3159)	F	<1	60.48	50.95	85.22
	p	>.05	<.0001	<.0001	<.0001
90AU					
News events[a]	β	.125	.412	NS	−.103
df=(1, 1008)	F	14.69	9.03	1.86	9.44
	p	<.001	<.01	>.05	<.01

[a]Only results for memory clarity of the personal context are shown; the effect of memory clarity of the event core was nonsignificant, $F < 1$.

retention interval variables had different effects in the two studies. Whereas retention interval was independently significant in both, the quadratic effect of retention interval was only reliable in the most recent study. It is not clear what caused this difference, but it seems that interevent memory is less important for the magnitude of inexact datings than for the rate of exact datings. Obviously, limiting the size of dating errors should be less memory-intensive than achieving exactly correct datings. However, it is somewhat surprising that intraevent memory appears to be more critical for error size than does interevent memory.

The news event study (90AU) yielded a more substantial gap between the mean errors for inexact datings of self-events and nonself-events ($ps <$ .0001). Unlike that found in the other-event studies, this gap remained after the retention interval and memory variables were included in the regression (see Table 9.5). Only the clarity of contextual memory predicted dating error magnitude for news and self-events, not clarity of the event core ($F < 1$), as was the case for the exact dating measure. The quadratic effect of retention interval was not reliable in the news event analysis.

The results for the magnitude of dating errors are very similar to those for exact datings. For both measures, the lower accuracy of temporal estimates for news cannot be accounted for exhaustively by inferior memory, unlike other-events, where controlling for memory eradicated the self–other difference. For both measures, memory of contextual information was a powerful determinant of temporal accuracy, whereas memory of the event core was entirely ineffectual. Only the quadratic effect of retention time on exact dating proportions was not consistently duplicated with the error magnitude measure. This suggests that error magnitude relies less acutely on interevent associations than do exact datings. When datings are inexact, the error magnitude may depend primarily on generic schemata and linear structures that are accessed directly from cues given by the contextual information of the target event.

Day-of-Week Accuracy

We argued that the day-of-week component of the dating errors is dependent mainly on reconstruction from the week schema and minimally on event memory. Information about the event is needed to place it in the schema, but extensive interevent associations should be of little avail. However, because the week schema is based on regularities of personal life, news events should exhibit lower day-of-week accuracy than self-events, unless their personal context is well remembered. However, because the week schema appears to be socially shared, the events of familiar others may behave like self-events.

DOW Error Distribution.   We deal first with the distribution of errors across the days of the week in terms of the reconstructive model presented in chapter 6. The percentage distributions around the correct day of the week obtained in two of our studies are shown in Fig. 9.2. The figure is

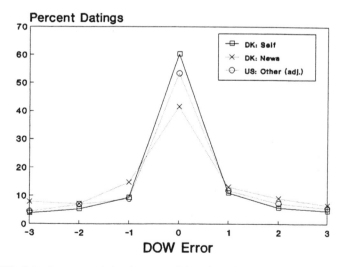

FIG. 9.2. Proportional distributions of day-of-week errors (DOW error) for self-events, other-events, and news events. (Data from 91OH and 90AU. Other-event proportions are adjusted to compensate for the different error level of self-events in the two studies.)

based on all observed responses, including those in the correct week (i.e., zero week error). Also, the error frequencies from the other-event study are adjusted to compensate for the slight difference between the error rates for self-events in the two studies. The shape of the curves for the three kinds of events are identical; only the height of the peaks varies. The percentage of DOW hits (i.e., zero DOW error) is considerably lower for news events than for self-events, whereas other-events are only slightly below self-events.

In the 90AU study, we derived predictions for the DOW distribution of news events in the same manner as described for self-events in chapter 6. That is, we collected day group choices from subjects and used the proportion of successful choices to calculate expected probabilities of DOW errors. The obtained day group choices were quite similar for self and news items, except that the rate of picking a single day of the week was lower for news (i.e., 20% as opposed to 40% for self-events) and the rate of unconstrained guessing was correspondingly higher (i.e., 45% for news, 25% for self-events). Successful choices of 2-day and 5-day groups were almost identical at about 15% and 20%, respectively, and choices of 3-day and 4-day groups were below 5% for both event types. Thus, because the percentages of the day groups have to add up to 100%, only one free parameter of the model shown in Fig. 6.5 needed to be changed, namely, a decrease of single-day choices by 20% for news; the 20% increase of guesses follows by mathematical necessity.

The 45% guessing rate estimated by this method is far below the 75% suggested by the strategy reports for day-of-week judgments that Friedman and Wilkins (1985) collected (see Table 9.1). A number of differences between the events in the two studies prevent easy comparisons (e.g., retention time, importance), but we believe the present method yields a better estimate of actual guessing because the subject is not forced to specify a strategy.

With the weights for day group sizes given previously, we calculated expected error rates, like those shown in Table 6.5. The fit of the predictions to the empirical data is shown in Fig. 9.3. The data did not deviate significantly from the predictions (evaluated by a chi-square test on the observed response frequencies for all 11 subjects, $\chi^2(6, N = 603) = 8.99, p > .10$).

That the models for self-events and news differ only in the frequency of guesses and single-day choices indicates that the structure of the week schema is basically the same for both event types but that it cannot be applied as often and at as high a level of precision for news events. This may happen either because there is less detail in the schema relevant to news than to self-events or because fewer relevant cues are available from memory of news event. We pursue this issue one step further in the next section.

DOW Hit Rate. The similarity of the distributions for the three kinds of events justify our use of the DOW hit rate—the height of the peak—as a summary measure of the error pattern. As noted earlier, to obtain a measure

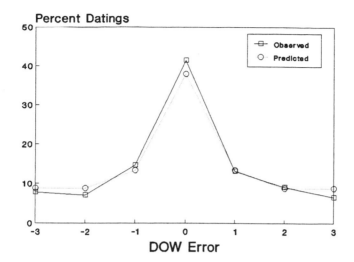

FIG. 9.3. News events: Predicted and observed DOW error proportions (from Larsen & Thompson, in press, Figure 5).

that is independent from exact datings and error magnitude, responses within ±3 days of error are removed from the computations.

The average hit rates obtained in our four double-diary studies are shown in Table 9.3. Not surprisingly, DOW hits were quite common in the brief diary period of 83KS; half of the self-event errors were on the correct day of the week, as were more than a third of the other-event errors. The self–other difference was significant, $p < .01$. DOW hits were almost as common in the three more extended studies, but the absolute superiority of self- over nonself-events was somewhat smaller, 5–7% as compared to the 11% gap reported in the 83KS data set. Nevertheless, all differences were significant at $p = .01$ or better. It is noteworthy that even for news events the DOW hit rate is far better than the 14% expected by chance.

As before, the contribution of event memory to dating was investigated by pooled within-subjects multiple regression analyses of data from the three extended studies (see Table 9.6). The results for the two other-event studies are rather inconsistent, except that the rating of memory clarity was a highly reliable predictor of DOW hit rate in both studies (though perhaps not as strongly as it was the case for exact datings and error magnitude). However, in one study retention time and quadratic retention time also predicted DOW hits, and the joint effect of these three variables preempted the effect of the self–other distinction. In the other study, retention time did not predict DOW hits whereas the self-other distinction maintained a reliable effect. In summary, intraevent memory is clearly important for DOW accuracy, but the roles of interevent memory and moderate distance from the self-schema are uncertain.

TABLE 9.6
DOW Hit Proportions for Self- and Nonself-Events:
Results of Repeated-Measures Multiple Regression Analyses

Nonself Events	Regr. Parameter	Independent Variables			
		Self- vs. Nonself	Retention Time	Retention Time 2	Memory Clarity
88OH Other-Events df=(1, 3503)	β	−.024	−.058	−.053	.109
	F	2.02	11.61	9.81	32.11
	p	>.05	<.001	<.002	<.0001
91OH Other-Events df=(1, 2516)	β	−.062	−.074	−.019	.068
	F	9.77	13.53	<1	9.51
	p	<.002	<.001	>.05	<.01
90AU News Events[a] df=(1, 772)	β	−.086	.356	NS	.142
	F	4.94	4.41	3.57	11.81
	p	<.05	<.05	>.05	<.001

[a]Only results for memory clarity of the personal context are shown; the effect of memory clarity of the event core was nonsignificant, $F < 1$.

In the news event study (90AU), a more complicated and surprising pattern of effects was found. Just like exact datings and error magnitude, DOW hits depended reliably on memory clarity of the personal context, whereas memory for the news itself was insignificant ($F < 1$). In addition, both linear retention interval and the self–news variable predicted DOW hits, though rather weakly ($ps < .05$). However, a significant interaction between event type and linear retention interval was obtained, $F(1, 771) = 6.03$, $p = .01$, $\beta = −.193$. Two points are noteworthy in this pattern. First, the interaction of retention interval and event type is one of the few effects showing that self-events and nonself-events behave differently in response to the classical variables of memory research (valence was another example). Second, the beta of the retention time effect suggests that the DOW hit rate increases with increasing time; this trend is also apparent from the averages in Table 9.3.

The Retention Interval × Event Type interaction is shown in Fig. 9.4. This figure reveals a crossover in the frequency of DOW hits between the two event types at very short retention intervals (i.e., within 2 months). Across the whole period, the tendency is for more DOW hits at longer intervals when self-events are concerned, whereas fewer DOW hits occur at longer intervals for news, particularly after 6 months have elapsed. For self-events, we suggest that the increasing trend of DOW hits is partly due to the removal

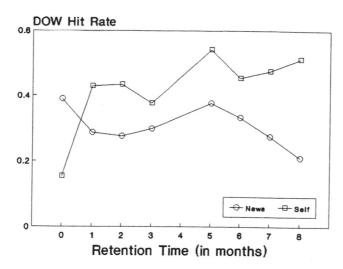

FIG. 9.4. DOW hit rate (excluding datings within ±3 days of the correct date) as a function of retention time for self-events and news. (Data from 90AU.)

of datings within the correct week. At short intervals, that is, events for which the right day of the week can be determined will also be associated with other pieces of temporal information, which will allow a successful estimate of the exact date of the event. Conversely, inexactly dated events will have little temporal information, insufficient to apply the week schema. As retention time increases, temporal information is degraded so that fewer events are dated exactly, but it presumably takes so little cueing to access the week schema that the DOW of this increasing number of inexact datings may still be right. Thus, the DOW hit rate increases.

If this interpretation is correct, why does it fail to hold for news events? The most obvious suggestion is that the need for contextual information is elevated for news because of low relevance of the personal week schema. When memory for the personal context of news is degraded by forgetting so that it cannot be dated exactly, it often falls below the threshold of cue information necessary to estimate the day of the week successfully. However, this divergence of news from events closer to the self must be regarded with caution because it was demonstrated only in this study.

We may now conclude that the day of the week is less often correctly reconstructed for nonself- than for self-events (though clearly above chance level). This difference is primarily due to lower intraevent memory, and for news, to low memory of the personal context. Day-of-week accuracy is only weakly dependent on interevent memory and therefore is little affected by forgetting.

The moderate dependence of DOW accuracy on event memory is in contrast to the other two measures of temporal accuracy. This finding supports the view that DOW hits result from the reconstructive application of a stable, generalized knowledge structure—a week schema. If the information pointing to the day of the week had been separately stored and retained, as a temporal code or tag, a clear effect of degradation of the memory trace over time would be expected. However, the stability observed in the relatively short time window of these experiments would hardly last indefinitely. Over intervals of years, the weekly activities of individuals are likely to change, leading to corresponding changes (i.e., updating) of the week schema. Our results suggest that the usual rate of such schema change is too slow to distort temporal memory in less than a year.

Previous studies have found little or no erosion of day-of-week accuracy for self-event memories (Huttenlocher et al., 1992; Thompson et al., 1993). The present results confirm these findings and extend the time frame and range of event content for which they can be regarded as valid. It may be suspected that the resistance of DOW hits to forgetting could be a methodological artifact because the subjects were provided with the text of their original diary record before dating each event. The diaries might have contained abundant cues for access to temporal schemata, masking any possible effect of forgetting. However, this seems unlikely because the proportion of DOW hits for self-events is very close to that reported by Huttenlocher et al. (1992), who gave minimal cues to their subjects.

Error Matrices. The day-of-week error patterns do not simply reflect errors that are multiples of one week; other, more complex error patterns also emerged. For example, the within-week error data presented in Table 9.7 suggest that subjects have the week parsed into several different components. Four of the traditional work days (i.e., Monday through Thursday) were fairly interchangeable in terms of the misdatings, although within this block of four there was some tendency to misdate events either one day long or one day short (e.g., Monday events were somewhat less likely to be misdated as occurring on Thursday than on Tuesday; Tuesday events were more likely to be misdated as occurring on Wednesday than on Monday).

This one-day error pattern breaks down on Thursdays, at least for self-events: Thursday events were relatively infrequently misdated as occurring on a Friday. Similarly, Sunday events were not frequently misdated as occurring on a Monday. Although these patterns may lead one to speculate (as did Huttenlocher et al., 1992) that the week can be parsed into a work week and a weekend, the breakdown appears to be more complex than that. Friday events were often thought to occur on Saturday but not Sunday. Similarly, Saturday events were thought to occur on Friday but not Sunday. This finding suggests that many of the diary entries for Friday and Saturday were seen as occurring on either of those days (e.g., student parties). By comparison, Sunday events were frequently misdated as occurring on Sat-

TABLE 9.7

Confusion Matrix of Days of the Week for Erroneously Dated Events
by Self-Events and Other Events. Columns Are Actual Days;
Rows Are Reported Days; Entries Are Conditional Probabilities

	Sun	Mon	Tue	Wed	Thu	Fri	Sat
				Self-Events			
Sun	38.1	6.0	3.4	4.2	2.0	2.6	6.8
Mon	6.7	22.9	17.2	12.5	8.9	5.8	3.4
Tue	4.9	16.0	24.7	14.9	16.6	8.5	5.1
Wed	8.1	25.6	21.8	31.5	26.7	14.3	7.1
Thu	5.3	14.8	22.6	19.9	27.1	12.5	9.7
Fri	9.9	9.5	8.8	10.4	11.7	37.5	24.0
Sat	26.9	5.2	1.6	6.6	6.8	18.8	43.9
				Other-Events			
Sun	26.5	7.5	3.4	3.4	5.0	5.9	10.5
Mon	7.6	16.3	15.9	13.6	10.0	10.3	5.9
Tue	5.8	20.3	20.9	19.3	13.1	10.3	3.2
Wed	12.5	23.0	19.7	25.2	21.2	14.3	10.4
Thu	13.5	9.7	19.7	20.9	24.0	11.8	3.7
Fri	9.9	14.0	12.6	12.8	17.2	34.3	25.0
Sat	24.2	9.2	8.0	4.7	9.5	13.2	41.4

urday but not on Friday. Thus, many of the Sunday events were probably
generic weekend events that could have occurred on either of the traditional
weekend days (e.g., watching football on TV). This complex pattern conflicts
with Huttenlocher et al.'s (1992) assertion that the within-week schema is
a simple 5 + 1 + 1 week days and the two weekend days. Instead, our data
suggest that subjects may have more complicated schemas that include not
only weekdays and weekends but also such groups as midweek (e.g., Tuesday, Wednesday, and Thursday) or end of week (e.g., Thursday and Friday).
The patterns of day-of-week choices directly expressed by subjects is consistent with this complexity. When asked to guess the days on which events
occurred, subjects most often chose 1-day, 2-day, or 5-day groups. The 2-day
groups were not exclusively weekends but rather represented pairs of days
that spanned the entire week (e.g., Monday + Tuesday, etc. See chapter 6,
especially Table 6.4).

Although the error patterns are fairly consistent in our data, there is some
variability across studies. The error data collected from Danish subjects suggest that the other work days are not often misdated as occurring on a
Friday, nor is a Friday often misdated as occurring on a Saturday or Sunday.
This may be an example of cross-cultural differences in time cycles: Denmark

has a 37-hour work week, and Friday afternoon has become a kind of a prologue to the weekend. Thus, one might expect the error data from Denmark to show a slightly different within-week error pattern than observed in the U.S. data, and that is exactly what occurred.

SUMMARY AND CONCLUSIONS

The Three Components of Dating

We have presented empirical evidence that relates the self-relevance of events to the three components of event dating performance that were distinguished in chapter 6: rate of exact datings, error magnitude of inexact datings, and rate of day-of-week hits. The pattern of results support our hypothesis that the three components represent a progression from strongly memory dependent (i.e., the exact datings) to weakly memory dependent (i.e., the DOW judgments). Clarity of memory for the particular event (i.e., intraevent memory) was a significant predictor of all three dating components, although its power decreased from the first to the third.

The independent contributions of linear and quadratic retention time point to the influence of some other aspect of event memory, which we propose is interevent memory (i.e., associations to other events and temporal landmarks; cf. Mandler, 1980). Both linear and quadratic time were very powerful predictors of exact datings, but only linear time was a consistent predictor of inexact dating errors. DOW accuracy was not consistently predicted by either of those variables. Thus, the three components of dating evince decreasing dependence on interevent as well as intraevent memory.

Self- and Nonself-events

Self-events were invariably dated more accurately than were nonself-events. For nonself-events coming from familiar other individuals, the lower level of dating was almost entirely accounted for by inferior intra- and interevent memory. This finding implies that the reconstructive processes are basically the same for self- and other-events, though fewer temporal cues, landmarks, and associations to other events in memory are available to assist in the dating of other-events.

Nonself-events coming from public news sources were also dated far above the chance level. Friedman and Wilkins' (1985) failure to find significant memory for the day of the week of news therefore does not hold during the first year of the lifetime of news memories. Still, news was dated less accurately than self-events, even when memory clarity and additional forgetting of interevent associations (i.e., episodic information) were controlled for. This result suggests that the schematic knowledge which is employed by the reconstructive process provides less information that is useful to constraining temporal estimates for news than for self-events.

Personal Context

In the news events study (90AU), subjects rated the clarity of event memory separately for the core of the event (i.e., what happened) and for the personal context in which the event took place (for news, the reception context). For all three components of dating, the analyses showed that context memory was a potent predictor of dating accuracy for news as well as for self-events, whereas event core memory was nowhere close to significance. This finding indicates that access to temporal knowledge is primarily gained through information retained about the personal context of events. The hypothesis proposed by Friedman (1993) that contextual information is generally of primary importance for the formation and application of temporal schemata is thus substantiated.

This agreement between the results for self-events and news may seem to suggest that these two event types are cognitively continuous. However, the personal context of news is qualitatively and causally distinct from the news itself. Reconstruction of the time of news therefore relies on schemata that have nothing to do with the news content but rather reflect regularities obtaining in the individual's personal life. In this sense, temporal memory for news is parasitic upon the temporal structure of self-related memories. If only the content of news is available for reconstruction, reference must be made to schemata that are specific to the public domain. This may only occasionally be possible, as for the political events that Brown (1990) showed to be referred to the chronological schema of U.S. presidential periods.

Why are the knowledge structures that mediate memory for time so dominantly autobiographical that temporal judgments for public events are forced to be parasitic? We suspect that this is an outcome of the ecology of the world of individual human beings which is reflected in their generic and episodic knowledge. Stated briefly, the *narrative singularity* of the individual's own life can be contrasted with the *narrative multiplicity* of the numerous other lives and event streams, of which news and stories let the individual catch a glimpse now and again—or now and never again.

CHAPTER TEN

Overview
and Summary

In this book, we have attempted to address some of the issues associated with memory for the events in one's life. In particular, we have been concerned with two aspects of memory. The first is *remembering what*, which involves one's ability to recall both the gist and the specific details of events. The second is *remembering when*, which we explored by asking our subjects to recall or reconstruct the date on which an event occurred.

In addition to having an emphasis on these two aspects of memory, this book has emphasized that both the memory reports of our subjects and the event dates that they provided could be due either to reproduction from memory (essentially, retrieval of a memory that contains much of the original stimulus information available in the event) or to reconstruction from memory (in which the memory report is substantially rebuilt from one or more of many available sources of information). We argue that the relative balance between reconstruction and reproduction differs for the memory ratings and temporal judgments. Event memory is initially highly reproductive but becomes increasingly reconstructive with lengthening retention interval; temporal judgments about events appear to be highly reconstructive, even for relatively recent events. Because of the apparent importance of reconstructive processes to our event dating results, we also extensively investigated the various sources of information that can be used to reconstruct event dates and the patterns of accuracy and error that are associated with those sources.

We think that the data obtained in our studies tell a nice story. However, we are concerned that the format of the previous chapters of this book may serve to obscure the general thematic consistency that we see in the data. Therefore, to provide a more coherent picture of the results, in this final chapter we recapitulate, review, and intertwine the major outcomes and implications of the earlier chapters. We also point to the limitations of our data and the paradigm and to some of the research that needs to be done in this area.

REMEMBERING WHAT:
SUMMARY, CONCLUSIONS, AND IMPLICATIONS

Retention Interval and Recall

Our event memory data are quite straightforward, producing few real surprises. Subjects' memories degrade with lengthening retention interval. When viewed in terms of the mean memory ratings, this decrease appears to be relatively gradual (see Figs. 1.2 and 3.1). The decrease is slightly more rapid over short retention intervals than over longer intervals and tends to reach a floor somewhere in the middle of the memory response scale. Compared to the relatively rapid decline of information over short retention intervals that is characteristic of typical Ebbinghaus memory curves, this gradual decline in early retention intervals might seem a bit odd. However, it becomes more understandable when one considers that the memory ratings reflect both memory for incidental event details and memory for the core details (or gist) of events. The gradual decline in rated memory and the mid-scale floor probably reflect subjects' recall for gist. This interpretation is consistent with the results of laboratory work suggesting that recall for gist persists across time (e.g., Bransford & Johnson, 1973).

For two reasons, it is a mistake to attribute this gradual decline to the memory rating measure that we used in most of our studies. First, as we illustrated in Fig. 1.1, standard cued recall measures for facts that are central to an event also show a similar gradual decline wth increasing event age (see also Linton, 1975). Second, analyses looking at the frequency with which subjects assigned perfect memory ratings (i.e., 6 and 7) to events indicated that the frequency of such ratings declined in a manner that resembles a typical Ebbinghaus function: a relatively rapid decline over short retention intervals, a slower decline over longer retention intervals (see Figs. 1.3 and 3.2). We suggest that these perfect recall data tend to reflect more accurately the rate at which peripheral event details are forgotten.

Event Characteristics and Recall

The data that we report in chapters 3 and 4 suggest that the characteristics of events are related to event recall. The results were quite consistent across studies. Events with higher rehearsal ratings were better recalled than were events with lower ratings. Events in which subjects physically participated were better recalled than were events that subjects merely encountered secondhand. Events stimulating high levels of initial mental involvement led to better recall than events with lower mental involvement. Atypical events (where atypical is defined in terms of event frequency or base rate) were better recalled than typical events. Person-atypical events (where atypical is defined in terms of unusualness for the person) were better recalled than person-typical events, and there is a hint in the data that person-typical events may be better remembered than events that are neither particularly person-typical nor person-atypical (similar to the incongruity effect in person memory found in the laboratory).

In chapter 4, we focused on whether the affective and emotional characteristics of events are related to recall for those events. Two particular characteristics are strongly related to event memory. One of these characteristics is event evaluative intensity: Events that are evaluatively intense are reported as better recalled than less intense events. The second of these characteristics is the magnitude of the emotional response produced by events: Events that are emotion-producing are reported as better recalled than nonemotion-producing events.

A third event characteristic, the valence, also appears to be related to event memory. Although some inconsistency arises in the existing research literature, that literature has suggested that pleasant events are better recalled than unpleasant events. The data that we obtained are consistent with this suggestion. Compared to the intensity and emotionality effects, the affective directionality effects are relatively weak. That is, as we show in Table 4.1, the direction of the affect–recall relation is usually positive (i.e, pleasant events are recalled better) for self-events, but the relation is not always statistically reliable.

Furthermore, one of the few surprises in our memory data were the outcomes suggesting that the relation between event valence and memory may depend on whether the events pertain to the self or to another person. Pleasant self-events are reported as better recalled than unpleasant self-events. For other-events, no recall advantage appears for pleasant events, and there is perhaps even a recall advantage for unpleasant events. However, only two data sets examined the valence–recall relation for other-events. One of those data sets showed no relation, whereas the other showed a significant advantage for unpleasant events. Clearly, additional research needs to examine this possible reversal of the valence–recall relation for other-events.

Although we extensively discussed the issue in chapters 2 and 4, we again emphasize that many of the memory effects that we report in this book are from regression models containing numerous simultaneous predictors. At any given level of the analysis (e.g., main effects, two-way interactions, etc.), we engaged in simultaneous evaluation of our predictors. Thus, any significant effects we report control for the other effects in each regression model. The practical implication of this procedure is straightforward: Affective intensity, affective direction, and emotionality all appear to affect memory independent of the other two predictors (and, for that matter, independent of the other predictors used in our models, such as the linear effects of event age, the quadratic effects of event age, event frequency, and event person-typicality). Thus, the data in this book contradict suggestions that valence effects in memory that have previously emerged in the literature were actually the result of an intensity confound (e.g., Banaji & Hardin, 1994).

In a similar spirit, we also attempted to assess the relation between event recall and the two cognitive processes of initial mental involvement and rehearsal. We were interested in whether these processes could account for the evaluative intensity, valence, and emotionality effects that we obtained. The valence–memory relations were generally significant, despite inclusion of both rehearsal and mental involvement in the regressions. Although not quite as resistant to the two process variables as the valence effect, the evaluative intensity–memory relation showed similar resistance. Finally, the results of our analyses suggest that rehearsal processes play little role in the mediation of the emotionality–recall relation: That relation was statistically reliable, despite the inclusion of rehearsal in the regression models. The best conclusion at this time is that although these two cognitive processes are strongly related to recall, they are not the sole mediators of the valence, intensity, and emotionality effects that we observed.

Subjects' Memory Predictions

Another aspect of the data that we investigated in this book concerns subjects' ability to predict their own recall. In our studies, subjects' predictions of their own memories were always statistically significant; in fact, relatively speaking, predicted recall was one of the more potent predictors of memory. However, this awareness is imperfect: In absolute terms, the proportion of variance accounted for by subjects' predictions of their memories was relatively small.

The notion that subjects' have insight—imperfect insight—into their own memories is also supported by the results of the analyses of the factors that predicted subjects' predictions of memory. For example, subjects thought that they would remember events that were rated as evaluatively extreme and that were positive. As we noted in chapter 4, these two event characteristics indeed predicted actual memory for personal events. However, subjects' predictions clearly are not always correct: Subjects predicted that they would better remember positive events that pertained to others, and, as the data in chapter 4 demonstrate, that prediction does not seem to hold true.

The Role of the Self in Event Recall

The self versus nonself theme in event recall was examined extensively in chapter 5 from the perspective of the self-schema. Self-events are recalled better than news events or others' events. Although this effect may occur for numerous reasons, we argue that one factor that significantly facilitates recall for self-events is the self-schema: It conveys both elaborative and organizational benefits that are probably not obtained from the cognitive representations that we have about other people or things. We especially favor the organizational (and hence the retrieval) benefits conveyed by the self as a prime cause of these persistent self-memories.

A number of lines of evidence from our studies implicate the organizational benefits of the self-schema. One of these lines of evidence comes from comparison of recall for self-events with recall for news events and for others' events. In several studies using different memory methodologies (e.g., Larsen, 1992b; Larsen & Plunkett, 1987; Larsen & Thompson, in press) memory for personal events was superior to memory for news events. As we argued in chapter 5, this difference occurred even though the news events selected for use in those studies tended to be more interesting and evocative than the personal events, which often tended toward the drab and routine. This outcome suggests that the nature of the event itself is not the key factor in the superiority of recall for self-events; it is the fact that those events are *self*-events that matters.

However, that series of studies leaves the exact mechanism(s) responsible for the superiority of self-event recall unclear. A second line of evidence, described in chapter 5, more strongly implicates the self-schema. We described the roommate studies, in which a recorder kept diaries for both him- or herself and for a roommate. Event recorders reported better recall for their own events than for the roommates' events. This difference persisted, even for those events that were *directly observed* by the diarykeepers. Hence, it was not simply the personal experience factor that served to determine the heightened recall for self-events. It can be argued that events that are directly observed should also be a part of the personal experiences of the diary-keepers and hence should be thought of as one type of self-event and should be remembered as well as other self-events. They weren't: An event perceived as one's own (i.e., an event that is related to the self-schema) clearly has an advantage in recall above and beyond the advantage bestowed by a person's being present at an event. This finding suggests that another factor is working to enhance recall for self-events. In our view, that factor is the organizational benefit conveyed by the self-schema.

This point is perhaps made even more strongly by a third line of evidence, one that comes from the initial mental involvement ratings and rehearsal ratings mentioned earlier in this chapter and is described in chapters 3 and 4. One easy explanation for self–other differences in recall is that people are initially more involved in self-events than other-events, pay more attention to self-events, and engage in greater amounts of elaborative mental activity (e.g., rehearsal) for those self-events. Thus, one might suspect that this heightened processing and elaboration may be responsible for the self–

other differences in memory that we observed. The data do not support this contention. In the 91OII data sets, the self–other difference in recall persisted, even when we controlled the memory ratings for initial mental involvement (see Betz & Skowronski, 1995). This was not due to a failure of the involvement measure: The mental involvement measure strongly predicted recall. The same argument applies to rehearsal (which also strongly predicted recall): The self–other difference in recall persisted, despite controlling for the rehearsal ratings. The conclusion from this study (and we again caution that it is only one study) is that recall is being affected by factors other than elaboration and rehearsal. We suggest that the critical factor is the organization provided by the self-schema.

REMEMBERING WHEN:
CONCLUSIONS AND IMPLICATIONS

Our explorations of the temporal judgments paralleled our explorations of the memory data in many ways. In general, the temporal judgments rendered by our subjects led to much more complexity than the memory data.

Retention Interval and Event Dating Performance

One of the things that we looked at was the relation between retention interval and event dating. As illustrated by the data in chapters 1 and 7, as events became older, the dates provided for those events became less accurate.

This straightforward outcome is complicated by several factors. In particular, the picture of decreasing accuracy with increasing retention interval changes depending on how one looks at the data. When viewed in terms of the magnitude of error (ignoring the direction of the error), then the data tend toward a linear (or perhaps a slightly negatively accelerating) decrease in dating accuracy with event age (Figs. 7.8, 7.9, and 7.10). When viewed in terms of exact dating accuracy (Figs. 1.3, 1.4, 7.1, 7.2, and 7.3; also see Table 6.6), then the function appears to be more Ebbinghaus-like, with a steep decline in the early retention intervals and relative stability thereafter.

A different picture emerges when the error magnitudes are plotted and the sign (or direction) of the errors is retained. In this case, one sees that the average signed error magnitude depends on the length of the retention interval and produces a characteristic pattern (Figs. 7.5, 7.6, and 7.7). Early in the interval, one sees evidence of time expansion: Subjects' estimates of event dates place them earlier than the actual date of occurrence for the event. Late in the interval, one sees evidence of telescoping: Subjects' estimates of event dates tend to be more recent than the actual date of occurrence for the event. At mid-interval, the date estimates tend to be relatively accurate. This characteristic error pattern is caused by the boundaries imposed by the starting and ending points of the diary study. As the earliest-date boundary moves back in time, the response function stretches backward with the boundary so that the relative frequency (and magnitude) of time expansion errors appears to increase. This boundary effect is another good example of a schematic influence on dating. That is, the effects represent a top-down effect based on the participants' knowledge of the diary interval.

Day-of-Week Errors

Another relation between dating error and time emerges when one looks at day-of-week error. Subjects' estimates often reflect errors that are multiples of one week (see Figs. 6.1 and 6.2). This tendency decreases with increasing event age, but it still remains remarkably stable across event age (see Fig. 1.8).

The day-of-week error patterns do not simply reflect errors that are multiples of one week; other, more complex error patterns also emerged. For example, the within-week error data presented in Table 9.7 suggest that subjects have the week parsed into several different components. The patterns of day-of-week choices directly expressed by subjects is consistent with this complexity. When asked to guess the days on which events occurred, subjects most often chose 1-day, 2-day, or 5-day groups.

In short, subjects appear to use the day (or days) of the week on which an event occurred to reconstruct their event dates, and this knowledge used in this reconstruction persists for a long period of time. The error patterns are consistent enough to be reliably modeled (see Table 6.5), and relatively simple models provide an excellent fit to the data (see Fig. 6.2).

Our belief that the within-week error pattern that we obtained in our studies reflects schematic knowledge about the days on which events in the real world occur is supported by two aspects of the data. First, these error patterns are persistent across time. One would not expect such persistence if the cues important to event dating were relatively fleeting incidental memory cues. Schematic knowledge tends to be much more long lasting.

A second factor implicating schematic knowledge as the source of the within-week error pattern is that although there are some small variations, the pattern of errors for self-events tends to resemble the pattern obtained for other-events and for public events (see Figs. 9.1, 9.2, 9.3, and 9.4). If event memory (rather than schematic knowledge) is driving the within-week error data, the poorer memories associated with others' events and public events should cause the within-week error pattern to be radically altered. The fact that the error pattern did not substantially change across self- and other-events implicates a source of knowledge that cuts across self-events, other-events, and public events. We believe that source to be schematic knowledge, which we think is extensively used in the reconstruction of the dates of events.

Sources or Strategies for Temporal Reconstruction

The notion that people have to reconstruct event dates suggests that they often have to access specific information sources consciously or use specific strategies in the process of reconstruction. Several such sources may exist: Some events may have cyclic temporal components that can aid dating (e.g., "I always go to church on Sunday"); other events may be related to important life landmarks (e.g., "it happened before the big flood"). We discussed the use of such strategies in chapter 6, chapter 7, and chapter 9. In chapters 6 and 9, we noted that people quite frequently use the cyclic information in their date reconstructions and that they frequently employed landmark strategy (see Tables 6.1, 6.2, and 9.1). In addition, people often reported that they could specify an approximate bounded time period in which an event occurred (e.g., "it was early in the quarter"). Furthermore, the frequency with which these strategies were used tended to be quite similar for self-events and other-events (see Table 9.2).

In chapters 7 and 9 (see Tables 7.2 and 9.1), we demonstrated that these information sources are related to accuracy and error in event dating. In general, when people reported retrieving a date from memory, they were highly accurate (though not perfectly so). People's dates were also highly accurate when they could date an event relative to a landmark event. Dating was less accurate for other sources. Finally, there is evidence (see Table 9.1) that the self–other difference in event dating discussed in chapter 9 may be a function of the information sources that subjects had available. Relative to self-events, in their reconstructions for other-events subjects often had less precise temporal information available, and consequently the dates that they provided for other-events were less accurate.

Event Characteristics and Dating Performance

We also presented data documenting how the characteristics of the events were systematically related to dating error and accuracy. We did this in three ways. First, we listed event samples and noted the dating error associated with those samples. Second, we conducted a content analysis of the data. The results of this analysis revealed that certain content categories were consistently associated with better event dating than were other categories. Finally, we used subjects' event ratings to explore event dating performance and found that events that were infrequent, person atypical, emotional, frequently rehearsed, and mentally involving were related to low error magnitude and high exact accuracy in dating.

The results of our mediational analyses suggested that these relations occurred largely because of event memory, which is one of the important sources of information that can be used to reconstruct an event date. That is, events that are positive, affectively extreme, infrequent, person-atypical, emotional, frequently rehearsed, and mentally involving are well-remembered events, and these variables often appear to be related to dating because of their effects on memory. However, continuing hints of other factors at work emerged throughout our analyses. These variables occasionally continued to predict event dating even when event memory was accounted for. By extension, then, one can assume that these variables are also associated with other factors, such as temporal schemata or direct date recall, that can serve to enhance event dating independent of event memory. This was particularly true for positive events—analyses involving the event valence variable were particularly immune to the inclusion of event memory in the regression models.

The Self-Schema in Event Dating Performance

In several studies, we investigated and compared event dating for self-events and nonself-events. Sensibly, self-events tended to be dated more accurately than nonself-events. When nonself-events came from familiar sources (as in the 88OH and 91OH diary studies), the lower level of event dating accuracy seemed to be entirely due to poorer event memory and poorer ability to relate the events to other events (e.g., landmarks) that could serve as dating aids (see Tables 9.2, 9.3, 9.4, and 9.5). That no interactions involving the self–other variable appeared in these studies further suggests that the basic processes underlying event dating were quite similar for self-events and other-events but fewer dating-relevant memory cues were available for other-events than for self-events.

We also presented data concerning people's ability to date events that were derived from news sources. Events from news sources were still dated less accurately than self-events, even when differential event memory was accounted for. However, the data also suggest that the personal context of an event is a strong predictor of dating accuracy, even for news events. These outcomes suggest that although memory is a contributor to the dating differences between self-events and news events, the self-event versus news event difference may also be due to other factors (e.g., the ease of remembering and using temporal schemata) that aid event dating. More generally, these outcomes suggest that Nelson's (1993) distinction between episodic and autobiographical events may have some validity. That is, even a news event can exhibit the characteristics of a self-event (at least with respect to dating performance) when that news event has been integrated into one's own life narrative.

This idea may help to explain the gender differences in event dating that we discussed in chapter 7—that females are more often exactly correct about event dates than males. Our preferred explanation, one that revolves around the different roles occupied by males and females, is quite consistent with Nelson's narrative view. To frame this hypothesis in Nelson's terms, the female's typical role in American society may cause females to be more likely to integrate date-relevant information into their personal narratives.

PRACTICAL APPLICATIONS:
IMPLICATIONS FOR SURVEY RESEARCH

Our focus in this book has been to emphasize the data describing event memory and event dating and to explore some of the psychological mechanisms that may underlie those data. However, we would be remiss if we did not point out some of the practical implications that emerge from the data. For example, one of the major methodological issues in a number of disciplines is the extent to which one can trust the responses that subjects provide to retrospective autobiographical questions. For example, "Where were you on the night of September 23rd?" "What was the make, model, and color of the car that drove away from the scene?" and "What was the date of your last visit to the physician?" are the types of questions that people are routinely asked as eyewitnesses or on surveys (for a set of excellent papers on this topic, see Schwarz & Sudman, 1994).

The data discussed in this book offer quite a mixed view of the extent to which one can trust the responses that are provided to these types of questions. For example, our data suggest that useful memory information can be obtained by the simple expedient of asking people to provide a self-report of their event memories. Our memory results map onto the results of laboratory research and other autobiographical memory research quite well, which suggests that such a self-report procedure can be quite useful in the discovery of general trends or patterns in the data.

However, it is also the case that our data offer several challenges to the assessment of memory by means of a retrospective survey methodology. As noted earlier, our memory data seem to reflect a scale anchoring bias: The slope of the forgetting function is different for studies with differing retention intervals. This bias likely reflects the fact that the definitions of the memory scale endpoints differ across studies. Furthermore, not all autobiographical memories are equivalent. Some seem primarily to reflect reproductive processes, whereas others primarily reflect reconstructive processes. As Brewer (1994) noted, many survey researchers previously assumed that subjects primarily used reproductive processes (e.g., memory for specific episodes) to respond to survey items. Thus, when asked how many times a person visited their physician in the last 5 years, it was commonly assumed that people attempted to recall and count their visits. Our data suggest that something different may happen: Respondents may use their generic or self-schemata to produce a response. For example, a person's self-knowledge may include the inference that they are health conscious, and this inference may be used to construct an (over)estimate of physician visits. The memories that are derived from these schemata are likely to have characteristics that are quite different from the memories that come from episodic recall (e.g., different decay functions, etc.) and are likely to be subject to different biases and errors.

Furthermore, although our data apply well to the discovery of general patterns and trends in memory, they cannot be easily applied to the evaluation of the veracity of an individual episodic memory (as in the flashbulb memory studies). As we noted earlier, the self-report technique is not a good one for discovering the kinds of biases that are likely to creep into retrospective episodic recall. The best that we can do is to point out that certain event characteristics (e.g., relative infrequency) and events that produce certain kinds of responses (e.g., emotionality) are more likely to lead to better memory than events with other characteristics (e.g., relative frequency) and that produce other kinds of responses (e.g., lack of emotionality).

Our data have rather strong implications for evaluating the veracity of retrospectively generated event dates. Generally speaking, one should look quite skeptically at the dates that are provided by subjects on survey instruments. This is especially true if the questions do not allow subjects to access written records of events and if the events are relatively routine and unexceptional (e.g., shopping trips). However, even events that are a bit more exceptional and unusual (e.g., visits to physicians' offices) are often subject to substantial error in dating, in part because temporal information is not often stored with event memories, and the resulting date reconstructions can often lead to error.

It is entirely reasonable to assume that providing or using anchor dates (e.g., asking for events occurring between August 1 and August 30) increases the accuracy of dating, but our data suggest that such boundaries may serve to introduce biases into the data. Specifically, such boundaries tend to produce telescoping effects for events near the lower boundary and time expansion for events near the more recent boundary. Because such tendencies may be natural consequences of limiting the direction of error near a boundary, there may be little a survey researcher can do to counteract such tendencies. Thus, the survey researcher is faced with a trade-off: Does the heightened accuracy that may accrue from presenting people with a bounded interval compensate for the bias introduced by the imposition of such boundaries?

However, the news on the event dating front is not all bad. People seem to have some degree of awareness of the extent to which their event dates can be trusted. It seems reasonable, then, that survey researchers can benefit from the simple expedient of asking respondents to place a confidence interval around the event dates that the respondents provide. If this procedure is perceived to be too difficult or too reactive, a number of alternatives are available. For example, because the sources of information that respondents use to construct event dates are consistently related to both dating error magnitude and exact accuracy, the assessment of such sources can serve as an indicator of the extent to which a date can be trusted.

In fact, from a practical perspective, an expansion of this idea might be one of the most important themes to be derived from our data. Time and time again, the data indicate that assessment of both event characteristics (e.g., valence, affective intensity) and psychological responses (e.g., emotionality, mental involvement) predict both memory and event dating. Such information can be useful in evaluating the potential validity of a retrospective report.

One example of this is the data comparing self-events and other-events. Proxy reports (e.g., reports provided about another person) tended to be less well recalled and less accurately dated than self-event reports. However, in evaluating the proxy event, one should assess the extent to which the self was involved in the others' event. Higher physical and mental involvement apparently leads to better memories and more accurate dates than do lower involvement levels.

FINAL THOUGHTS

In this book, we have been concerned with both the substantive and temporal aspects of autobiographical memory. Although many theorists and researchers do not see memory for events and memory for time as connected topics, in the context of autobiographical memory—a person's memories for events she or he has actually experienced—these two aspects of memory are inseparable. That is, in the study of autobiographical memory, it is difficult if not impossible to separate the study of memory for what from the study of memory for when.

In many ways, the very notion of autobiographical memory is unthinkable without some ultimate reference to the time at which the event occurred. Indeed, in Nelson's (1993) view of memory systems, autobiographical memory is precisely the one that has (and is even defined by having) a temporal structure to it. As indicated by the data in this book, we do not precisely recall the temporal location of events, far from it. However, our autobiographical memories have a temporal aspect to them, and groups of events often seem to cohere into a chronologically ordered, continuous past reality, frequently reflecting the eras in an individual's life (e.g., grade school, college, high school, etc.). The perception of development and change that comes from these memories may be an important element—indeed, may be a defining part of—the sense of self.

We push this point a bit further. We suspect that an individual with no retrospective sense of time would undoubtedly be a severely disordered personality. Memories from the perspective of one's youth would be juxtaposed with contemporary memories, and that would likely be confusing, indeed. Normal functioning in society demands that the events in one's own life have some sense of temporal ordering to them (whether this temporal ordering is correct or not may not matter).

Given the apparent importance of the sense of time and change to the development of the self, we believe that the study of memory for when an event occurred has not received nearly the attention it deserves. Experimental psychology has devoted much effort to understanding the factors that affect the content of memories but relatively little effort to understanding the temporal aspects of memories. This focus on remembering what is not entirely irrelevant to the study of autobiographical memory. After all, because of (what we believe to be) the highly reconstructive nature of temporal memory, remembering what often is a big contributor to remembering when. However, in the grand scheme of things, we do not well understand much about our sense of temporal order and temporal change. It is our hope that the studies presented in this book make a contribution to our understanding of these topics and help to stimulate further research on autobiographical memory.

Measures Used
in the Diary Studies

For the reader interested in the details of our studies, we provide a description of the measures used in collecting and testing the diaries. The measures used varied from study to study. The main measures used for each data set are specified in Tables A, B, and C, which specify the ratings made at time of recording, the ratings (or recall) for content, and the ratings (or recall) for temporal location, respectively.

The descriptions that follow include all the measures in our diary studies. However, the descriptions do not include the manipulations (e.g., calendar present or not present) used in the dairy studies. We have also excluded the designations of type of event (e.g., participant vs. observed event) even though the participants were required to make judgments regarding those types in some of our studies.

INITIAL RATINGS (AND DATE)

At the time the diary entries were made, the participant recorded the date of the event. In addition, each participant provided a number of ratings for each event, including a metamemory measure (how well will you remember this event?). Those ratings are described in this section.

Metamemory (memorability). Participants rated how well they thought they would remember the event. The scale ranged from 1 to 3 with a rating of 3 corresponding to *If I were asked about this event a year from now, I'd probably remember it* and a rating of 1 corresponding to *If I were asked about this event two weeks from now, I'd probably have forgotten it.* The rating of 2 was used for events that fell somewhere between those two extremes.

217

TABLE A
Data Sets and Ratings Made at Time of Recording. The Data Sets
Were Collected at Kansas State University (KS), The Ohio State University
at Newark (OS), and Aarhus University (AU).

Data Set	N	Rating			
		Metamemory	Pleasantness	Emotionality	Frequency
79KS	32	X			
80KS	30	X	X		
81KS	21	X			
83KS	23	X			
86KS	35	X	X		
86AU	1		X	X	X
87KS	43	X	X		
88OH	62	X	X		
89KS	33	X	X	X	X
89OH	30	X	X		
90KS	6	X	X	X	X
90AU	12		X	X	X
91KS	25	X	X	X	X
91OH	47		X		
92KS	38	X	X	X	X
Total	428				

TABLE B
Data Sets and Ratings (or Recall) for Content at Time of Test.
The Data Sets Were Collected at Kansas State University (KS),
The Ohio State University at Newark (OS), and Aarhus University (AU).
Ratings or Recall Are for Memory (M), Rehearsal (R), Location (L),
Who With (WW), and Source (S). The Maximum Retention Interval
in Weeks (RI) is Also Included for Each Study.

Data Set	N	Rating					
		RI	M	R	L	W	S
79KS	32	16	X	S			
80KS	30	14	X	S			
81KS	21	8	X	S			
83KS	23	14	X	S			
86KS	35	13	X				
86AU	1	48	X	S	X	X	X
87KS	43	14	X				
88OH	62	11	X				
89KS	33	15	X				
89OH	30	10	X				
90KS	6	129	X	N	X	X	
90AU	12	60	X	S			X
91KS	25	15	X	N			
91OH	47	11	X	S			
92KS	38	15	X				
Total	428						

TABLE C
Data Sets and Ratings (or Recall) for Temporal Location at Time of Test.
The Data Sets Were Collected at Kansas State University (KS),
The Ohio State University at Newark (OS), and Aarhus University (AU).
Ratings or Recall Are for Dating Error (DE), Estimated Accuracy (EA),
Dating Strategy (DS), and Time of Week (TOW).

Data Set	N	Rating			
		DE	EA	DS	TOW
79KS	32	X			
80KS	30	X			
81KS	21	X			
83KS	23	X			
86KS	35	X			
86AU	1	X	X		
87KS	43	X			
88OH	62	X			
89KS	33	X	X	X	
89OH	30	X	X	X	
90KS	6	X	X	X	X
90AU	12	X			X
91KS	25	X			X
91OH	47	X	X	X	
92KS	38	X	X		X
Total	428				

Pleasantness. The pleasantness of the event was rated on a scale ranging from −3 to +3. A rating of −3 was for extremely unpleasant events such as the death of a loved one or the termination of a close personal relationship. A rating of +3 was for extremely pleasant events such as getting engaged. The other ratings were characterized with verbal descriptions as follows: −2 = very unpleasant, −1 = unpleasant, 0 = neutral, +1 = pleasant, and +2 = very pleasant.

Frequency. This was a rating of how often this *type* of event occurred. The seven-point scale provided a range from once per day to once in a lifetime and was described as follows: 1 = 1/day, 2 = 1/week, 3 = 1/month, 4 = 2/year, 5 = 1 in 3 years, 6 = 1 in 15 years, and 7 = 1 in a lifetime.

Emotional involvement. The emotional involvement scale was a five-point scale given the following labels: 1 = nothing, 2 = little, 3 = moderate, 4 = considerable, and 5 = extreme.

Centrality. Participants were told that they were to rate how central that event was to their life. The centrality scale ranged from 1 to 3 with 1 = not central, 2 = in between, and 3 = central.

Importance. Participants were told to rate the personal importance of the event on a seven-point scale. The endpoints of the scale were given verbal labels with 1 identified as *trivial* and 7 identified as *very important.*

Judgments about roommates' events. In a few studies, participants recorded events for other people, usually roommates. In those studies, the participants filled out the same set of judgments about the roommates' events that they had used for their own events. The scales described in this section were used for both sets of events.

MEMORY TEST MEASURES

During the memory test, each participant responded to a series of questions about his or her memory for the event. We describe the memory test measures in this section.

Memory. Participants rated how well they remembered the event on a 7-point scale. A rating of 1 indicated that they did not remember the event at all. A rating of 7 indicated that they remembered the event perfectly. Participants were told that, if there were a conversation in the event, a rating of 7 indicated that they could repeat the conversation essentially word for word. The verbal descriptions attached to the other numbers in the memory rating were: 2 = barely at all, 3 = not so well, 4 = fairly well, 5 = very well, and 6 = almost perfectly.

Memory for roommates' events. In a few studies, participants recorded events for others (usually roommates) and were asked to give memory ratings for those events. The preceding scale was used for those judgments.

Test pleasantness. This scale was the same as the pleasantness scale used while recording the event (–3 to +3) but was intended to represent the pleasantness at the time of the memory test.

Rehearsal. In early studies, participants gave an estimate of the amount of rehearsal using a six-point scale. In later studies, participants gave a number representing their estimate of the number of rehearsals. That difference is represented in Table B by placing either an S (six-point scale) or an N (numeric estimate) under the rehearsal category to designate which procedure was used.

In those studies using the six-point scale, the participants were given a scale with both numeric and descriptive labels. The scale was described as follows: 1 = never (0), 2 = rarely(1–2), 3 = a few times (3–5), 4 = several times (6–10), 5 = quite often (11–20), and 6 = very often (over 20).

Prior rehearsals. In one study, participants were asked to estimate the number of times they thought about or talked about the event before it occurred. They used a six-point scale with both numeric and descriptive labels. The scale was described as follows: 1 = never (0), 2 = rarely(1–2), 3 = a few times (3–5), 4 = several times (6–10), 5 = quite often (11–20), and 6 = very often (over 20).

Who with. In some studies, participants were required to indicate who was with them during the event. During the test, they were asked to recall that information.

Location. In some studies, participants were required to give the location of the event. During the test, they were asked to recall that information.

Source. In studies involving news events, subjects were required to recall the source of the information.

Estimated date. In most studies, participants were given a calendar containing no information other than date and day of the week. Using that information, they were asked to estimate the date of the event. The only exception was the 1987 study in which the presence or absence of a calendar was one of the manipulations. Thus, half of the participants in that study did not have a calendar present when estimating the dates of events.

Exact date judgment. In some studies, participant were asked to indicate whether they thought the date they had picked was the exact date of the event.

Estimated dating error. In several studies, participants were asked to give their probable error in dating events. In early studies, participants gave an estimate of the probable error using a five-point scale. In later studies, participants gave a number representing their estimate of the number of days in error. That difference is represented in Table B by placing either an S (five-point scale) or an N (numeric estimate) under the estimated dating error category to designate which procedure was used.

In those studies using the five-point scale, the participants were given a scale with descriptive labels. The descriptions were as follows: 1 = exact date, 2 = within a day, 3 = within a week, 4 = within a month, and 5 = more than a month error.

Confidence. Participants frequently were asked to state their confidence in an estimate (e.g., the date, the day of week, the month). The confidence rating was done on a five-point scale ranging from *no confidence* (1) to *completely confident* (5).

Dating strategy. On occasion, participants were asked to specify the strategy by which they estimated the date of each event. Pretesting determined that there were seven strategies that were typically used. Participants were asked either to specify one of those seven strategies or to specify "other." They used a numeric code for this task: 1 = knew exact date, 2 = specific reference event (i.e., reference to another event), 3 = general reference event (i.e., reference to a period such as summer), 4 = number of intervening events (since the event to be dated), 5 = clarity of memory, 6 = prototypic date (e.g., know that Monday is bowling night), 7 = guess, and 8 = other.

Time of week. Time of week was estimated in two different ways. In the 1991 study, participants made a judgment using one of six possibilities, coded as follows: 0 = no information, 1 = exact day, 2 = weekend, 3 = weekday, 4 = early in week, 5 = middle of week, 6 = end of week. In other studies, participants circled the day or range of days of the week during which the event might have occurred. If they had no information on which to base their judgment about the day of week, they circled all seven days.

References

Archer, E. J. (1960). A re-evaluation of the meaningfulness of all possible CVC trigrams. *Psychological Monographs, 74*, (10, Whole No. 497).

Auriat, N. (1992). Autobiographical memory and survey methodology: Furthering the bridge between two disciplines. In M. A. Conway, D. C. Rubin, H. Spinnler, & W. A. Wagenaar (Eds.), *Theoretical perspectives on autobiographical memory* (pp. 295–312). Dordrecht: Kluwer.

Baddeley, A. D., Lewis, V., & Nimmo-Smith, I. (1978). When did you last . . . ? In M. M. Gruneberg & R. N. Sykes (Eds.), *Practical aspects of memory* (pp. 77–83). New York: Academic Press.

Baddeley, A., Mahadevan, R., & Thompson, C. (1992). *Exploring the memory of a memorist: Basic capacity or acquired expertise?* Unpublished manuscript.

Bahrick, H. P., & Karis, D. (1982). Long-term ecological memory. In C. R. Puff (Ed.), *Handbook of research methods in human memory and cognition.* New York: Academic Press.

Banaji, M. R. (1986). *Affect and memory: An experimental investigation.* Unpublished doctoral dissertation, The Ohio State University, Columbus.

Banaji, M. R., & Crowder, R. G. (1989). The bankruptcy of everyday memory. *American Psychologist, 44*, 1185–1193.

Banaji, M. R., & Hardin, C. (1994). Affect and memory in retrospective reports. In S. Sudman & N. Schwarz (Eds.), *Autobiographical memory and the validity of retrospective reports.* New York: Springer-Verlag.

Barsalou, L. W. (1988). The content and organization of autobiographical memories. In U. Neisser & E. Winograd (Eds.), *Remembering reconsidered: Ecological and traditional approaches to the study of memory* (pp. 193–243). New York: Cambridge University Press.

Bellezza, F. S. (1984). The self as a mnemonic device: The role of internal cues. *Journal of Social and Personality Psychology, 47*, 506–516.

Bellezza, F. S., & Hoyt, S. K. (1992). The self-reference effect and mental cueing. *Social Cognition, 10*, 51–78.

Bem, D. J. (1972). Self-perception theory. In L. Berkowitz (Ed.), *Advances in experimental social psychology* (Vol. 6, pp. 2–62). New York: Academic Press.

Betz, A. L., & Skowronski, J. J. (1995). *Social memory in everyday life II: Factors related to temporal dating and recall of self-events and other-events.* Manuscript under review.

Boswell, J. (1980). *Life of Johnson*. Harmondsworth. Penguin. (Originally published 1791)

Bower, G. H., & Gilligan, S. G. (1979). Remembering information related to one's self. *Journal of Research in Personality, 13*, 420–432.

Bower, G. H., & Mayer, J. D. (1985). Failure to replicate mood-dependent retrieval. *Bulletin of the Psychonomic Society, 3*, 39–42.

Bower, G. H., Monteiro, K. P., & Gilligan, S. G. (1978). Emotional mood as a context for learning and recall. *Journal of Verbal Learning and Verbal Recall, 17*, 573–585.

Bower, G. H., & Winzenz, D. (1970). Comparison of associative learning strategies. *Psychonomic Science, 20*, 119–120.

Bradburn, N. M., Rips, L. J., & Shevell, S. K. (1987). Answering autobiographical questions: The impact of memory and inference on surveys. *Science, 236*, 151–167.

Bransford, J. D., & Johnson, M. K. (1973). Considerations of some problems of comprehension. In W. G. Chase (Ed.), *Visual information processing*. New York: Academic Press.

Brewer, W. F. (1986). What is autobiographical memory? In D. C. Rubin (Ed.), *Autobiographical memory* (pp. 25–49). New York: Cambridge University Press.

Brewer, W. F. (1988). Memory for randomly sampled autobiographical events. In U. Neisser & E. Winograd (Eds.), *Remembering reconsidered: Ecological and traditional approaches to the study of memory* (pp. 21–90). New York: Cambridge University Press.

Brewer, W. F. (1994). Autobiographical memory and survey research. In N. Schwarz & S. Sudman (Eds.), *Autobiographical memory and the validity of retrospective reports* (pp. 11–20). New York: Springer-Verlag.

Brown, J., & Taylor, S. E. (1986). Affect and the processing of personal information: Evidence for mood-activated self-schemata. *Journal of Experimental Social Psychology, 22*, 436–452.

Brown, N. R. (1990). Organization of public events in long-term memory. *Journal of Experimental Psychology: General, 119*, 297–314.

Brown, N. R., Rips, L. J., & Shevell, S. K. (1985). The subjective dates of natural events in very-long-term memory. *Cognitive Psychology, 17*, 139–177.

Brown, P., Keenan, J. M., & Potts, G. R. (1986). The self-reference effect with imagery encoding. *Journal of Personality and Social Psychology, 51*, 897–906.

Brown, R., & Kulik, J. (1977). Flashbulb memories. *Cognition, 5*, 73–99.

Bruce, D., & van Pelt, M. (1989). Memories of a bicycle tour. *Applied Cognitive Psychology, 3*, 137–156.

Campbell, D. T., & Fiske, D. W. (1959). Convergent and discriminate validation of the multitrait-multimethod matrix. *Psychological Bulletin, 47*, 15–38.

Cantor, N., & Kihlstrom, J. F. (1987). *Personality and social intelligence*. Englewood Cliffs, NJ: Prentice-Hall.

Ceci, S. J., & Loftus, E. F. (1994). 'Memory work': A royal road to false memories? *Applied Cognitive Psychology, 8*, 351–364.

Chase, W. G., & Ericsson, K. A. (1981). Skilled memory. In J. R. Anderson (Ed.), *Cognitive skills and their acquisition* (pp. 141–180). Hillsdale, NJ: Lawrence Erlbaum Associates.

Chase, W. G., & Ericsson, K. A. (1982). Skill and working memory. In G. H. Bower (Ed.), *The psychology of learning and motivation* (Vol. 16, pp. 1–58). New York: Academic Press.

Cialdini, R. B. (1980). Full cycle social psychology. In L. Bickman, (Ed.), *Applied social psychology annual* (Vol. 1, pp. 21–47). Beverly Hills, CA: Sage.

Clark, M. S., Milberg, S., & Ross, J. (1983). Arousal cues arousal-related material in memory: Implications for understanding effects of mood on memory. *Journal of Verbal Learning and Verbal Behavior, 22*, 633–649.

Cohen, J., & Cohen, P. (1983). *Applied multiple regression/correlation analysis for the behavioral sciences* (2nd edition). Hillsdale, NJ: Lawrence Erlbaum Associates.

Cohler, B. J. (1993). A commentary on Lindsay and Read from psychoanalytic perspectives. *Applied Cognitive Psychology, 8*, 365–378.

Colgrove, F. W. (1899). Individual memories. *American Journal of Psychology, 10*, 228–255.

Conway, M. A. (1990). *Autobiographical memory: An introduction.* Philadelphia: Open University Press.

Conway, M. A., Anderson, S. J., Larsen, S. F., Donnelly, C. M., McDaniel, M. A., McClelland, A. G. R., Rawles, R. E., & Logie, R. H. (1994). The formation of flashbulb memories. *Memory and Cognition, 22,* 326–343.

Conway, M. A., & Rubin, D. C. (1993). The structure of autobiographical memory. In A. F. Collins, S. E. Gathercole, M. A. Conway, & P. E. Morris (Eds.), *Theories of memory* (pp. 103–137). Hove, UK: Lawrence Erlbaum Associates.

Craik, F. I. M., & Lockhart, R. S. (1972). Levels of processing: A framework for memory research. *Journal of Verbal Learning and Verbal Behavior, 11,* 671–684.

Craik, F. I. M., & Tulving, E. (1975). Depth of processing and the retention of words in episodic memory. *Journal of Experimental Psychology: General, 104,* 268–294.

Craik, F. I. M., & Watkins, M. J. (1973). The role of rehearsal in short-term memory. *Journal of Verbal Learning and Verbal Behavior, 12,* 599–607.

Crovitz, H. F., & Shiffman, H. (1974). Frequency of episodic memories as a function of their age. *Bulletin of the Psychonomic Society, 38,* 517–518.

Dalgleish, T., & Watts, F. N. (1990). Biases of attention and memory in disorders of anxiety and depression. *Clinical Psychology Review, 10,* 589–604.

Davis, P. J. (1987). Repression and the inaccessibility of affective memories. *Journal of Personality and Social Psychology, 53,* 585–593.

Diener, E., Larsen, R. J., Levine, S., & Emmons, R. A. (1985). Intensity and frequency: Dimensions underlying positive and negative affect. *Journal of Personality and Social Psychology, 48,* 1253–1265.

Dreben, E. K., Fiske, S. T., & Hastie, R. (1979). The independence of evaluative and item information: Impression and recall order effects in behavior-based impression formation. *Journal of Personality and Social Psychology, 37,* 1758–1768.

Dudycha, G. J., & Dudycha, M. M. (1941). Childhood memories: A review of the literature. *Psychological Bulletin, 38,* 668–682.

Ebbinghaus, H. E. (1964). *Memory: A contribution to experimental psychology.* New York: Dover. (Originally published 1885; translated 1913)

Ericsson, K. A. (1988). Analysis of memory performance in terms of memory skill. In R. J. Sternberg (Ed.), *Advances in the psychology of human intelligence* (Vol. 4, pp. 137–179). Hillsdale, NJ: Lawrence Erlbaum Associates.

Ericsson, K. A., & Chase, W. G. (1982). Exceptional memory. *American Scientist, 70,* 607–615.

Ericsson, K. A., & Simon, H. A. (1984). *Protocol analysis: Verbal reports as data.* Cambridge, MA: MIT Press.

Fiske, S. (1980). Attention and weight in person perception: The impact of negative and extreme behavior. *Journal of Personality and Social Psychology, 38,* 889–906.

Fivush, R., & Hudson, J. A. (Eds.). (1990). *Knowing and remembering in young children.* New York: Cambridge University Press.

Fivush, R., & Reese, E. (1991, July). *Parental style for talking about the past.* Paper presented at the International Conference on Memory, Lancaster, England.

Freud, S. (1900/1965). The interpretation of dreams. *The standard edition of the complete psychological works of Sigmund Freud* (Vols. 4 and 5). London: Hogarth Press.

Friedman, W. J. (1987). A follow-up to "Scale effects in memory for the time of events": The earthquake study. *Memory and Cognition, 15,* 518–520.

Friedman, W. J. (1993). Memory for the time of past events. *Psychological Bulletin, 113,* 44–66.

Friedman, W. J., & Wilkins, A. J. (1985). Scale effects in memory for the time of past events. *Memory and Cognition, 13,* 168–175.

Galton, F. (1879). Psychometric experiments. *Brain, 2,* 149–162.

Ganellen, R. J., & Carver, C. S. (1985). Why does self-reference promote incidental coding? *Journal of Experimental Social Psychology, 21,* 284–300.

Gergen, K. (1982). From self to science: What is there to know? In J. Suls (Ed.), *Psychological perspectives on the self* (Vol. 1, pp. 129–149). Hillsdale, NJ: Lawrence Erlbaum Associates.

Gibson, J. J. (1979). *The ecological approach to visual perception*. Boston: Houghton Mifflin.

Glaze, J. A. (1928). The association value of nonsense syllables. *Journal of Genetic Psychology, 35*, 255–267.

Glenberg, A. M. (1987). Temporal context and recency. In D. S. Gorfein & R. R. Hoffman (Eds.), *Memory and learning: The Ebbinghaus Centennial Conference* (pp. 173–190). Hillsdale, NJ: Lawrence Erlbaum Associates.

Goldsmith, L. R., & Pillemer, D. B. (1988). Memories of statements spoken in everyday contexts. *Applied Cognitive Psychology, 2*, 273–286.

Greenwald, A. G. (1980). The totalitarian ego: Fabrication and revision of personal history. *American Psychologist, 35*, 603–618.

Greenwald, A. G., & Pratkanis, A. R. (1984). In R. S. Wyer & T. K. Srull (Eds.), *Handbook of social cognition* (Vol. 3, pp. 129–178). Hillsdale, NJ: Lawrence Erlbaum Associates.

Halpin, J. A., Puff, C. R., Mason, H. F., & Martson, S. P. (1984). Self-reference and incidental recall by children. *Bulletin of the Psychonomic Society, 22*, 87–89.

Hansen, C. H., & Hansen, R. D. (1988). Finding the face in the crowd: An anger superiority effect. *Journal of Personality and Social Psychology, 54*, 917–924.

Hansen, T. (1993). *Day of week and hour of day in memory for everyday events.* Unpublished master's thesis, University of Aarhus, Denmark.

Hardin, C., & Banaji, M. R. (1990). *Affective intensity and valence in memory.* Paper presented at the annual convention of the American Psychological Association, Boston, MA.

Hastie, R. (1980). Memory for behavior information that confirms or contradicts a personality impression. In R. Hastie, T. M. Ostrom, E. B. Ebbesen, R. S. Wyer, D. L. Hamilton, & D. E. Carlson (Eds.), *Person memory: The cognitive basis of social perception* (pp. 155–177). Hillsdale, NJ: Lawrence Erlbaum Associates.

Hastie, R. (1984). Causes and effects of causal attribution. *Journal of Personality and Social Psychology, 46*, 44–56.

Höffding, H. (1891). *Outlines of psychology.* London: Macmillan. (Originally published 1885)

Holmes, D. S. (1970). Differential change in affective intensity and the forgetting of unpleasant personal experiences. *Journal of Personality and Social Psychology, 3*, 234–239.

Holmes, D. S. (1990). The evidence for repression: An examination of sixty years of research. In J. L. Singer (Ed.), *Repression and dissociation: Implications for personality theory, psychopathology and health* (pp. 85–102). Chicago: University of Chicago Press.

Hudson, J. A. (1986). Memories are made of this: General event knowledge and the development of autobiographical memory. In K. Nelson (Ed.), *Event knowledge: Structure and function in development* (pp. 97–118), Hillsdale, NJ: Lawrence Erlbaum Associates.

Hudson, J. A. (1990). The emergence of autobiographic memory in mother–child conversation. In R. Fivush & J. A. Hudson (Eds.), *Knowing and remembering in young children* (pp. 166–196). New York: Cambridge University Press.

Huttenlocher, J., Hedges, L., & Bradburn, N. (1990). Reports of elapsed time: Bounding and rounding processes in estimation. *Journal of Experimental Psychology: Learning, Memory, & Cognition, 16*, 196–213.

Huttenlocher, J., Hedges, L., & Prohaska, V. (1992). Memory for day of the week: A 5 + 2 day cycle. *Journal of Experimental Psychology: General, 121*, 313–325.

Isen, A. M. (1984). Toward understanding the role of affect in cognition. In R. S. Wyer & T. K. Srull (Eds.), *Handbook of social cognition* (Vol. 3, pp. 179–236). Hillsdale, NJ: Lawrence Erlbaum Associates.

Jackson, J. L. (1990). A cognitive approach to temporal information processing. In R. A. Block (Ed.), *Cognitive models of psychological time* (pp. 153–180). Hillsdale, NJ: Lawrence Erlbaum Associates.

James, W. (1950). *The principles of psychology* (Vol. 1). New York: Dover. (Originally published 1890)

Jepson, C., & Chaiken, S. (1990). Chronic issue-specific fear inhibits systematic processing of persuasive communications. *Journal of Social Behavior and Personality, 5*, 61–84.

Keenan, J. M., & Bailett, S. D. (1980). Memory for personally and socially significant events. In R. S. Nickerson (Ed.), *Attention and human performance* (Vol. 8, pp. 651–669). Hillsdale, NJ: Lawrence Erlbaum Associates.

Kendzierski, D. (1980). Self-schema and scripts: The recall of self-referent and scriptal information. *Personality and Social Psychology Bulletin, 6*, 23–29.

Kihlstrom, J. F., & Cantor, N. (1984). Mental representations of the self. In L. Berkowitz (Ed.), *Advances in experimental social psychology* (Vol. 15, pp. 2–47). New York: Academic Press.

Kihlstrom, J. F., Cantor, N., Albright, J. S., Chew, B. R., Klein, S. B., & Niedenthal, B. M. (1988). Information processing and the study of the self. In L. Berkowitz (Ed.), *Advances in experimental social psychology* (Vol. 17, pp. 2–47). New York: Academic Press.

Kihlstrom, J. F., & Harackiewicz, J. M. (1982). The earliest recollection: A new survey. *Journal of Personality, 50*, 134–148.

Klein, S. B., & Kihlstrom, J. F. (1986). Elaboration, organization, and the self-reference effect in memory. *Journal of Experimental Psychology: General, 115*, 26–38.

Klein, S. B., & Loftus, J. (1989). The nature of self-referent encoding: The contributions of elaborative and organizational processes. *Journal of Personality and Social Psychology, 55*, 5–11.

Klein, S. B., & Loftus, J. (1993). The mental representation of trait and autobiographical information about the self. In T. K. Srull & R. S. Wyer (Eds.), *Advances in social cognition: The mental representation of trait and autobiographical knowledge about the self* (Vol. 5, pp. 1–50). Hillsdale, NJ: Lawrence Erlbaum Associates.

Klinger, E., Barta, S. G., & Maxeiner, M. E. (1980). Motivational correlates of thought content frequency and commitment. *Journal of Personality and Social Psychology, 39*, 1222–1237.

Kreitler, H., & Kreitler, S. (1968). Unhappy memories of "the happy past": Studies in cognitive dissonance. *British Journal of Psychology, 59*, 157–166.

Kuiper, N. A., & Rogers, T. B. (1979). Encoding of personal information: Self-other differences. *Journal of Personality and Social Psychology, 37*, 499–514.

Larsen, S. F. (1988). Remembering without experiencing: Memory for reported events. In U. Neisser & E. Winograd (Eds.), *Remembering reconsidered: Ecological and traditional approaches to the study of memory* (pp. 326–355). New York: Cambridge University Press.

Larsen, S. F. (1992a). Personal context in autobiographical and narrative memories. In M. A. Conway, D. C. Rubin, W. Wagenaar, & H. Spinnler (Eds.), *Theoretical perspectives on autobiographical memory* (pp. 53–71). Amsterdam: Kluwer.

Larsen, S. F. (1992b). Potential flashbulbs: Memories of ordinary news as the baseline. In E. Winograd and U. Neisser (Eds.), *Affect and accuracy in recall: Studies of flashbulb memories* (pp. 32–64). New York: Cambridge University Press.

Larsen, S. F., & Plunkett, K. (1987). Remembering experienced and reported events. *Applied Cognitive Psychology, 1*, 15–26.

Larsen, S. F., & Thompson, C. P. (in press). Reconstructive memory in the dating of personal and public events. *Memory and Cognition.*

Larsen, S. F., Thompson, C. P., & Hansen, T. (in press). Time in autobiographical memory. In D. C. Rubin (Ed.), *Constructing our past.* New York: Cambridge University Press.

Leonesio, R. J., & Nelson, T. O. (1990). Do different metamemory judgments tap the same underlying aspects of memory? *Journal of Experimental Psychology: Learning, Memory & Cognition, 16*, 464–470.

Lewis, H. B. (1990). Shame, repression, field dependence and psychopathology. In J. L. Singer (Ed.), *Repression and dissociation: Implications for personality theory, psychopathology and health* (pp. 233 258). Chicago: University of Chicago Press

Lieury, A., Aiello, B., Lepreux, D., & Mellet, M. (1980). Le rôle des repères dans la récuperation et la datation des souvenirs. *Année Psychologique, 80*, 149–167.

Lieury, A., Richer, E., & Weeger, I. (1978). Les événements privés et publics dans les souvenirs. *Bulletin de Psychologie, 32*, 41–48.

Lindsay, D. S. (1993). Eyewitness suggestibility. *Current Directions in Psychological Science, 2*, 86–89.

Lindsay, D. S., & Read, J. D. (1993). Psychotherapy and memories of childhood sexual abuse: A cognitive perspective. *Applied Cognitive Psychology, 8*, 281–337.

Linton, M. (1975). Memory for real-world events. In D. A. Norman & D. E. Rumelhart (Eds.), *Explorations in cognition* (pp. 376–404). San Francisco: Freeman.

Linville, P. W., & Carlston, D. E. (1994). Social cognition of the self. In P. Devine, D. L. Hamilton, & T. M. Ostrom (Eds.), *Social cognition: Impact on social psychology* (pp. 143–193). New York: Academic Press.

Loftus, E. F. (1993). When a lie becomes memory's truth: Memory distortion after exposure to misinformation. *Current Directions in Psychological Science, 1*, 121–123.

Loftus, E. F., & Marburger, W. (1983). Since the eruption of Mt. St. Helens, has anyone beaten you up? Improving the accuracy of retrospective reports with landmark events. *Memory and Cognition, 11*, 114–120.

Lord, C. G. (1980). Schemas and images as memory aids: Two modes of processing social information. *Journal of Personality and Social Psychology, 38*, 257–269.

Maki, R. H., & McCaul, K. D. (1985). The effects of self-reference versus other reference on the recall of traits and nouns. *Bulletin of the Psychonomic Society, 23*, 169–172.

Mandler, G. (1980). Recognizing: The judgment of previous occurrence. *Psychological Review, 87*, 252–271.

Markus, H. (1977). Self-schemata and processing information about the self. *Journal of Personality and Social Psychology, 35*, 63–74.

Matlin, M. W., & Stang, D. J. (1978). *The Pollyanna principle.* Cambridge, MA: Schenkman.

Mayer, J. D., & Salovey, P. (1988). Personality moderates the interaction of mood and cognition. In K. Fiedler & J. Forgas (Eds.), *Affect, cognition, and social behavior* (pp. 87–99). Gottingen, Federal Republic of Germany: Hogrefe.

McCaul, K. D., & Maki, R. H. (1984). Self-reference versus desirability ratings and memory for traits. *Journal of Personality and Social Psychology, 47*, 953–955.

McCormack, P. D. (1979). Autobiographical memory in the aged. *Canadian Journal of Psychology, 33*, 118–124.

McGuire, W. J. (1969). The nature of attitudes and attitude change. In G. Lindzey & E. Aronson (Eds.), *Handbook of social psychology* (2nd ed., Vol. 3, pp. 136–314). Reading, MA: Addison-Wesley.

McKoon, G., Ratcliff, R., & Dell, G. S. (1986). A critical evaluation of the semantic-episodic distinction. *Journal of Experimental Psychology: Learning, Memory, & Cognition, 12*, 295–306.

Meltzer, H. (1930). The present status of experimental studies on the relationship of feelings to memory. *Psychological Review, 37*, 124–139.

Michon, J. A., Pouthas, V., & Jackson, J. L. (1988). *Guyau and the idea of time.* New York: North-Holland.

Murdock, B. B. (1974). *Human memory: Theory and data.* Hillsdale, NJ: Lawrence Erlbaum Associates.

Neisser, U. (1982). Memory: What are the important questions? In U. Neisser (Ed.), *Remembering in natural contexts* (pp. 3–19). San Francisco: Freeman.

Neisser, U., & Harsch, N. (1992). Phantom flashbulbs: False recollections of hearing the news about Challenger. In E. Winograd & U. Neisser (Eds.), *Affect and accuracy in recall: Studies of "flashbulb" memories* (pp. 9–31). New York: Cambridge University Press.

Neisser, U., Winograd, E., & Weldon, M. S. (November, 1991). *Remembering the earthquake: "What I experienced" versus "How I heard the news."* Paper presented at the meeting of the Psychonomic Society, San Francisco.

Nelson, K. (1978). How young children represent knowledge of their world in and out of language. In R. S. Siegler (Ed.), *Children's thinking: What develops?* (pp. 225–273). Hillsdale, NJ: Lawrence Erlbaum Associates.

Nelson, K. (1989). *Narratives from the crib.* Cambridge, MA: Harvard University Press.

Nelson, K. (1993). The psychological and social origins of autobiographical memory. *Psychological Science, 4,* 7–14.

Nelson, K., & Gruendel, J. (1981). Generalized event representations: Basic building blocks of cognitive development. In M. Lamb & A. Brown (Eds.), *Advances in developmental psychology* (Vol. 1, pp. 131–158). Hillsdale, NJ: Lawrence Erlbaum Associates.

Nisbett, R. E., & Wilson, T. D. (1977). Telling more than we can know: Verbal reports on mental processes. *Psychological Review, 84,* 231–259.

Packman, J. L., & Battig, W. F. (1978). Effects of different kinds of semantic processing on memory for words. *Memory and Cognition, 6,* 502–508.

Peeters, G., & Czapinski, J. (1990). Positive–negative asymmetry in evaluations: The distinction between affective and informational negativity effects. *European Review of Social Psychology, 1,* 33–60.

Pezdek, K. (1993). The illusion of illusory memory. *Applied Cognitive Psychology, 8,* 339–350.

Pillemer, D. B. (1984). Flashbulb memories of the assassination attempt on President Reagan. *Cognition, 16,* 63–80.

Pillemer, D. B., & White, S. H. (1989). Childhood events recalled by children and adults. In H. W. Reese (Ed.), *Advances in child development and behavior* (Vol. 21, pp. 297–340). New York: Academic Press.

Rapaport, D. (1942). *Emotions and memory.* Baltimore: Williams & Wilkins. (Republished without modification in 1950)

Ratner, H. H. (1980). The role of social context in memory development. In M. Perlmutter (Ed.), *Children's memory: New directions for child development* (Vol. 10, pp. 49–68). San Francisco: Jossey-Bass.

Reason, J., & Lucas, D. (1984). Using cognitive diaries to investigate naturally occurring memory blocks. In J. E. Harris & P. E. Morris (Eds.), *Everyday memory, actions and absent-mindedness.* New York: Academic Press.

Reisberg, D., Heuer, F., McLean, J., & O'Shaughnessy, M. (1988). The quantity, not the quality, of affect predicts memory vividness. *Bulletin of the Psychonomic Society, 26,* 100–103.

Robinson, J. A. (1976). Sampling autobiographical memory. *Cognitive Psychology, 8,* 578–595.

Robinson, J. A. (1980). Affect and retrieval of personal memories. *Motivation and Emotion, 4,* 149–174.

Robinson, J. A. (1986). Temporal reference systems and autobiographical memory. In D. C. Rubin (Ed.), *Autobiographical memory* (pp. 159–188). New York: Cambridge University Press.

Robinson, J. A. (1992). First experience memories: Contexts and functions in personal histories. In M. A. Conway, D. C. Rubin, H. Spinnler, & W. A. Wagenaar (Eds.), *Theoretical perspectives on autobiographical memory* (pp. 223–240). Dordrecht: Kluwer.

Roenker, D. L., Thompson, C. P., & Brown, S. C. (1971). A comparison of measures for the estimation of clustering in free recall. *Psychological Bulletin, 10,* 45–48.

Rogers, T. B., Kuiper, N. A., & Kirker, W. S. (1977). Self-reference and the encoding of personal information. *Journal of Personality and Social Psychology, 35,* 677–688.

Ross, B. M. (1991). *Remembering the personal past: Descriptions of autobiographical memory.* New York: Oxford University Press.

Ross, L. (1977). The intuitive psychologist and his shortcomings: Distortions in the attribution process. In L. Berkowitz (Ed.), *Advances in experimental social psychology* (Vol. 10, pp. 173–220). New York: Academic Press.

Rubin, D. C. (1982). On the retention function for autobiographical memory. *Journal of Verbal Learning and Verbal Behavior, 16,* 611–621.

Rubin, D. C., & Baddeley, A. (1989). Telescoping is not time compression: A model of the dating of autobiographical events. *Memory and Cognition, 17,* 653–661.

Rubin, D. C., Wetzler, S. E., & Nebes, R. D. (1986). Autobiographical memory across the lifespan. In D. C. Rubin (Ed.), *Autobiographical memory* (pp. 202–224). Cambridge, England: Cambridge University Press.

Rundus, D. (1971). Analysis of rehearsal processes in free recall. *Journal of Experimental Psychology, 89,* 63–77.

Salancik, G. R. (1974). Inference of one's attitude from behavior recalled under linguistically manipulated cognitive sets. *Journal of Experimental Social Psychology, 10,* 415–427.

Schachtel, E. (1947). On memory and childhood amnesia. *Psychiatry, 10,* 1–26.

Schacter, D. L. (1992). Understanding implicit memory. *American Psychologist, 47,* 559–569.

Schwarz, N. (1990). Feelings as information: Informational and motivational functions of affective states. In E. T. Higgins & R. M. Sorrentino (Eds.), *Handbook of motivation and cognition* (Vol. 2, pp. 527–561). New York: Guilford.

Schwarz, N., & Sudman, S. (Eds.). (1994). *Autobiographical memory and the validity of retrospective reports.* New York: Springer-Verlag.

Singer, J. L. (Ed.). (1990). *Repression and dissociation: Implications for personality theory, psychopathology and health.* Chicago: University of Chicago Press.

Skowronski, J. J., Betz, A. L., Thompson, C. P., & Larsen, S. F. (1995). Long-term performance in autobiographical event dating: Patterns of accuracy and error across a two-and-a-half year time span. In A. L. Healy & L. B. Bourne (Eds.), *Acquisition and long-term retention of knowledge and skills: The durability and specificity of cognitive procedures* (pp. 206–233). Newbury Park, CA: Sage.

Skowronski, J. J., Betz, A. L., Thompson, C. P., & Shannon, L. (1991). Social memory in everyday life: Recall of self-events and other-events. *Journal of Personality and Social Psychology, 60,* 831–843.

Skowronski, J. J., & Carlston, D. E. (1987). Social judgment and social memory: The role of cue diagnosticity in negativity, positivity, and extremity biases. *Journal of Personality and Social Psychology, 52,* 689–699.

Skowronski, J. J., & Thompson, C. P. (1990). Reconstructing the dates of events: Gender differences in accuracy. *Applied Cognitive Psychology, 4,* 371–381.

Slamecka, N. J., & Graf, P. (1978). The generation effect: Delineation of a phenomenon. *Journal of Experimental Psychology: Human Learning and Memory, 4,* 592–604.

Squire, L. R. (1992). Memory and the hippocampus: A synthesis from findings with rats, monkeys, and humans. *Psychological Review, 99,* 195–231.

Squire, L. R., & Slater, P. C. (1975). Forgetting in very long-term memory as assessed by an improved questionnaire technique. *Journal of Experimental Psychology: Human Learning and Memory, 104,* 50–54.

Taylor, S. E. (1991). Asymmetrical effects of positive and negative events: The mobilization-minimization hypothesis. *Psychological Bulletin, 110,* 67–85.

Thomas, D. L., & Diener, E. (1990). Memory accuracy in the recall of emotions. *Journal of Personality and Social Psychology, 59,* 291–297.

Thompson, C. P. (1982). Memory for unique personal events: The roommate study. *Memory and Cognition, 10,* 324–332.

Thompson, C. P. (1985a). Memory for unique personal events: Effects of pleasantness. *Motivation and Emotion, 9,* 277–289.

Thompson, C. P. (1985b). Memory for unique personal events: Some implications of the self-schema. *Human Learning, 4,* 267–280.

Thompson, C. P., & Cowan, T. (1986). A nicer interpretation of a Neisser recollection. *Cognition, 22,* 199–200.

Thompson, C. P., Cowan, T., & Frieman, J. (1993). *Memory search by a memorist.* Hillsdale, NJ: Lawrence Erlbaum Associates.

Thompson, C. P, Cowan, T., Frieman, J., Mahadevan, R. S., Vogl, R. J., & Frieman, J. (1991). Rajan: A study of a memorist. *Journal of Memory and Language, 30,* 702–724.

Thompson, C. P., Skowronski, J. J., & Betz, A. L. (1993). The use of partial temporal information in dating personal events. *Memory and Cognition, 21,* 352–360.

Thompson, C. P., Skowronski, J. J., & Lee, D. J. (1988a). Reconstructing the date of a personal event. In M. M. Gruneberg, P. E. Morris, & N. Sykes (Eds.), *Practical aspects of memory: Current research and issues* (Vol. 1, pp. 241–246). New York: Academic Press.

Thompson, C. P., Skowronski, J. J., & Lee, D. J. (1988b). Telescoping in dating naturally occurring events. *Memory and Cognition, 16,* 461–468.

Thomson, R. H. (1930). An experimental study of memory as influenced by feeling tone. *Journal of Experimental Psychology, 13,* 462–467.

Tulving, E. (1972). Episodic and semantic memory. In E. Tulving & W. Donaldson (Eds.), *Organization of memory* (pp. 381–403). New York: Academic Press.

Tulving, E. (1983). *Elements of episodic memory.* Oxford, England: Clarendon.

Tulving, E., & Watkins, M. J. (1973). Continuity between recall and recognition. *American Journal of Psychology, 86,* 739–748.

Underwood, B. J., Ham, M., & Ekstrand, B. (1962). Cue selection in paired-associate learning. *Journal of Experimental Psychology, 64,* 405–409.

Wagenaar, W. A. (1986). My memory: A study of autobiographical memory over six years. *Cognitive Psychology, 18,* 225–252.

Warren, M. W., Chattin, D., Thompson, D. D., & Tomsky, M. T. (1983). The effects of autobiographical elaboration on noun recall. *Memory and Cognition, 11,* 445–455.

Warrington, E. K., & Silberstein, M. S. (1970). A questionnaire technique for investigating very long-term memory. *Quarterly Journal of Experimental Psychology, 22,* 508–512.

Wegner, D. M., & Vallacher, R. R. (1986). Action Identification. In R. M. Sorrentino & E. T. Higgins (Eds.), *Handbook of motivation and cognition: Foundations of social behavior* (pp. 550–582). New York: Guilford.

White, R. T. (1982). Memory for personal events. *Human Learning, 1,* 171–183.

Whitrow, G. J. (1975). *The nature of time.* New York: Penguin.

Wilson, T. D., Hull, J. G., & Johnson, J. (1981). Awareness and self-perception: Verbal reports on internal states. *Journal of Personality and Social Psychology, 40,* 53–71.

Winograd, E., & Soloway, R. M. (1985). Reminding as a basis for temporal judgment. *Journal of Experimental Psychology: Learning, Memory, & Cognition, 11,* 65–74.

Yntema, D. B., & Trask, F. P. (1963). Recall as a search process. *Journal of Verbal Learning and Verbal Behavior, 2,* 65–74.

Zajonc, R. B. (1960). The process of cognitive tuning in communication. *Journal of Abnormal and Social Psychology, 61,* 159–167.

Author Index

A

Aiello, B., 184, 227
Albright, J. S., 98, 226
Anderson, S. J., 6, 224
Archer, E. J., 22, 222
Auriat, N., 113, 122, 222

B

Baddeley, A. D., 102, 106, 109, 131, 132, 222, 229
Bahrick, H. P., 24, 57, 222
Bailett, S. D., 89, 226
Banaji, M. R., 22, 67, 68, 76, 143, 207, 222, 225
Barsalou, L. W.,105, 108, 222
Barta, S. G., 72, 226
Battig, W. F., 89, 228
Bellezza, F. S., 70, 88, 89, 222
Bem, D. J., 98, 222
Betz, A. L., 27, 34, 38, 72, 74, 87, 90, 94, 95, 99, 106, 110, 112, 114, 122, 131, 134, 180, 186, 200, 209, 222, 226
Boswell, J., 104, 223
Bower, G. H., 68, 71, 73, 87, 88, 89, 90, 223
Bradburn, N. M., 33, 131, 223, 225
Bransford, J. D., 42, 64, 205, 223

Brewer, W. F., 23, 24, 68, 101, 102, 105, 213, 223
Brown, J., 73, 223
Brown, N. R., 102, 105, 183, 184, 185, 192, 203, 223
Brown, P., 70, 223
Brown, R., 23, 223
Brown, S. C., 90, 228
Bruce, D., 102, 107, 223

C

Campbell, D. T., 66, 223
Cantor, N., 73, 98, 223, 226
Carlston, D. E., 68, 82, 84, 99, 227, 229
Carver, C. S., 88, 224
Ceci, S. J., 68, 223
Chaiken, S., 70, 226
Chase, W. G., 85, 86, 91, 223, 224
Chattin, D., 88, 89, 230
Chew, B. R., 98, 226
Cialdini, R. B., 22, 223
Clark, M. S., 67, 223
Cohen, J., 37, 223
Cohen, P., 37, 223
Cohler, B. J., 68, 223
Colgrove, F. W., 163, 223
Conway, M. A., 6, 57, 108, 224
Cowan, T. M., 23, 34, 85, 229, 230

231

Craik, F. I. M., 26, 85, 86, 87, 224
Crovitz, H. F., 23, 224
Crowder, R. G., 22, 222
Czapinski, J., 70, 228

D

Dalgleish, T., 70, 224
Davis, P. J., 69, 224
Dell, G. S., 2, 227
Diener, E., 75, 224, 229
Donnelly, C. M., 6, 224
Dreben, E. K., 68, 82, 224
Dudycha, G. J., 23, 24, 224
Dudycha, M. M., 23, 24, 224

E

Ebbinghaus, H. E., 9, 21, 29, 30, 39, 40, 42,
      86, 102, 129, 161, 205, 209, 224
Ekstrand, B., 26, 230
Emmons, R. A., 75, 224
Ericsson, K. A., 85, 86, 91, 185, 223, 224

F

Fiske, D. W., 66, 223
Fiske, S., 71, 99, 224
Fiske, S. T., 68, 82, 224
Fivush, R., 2, 3, 224
Freud, S., 68, 69, 224
Friedman, W. J., 102, 105, 107, 108, 109,
      111, 164, 185, 186, 187, 196, 202,
      203, 224
Frieman, J., 34, 85, 230

G

Galton, F., 23, 224
Ganellen, R. J., 88, 224
Gergen, K., 98, 225
Gibbons, J., 32
Gibson, J. J., 103, 225
Gilligan, S. G., 68, 73, 87, 88, 89, 90, 223
Glaze, J. A., 22, 225
Glenberg, A. M., 105, 225
Goldsmith, L. R., 46, 225
Graf, P., 26, 229

Greenwald, A. G., 84, 98, 225
Gruendel, J., 2, 3, 228

H

Halpin, J. A., 88, 225
Ham, M., 26, 230
Hansen, C. H., 71, 225
Hansen, R. D., 71, 225
Hansen, T., 104, 113, 115, 225, 226
Harackiewicz, J. M., 23, 24, 226
Hardin, C., 67, 68, 76, 143, 207, 222, 225
Harsch, N., 6, 23, 227
Hastie, R., 68, 71, 82, 98, 224, 225
Hedges, L., 33, 115, 116, 118, 119, 120, 131,
      200, 201, 225
Heuer, F., 75, 228
Höffding, H., 101, 105, 225
Holmes, D. S., 67, 68, 69, 225
Hoyt, S. K., 70, 222
Hudson, J. A., 2, 3, 224, 225
Hull, J. G., 49, 230
Huttenlocher, J., 33, 115, 116, 118, 119, 120,
      131, 200, 201, 225

I

Isen, A. M., 72, 73, 225

J

Jackson, J. L., 102, 105, 225, 227
James, W., 101, 104, 226
Jepson, C., 70, 226
Johnson, J., 49, 230
Johnson, M. K., 42, 64, 205, 223

K

Karis, D., 24, 57, 222
Keenan, J. M., 70, 89, 223, 226
Kendzierski, D., 88, 226
Kihlstrom, J. F., 23, 24, 73, 87, 88, 90, 91,
      98, 223, 226
Kirker, W. S., 70, 83, 88, 228
Klein, S. B., 73, 87, 88, 90, 91, 98, 226
Klinger, E., 72, 226
Kreitler, H., 68, 226

Kuiper, N. A., 70, 83, 88, 90, 226, 228
Kulik, J., 23, 223

L

Larsen, S. F., 6, 23, 28, 35, 75, 95, 96, 97,
    104, 110, 112, 113, 115, 117, 119,
    120, 183, 184, 189, 208, 224, 226, 229
Lee, D. J., 105, 106, 110, 131, 179, 186, 230
Leonesio, R. J., 28, 64, 226
Lepreux, D., 184, 227
Levine, S., 75, 224
Lewis, H. B., 72, 226
Lewis, V., 102, 109, 222
Lieury, A., 183, 184, 185, 227
Lindsay, D. S., 23, 68, 227
Linton, M., 23, 24, 68, 78, 86, 102, 109, 205,
    227
Linville, P. W., 84, 227
Lockhart, R. S., 85, 86, 87, 224
Loftus, E. F., 7, 23, 68, 91, 185, 223, 225
Loftus, J., 73, 102, 224
Logie, R. H., 6, 224
Lord, C. G., 88, 89, 227
Lucas, D., 24, 228

M

Mahadevan, R., 34, 109, 222, 230
Maki, R. H., 88, 89, 227
Mandler, G., 202, 227
Marburger, N., 7, 102, 185, 227
Markus, H., 73, 227
Martson, S. P., 88, 225
Mason, H. F., 88, 225
Matlin, M. W., 67, 68, 69, 70, 72, 78, 82, 227
Maxeiner, M. E., 72, 226
Mayer, J. D., 73, 223, 227
McCaul, K. D., 88, 89, 227
McClelland, A. G. R., 6, 224
McCormack, P. D., 42, 227
McDaniel, M. A., 6, 224
McGuire, W. J., 70, 227
McKoon, G., 2, 227
McLean, J., 75, 228
Mellet, M., 184, 227
Meltzer, H., 67, 227
Michon, J. A., 105, 227
Milberg, S., 67, 223
Monteiro, K. P., 73, 223

Murdock, B. B., 106, 227

N

Nebes, R. D., 23, 42, 57, 229
Neisser, U., 6, 22, 23, 29, 232, 233
Nelson, K., 2, 3, 4, 18, 101, 102, 122, 182,
    228
Nelson, T. O., 28, 64, 226
Niedenthal, B. M., 98, 226
Nimmo-Smith, I., 102, 109, 222
Nisbett, R. E., 28, 49, 228

O

O'Shaughnessy, M., 75, 228

P

Packman, J. L., 89, 228
Peeters, G., 70, 228
Pezdek, K., 68, 228
Pillemer, D. B., 2, 3, 46, 57, 225, 228
Plunkett, K., 35, 95, 97, 208, 226
Potts, G. R., 70, 223
Pouthas, V., 105, 227
Pratkanis, A. R., 98, 225
Prohaska, V., 33, 115, 116, 118, 119, 120,
    200, 201, 225
Puff, C. R., 88, 225

R

Rapaport, D., 67, 228
Ratcliff, R., 2, 227
Ratner, H. H., 3, 228
Rawles, R. E., 6, 224
Read, J. D., 68, 227
Reason, J., 24, 228
Reese, E., 3, 224
Reisberg, D., 75, 228
Richer, E., 183, 227
Rips, L. J., 102, 131, 223
Robinson, J. A., 23, 68, 108, 122, 228
Roenker, D. L., 90, 228
Rogers, T. B., 70, 83, 84, 88, 90, 226, 228
Ross, B. M., 68, 228
Ross, J., 67, 223

Ross, L., 98, 228
Rubin, D. C., 23, 42, 57, 102, 106, 108, 131, 132, 224, 229
Rundus, D., 26, 229

S

Salancik, G. R., 98, 229
Salovey, P., 73, 227
Schachtel, E., 3, 229
Schacter, D. L., 1, 229
Schwarz, N., 71, 213, 229
Shannon, L., 27, 34, 38, 74, 87, 90, 94, 95, 99, 114, 180, 229
Shevell, S. K., 102, 131, 223
Shiffman, H., 23, 224
Silberstein, M. S., 183, 230
Simon, H. A., 185, 224
Singer, J. L., 69, 229
Skowronski, J. J., 27, 34, 38, 68, 72, 74, 82, 87, 90, 94, 95, 97, 99, 105, 106, 110, 112, 114, 122, 131, 134, 157, 159, 179, 180, 186, 200, 209, 222, 229, 230
Slamecka, N. J., 26, 229
Slater, P. C., 183, 229
Soloway, R. M., 106, 230
Squire, L. R., 1, 183, 229
Stang, D. J., 67, 68, 69, 72, 78, 82, 227
Sudman, S., 213, 229

T

Taylor, S. E., 70, 71, 72, 73, 223, 229
Thomas, D. L., 75, 229
Thompson, C. P., 23, 27, 28, 34, 38, 74, 85, 87, 88, 89, 90, 91, 93, 94, 95, 96, 97, 99, 104, 105, 106, 110, 113, 114, 115, 117, 119, 120, 122, 131, 134, 143, 157, 159, 163, 164, 168, 179, 180, 186, 189, 200, 208, 222, 226, 228, 229, 230
Thompson, D. D., 88, 89, 230
Thomson, R. H., 163, 230
Tomsky, M. R., 88, 89, 230

Trask, F. P., 105, 230
Tulving, E., 2, 27, 85, 101, 102, 105, 224, 230

U

Underwood, B. J., 26, 230

V

Vallacher, R. R., 71, 230
van Pelt, M., 102, 107, 223
Vogl, R. J., 34, 230

W

Wagenaar, W. A., 24, 49, 68, 78, 102, 105, 230
Warren, M. W., 88, 89, 230
Warrington, E. K., 183, 230
Watkins, M. J., 26, 27, 86, 224, 230
Watts, F. N., 70, 224
Weeger, I., 183, 227
Wegner, D. M., 71, 230
Weldon, M. S., 6, 228
Wetzler, S. E., 23, 42, 229
White, R. T., 24, 102, 107, 230
White, S. H., 2, 3, 228
Whitrow, G. J., 103, 230
Wilkins, A. J., 102, 107, 185, 196, 202, 224
Wilson, T. D., 28, 49, 51, 228, 230
Winograd, E., 6, 106, 228, 230
Winzenz, D., 71, 223

Y

Yntema, D. B., 105, 230

Z

Zajonc, R. B., 26, 230

Subject Index

A

Absolute error magnitude, 125, 126, 136, 149, 151
Accessibility principle, 105
Accuracy, 5, 10, 14, 15, 20, 28, 29, 34, 37, 69, 70, 97, 107, 112, 121, 124–128, 130, 131, 136–139, 142–144, 147–152, 154, 156–165, 168, 171, 172, 174, 176, 178–180, 187–189, 194, 195, 197, 199, 200, 202–204, 209, 211, 212, 214, 215
Accuracy predictions, 124
Adjusted exact data, 129
Amnesia, 2, 3, 20, 97, 183
Anchoring processes, 32, 126
Autobiographical memory, 1–4, 6, 18, 19, 21–24, 35, 38, 57, 74, 78, 95, 97, 102, 103, 106–108, 122, 182, 213, 215, 216
  use of diaries in assessment of, 19, 35, 217
Autobiographical memory research
  implications of recording an event, 26
  problems in event selection, 24, 26, 101
  problems in verifying memories in, 23
  problems of verification in, 23

B

Boundaries, 7, 108, 131, 132, 161, 210, 214

C

Calendar, 7, 22, 32, 33, 96, 103–105, 107, 115, 119, 142, 159, 164, 183, 217, 221
Childhood amnesia
  schema change model and, 3
  social interaction model and, 3
Clarity of memory, 97, 148, 193, 202, 221
Class of events, 6
Cognitive calendar, 104
Confidence, 29, 44, 105, 149, 214, 221
Content analyses, 46, 138
Content of events and dating accuracy, 137
Core details, 9, 205
Cross-cultural differences, 201

D

Dating, 4, 10, 11, 13–16, 20, 29, 32–34, 37, 105–107, 109–113, 117, 120–139, 142–166, 168, 170–172, 174, 176, 178–189, 191, 193–195, 197, 200, 202–204, 209–215, 221
Dating accuracy, 10, 14, 20, 29, 34, 37, 107, 112, 124–128, 130, 136–139, 142–144, 148, 149, 151, 152, 157, 159, 160, 162–165, 168, 171, 172, 174, 178–180, 187, 189, 203, 209, 212

Dating error, 16, 34, 37, 123–126, 132–139,
        142, 146–151, 153, 155–157, 160,
        161, 165, 166, 170, 171, 179, 193,
        194, 210, 211, 215, 221
Day-of-week effect, 6, 11–17, 32, 33, 111,
        113, 116, 185, 189, 195, 200–202, 210
Declarative memory, 1
Depth of processing, 86, 112
DOW, 113, 117, 119–121, 189, 193,
        195–200, 202
DOW hit rate, 196–199
Duration, 34, 106, 107, 109, 111, 112, 119,
        122, 123
Dynamic time, 103

E

Ecological time, 103
Elaborative rehearsal, 26, 71, 72, 86, 87
Episodic memory, 1–4, 101, 102, 108,
        121–123, 183, 214
Error distribution, 16, 114, 122, 123, 193, 195
Event description, 28, 39
Event emotionality, 143, 146, 153–155
Event frequency, 55, 62, 64, 78, 79, 81,
        143–145, 153, 155, 156, 206, 207
Event intensity, 38, 55, 66, 166, 178
Event involvement, 62, 66
Event memory
    attention and, 71
    effects of retention interval on, 22, 28,
        29, 40, 42, 45, 64–66, 83, 88, 97, 101,
        104, 111, 112, 191–193, 197, 198,
        202, 213
    elaborative processing and, 71, 91
    emotionality and, 30, 31, 55, 57, 79, 82,
        108, 143, 144, 146, 147, 153–157,
        206, 207, 214, 215
    encoding and, 24, 25, 43, 68, 69, 71, 73,
        83–88, 90, 91, 97, 100, 105
    evaluative intensity and, 67, 68, 74–76,
        78–82, 163–166, 168, 170–172, 174,
        176, 178–180, 206, 207
    event frequency and, 30, 31, 37, 43, 45,
        55, 62, 64, 69, 72, 76, 78, 79, 81, 82,
        97, 108, 111, 115, 119–121, 124, 125,
        129, 137, 143–145, 153–156, 161,
        172, 176, 178, 189, 193, 196, 198,
        205–207, 210, 211, 214, 219
    event valence and, 19, 20, 30, 31, 33, 37,
        38, 53, 55, 62, 66–70, 72–76, 78–82,

        89, 98–100, 143, 149, 152–157,
        162–166, 168, 170–172, 174, 176,
        178–180, 198, 206, 207, 212, 215,
        219, 220
    involvement and, 19, 30, 37, 39, 55, 59,
        60, 62, 64, 66, 78, 80, 81, 84, 85, 94,
        143, 144, 147, 148, 206–209, 215, 219
    memory for context and, 1, 22, 26, 71,
        79, 83, 91–93, 95–97, 144, 146, 147,
        155, 184–186, 191–193, 195, 198,
        199, 203, 212, 215
    memory search and retrieval and, 8, 10,
        20
    mood as a cue for, 72, 73
    news events and, 2–5, 20, 91, 95–97, 100,
        105, 182, 184, 185, 188, 189,
        191–193, 195–197, 199, 203, 207,
        208, 212, 213, 221
    other-events and, 76, 78, 80, 92–96, 98,
        99, 105, 106, 170, 171, 180, 181, 183,
        194, 196, 197, 220
    person expectancies and, 19, 30, 31, 39,
        55, 62–64, 76, 79–81, 98, 99, 124,
        125, 143–146, 153–157, 198, 207
    person-expectancies and, 64, 99, 145,
        154, 206
    rehearsal and, 108
    repression and, 68, 69, 72, 82
    reproduction and, 4–6, 8, 9, 18, 204, 213
    role of encoding efficiency in valence
        effects, 69
    the self and, 70, 73
    self-events and, 20, 27, 33, 34, 62, 63, 75,
        76, 78–83, 91, 94–100, 102, 107, 126,
        139, 158, 159, 170, 180–187, 191,
        193–196, 198–200, 202, 203, 206,
        208, 210–212, 215
    self-reference and, 83–85, 87–91, 96, 101
    and structures for retrieval, 106, 108, 111,
        112, 117–119, 121, 191–193, 195–199,
        202
Event pleasantness, 20, 31, 38, 53, 55,
        74–76, 99, 155
Event rehearsal, 19, 32, 39, 55, 57, 71, 81,
        143, 148
Event valence, 30, 31, 69, 75, 76, 78–82,
        143, 152–157, 162, 163, 165, 166,
        168, 170–172, 174, 176, 178, 180,
        206, 212
Exact dating, 111, 126–131, 133, 135–139,
        142–148, 154, 156, 158–161, 165,
        171, 172, 174, 178, 191, 193–195, 209

Exact hit rate measure, 125
Expectancies, 83, 94, 98
Explicit memory, 1

F

Familiarity, 69, 89, 92, 101, 192
Female dating, 160
Final memory ratings, 30–32, 49, 51–55, 57,
    61, 63, 65
First event memories, 108
Forgetting, 9, 19, 20, 27, 30, 32, 39, 40,
    42–44, 58, 64, 66, 97, 119–121, 125,
    161, 192, 193, 199, 200, 202, 213
Frequency rating, 79, 153–155

G

Gender differences, 20, 125, 157, 212
Generic event memory, 2–4, 108, 122, 123
Gist recall, 42
Guessing, 110–112, 116, 149, 185, 186, 196

H

Hour, 107, 109–111, 113, 185, 202

I

Idiosyncratic differences, 46
Implicit memory, 1
Imprecision in prediction, 51
Information source, 148, 150–152
Initial memory ratings, 31, 32, 49, 51–55, 65
Initial mental involvement, 30, 55, 62, 64,
    80, 81, 143, 144, 147, 148, 206–209
Inter-event memory, 192, 202
Intra-event memory, 192, 193

L

Life periods, 122, 182
Linear landmark, 112
Linear time, 109, 202
List-learning, 42, 101

M

Memory measures
    cued recall, 22, 27, 28, 96, 205
    free recall, 27, 40, 87
    memory ratings, 2, 19, 21, 22, 28, 29, 33,
        34, 40, 44, 57, 65, 66, 105, 111, 212,
        215
    recognition, 22, 27, 40, 89, 96, 101, 192
Mobilization-minimization theory, 71
Mood repair hypothesis, 1, 7, 12, 25, 72,
    107, 109–111, 113, 122, 127, 134,
    137, 185, 219, 221
Multiple regression, 21, 37, 38, 125, 165, 197
    dummy coding to control for
        within-subject effects in, 37, 40
    interpreting results of, 29, 44, 66

N

Naturalistic research, 187
News, 4, 20, 83, 91, 95–97, 100, 105, 182,
    184, 185, 187–189, 191–199, 202,
    203, 207, 208, 212, 214, 221

O

Objective time, 103
Order code, 106

P

Perfect memory measure, 43, 125
Personal context, 97, 184–186, 191, 193,
    195, 198, 199, 203, 212
Personal events, 6, 7, 25, 40, 65, 83, 85–87,
    90–92, 94, 97, 100, 102, 104–106,
    185, 193, 207, 208
Personal memories, 64, 95, 97, 100, 101, 184
Person-atypical, 64, 99, 145, 146, 161, 206,
    211, 212
Procedural memory, 1

R

Raw error magnitude, 125
Recall for self-events, 91, 95, 208
Reception context, 96, 184, 203

Reconstruction of memory, 4–6, 8, 9, 14,
    18, 20, 29, 33, 101, 104, 106–108,
    112, 113, 119, 121–125, 130, 139,
    142, 148, 164, 165, 168, 170–172,
    176, 178–186, 188, 189, 191, 192,
    195, 200, 202–204, 210, 211, 213, 216
Rehearsal, 4, 6, 19, 26, 30–32, 39, 55,
    57–59, 64, 69, 71, 72, 80, 81, 85–87,
    92–95, 100, 143, 144, 146–148, 205,
    207–209, 220
Rehearsal ratings, 31, 32, 57, 59, 64, 205,
    208, 209
Relativistic ratings, 44
Retention interval, 8–10, 17, 19, 28–30, 32,
    35, 39, 40, 42–44, 49, 51, 53, 55,
    57–59, 61, 62, 64, 66, 93, 96, 111,
    119, 124–137, 148–153, 155, 161,
    166, 191, 192, 194, 198, 204, 205, 209
Retrieval structure, 85–87

S

Scale effects, 107
Self-reference effect
    organization versus elaboration in, 84, 87,
        88, 90, 91, 100, 209
Self relevance, 182, 183
Self-schema, 19, 20, 83–98, 100, 182, 197,
    207–209, 212
    expert performance and, 85, 91, 100
Semantic memory, 2
Serial order, 102
State-dependent memory, 67, 73, 79
Static time, 103
Strategy reports, 110, 120, 185, 186, 196
Subjective reports, 20, 109, 112, 184–186,
    193

T

Task diligence, 44
Telescoping, 20, 131–134, 161, 209, 214

Temporal cues, 106, 191, 202
Temporal information, 6, 13, 15, 20, 33,
    106, 113, 114, 148, 186, 199, 211, 214
Temporal memory
    effect of retention interval on, 72
    general world knowledge and
        reconstruction of, 4, 7, 139, 164
    individual differences in, 5, 14, 15, 18,
        19, 46, 127, 128, 161
    landmark events in reconstruction of, 7,
        20, 107, 109–111, 123
    role of event memory in reconstruction
        of, 4, 6, 18, 105, 118
    role of temporal traces in, 107, 108, 119
    schemata in reconstruction of, 2, 3
    strategies for reconstruction, 6
    strategies for reconstruction of, 4, 33, 179
    temporal boundaries in reconstruction of,
        101
Temporal reconstruction, 20, 107, 108, 124,
    183, 185, 192, 211
Temporal schema, 5, 9, 11, 18, 107, 113,
    121, 122, 125, 138, 191
Temporal symbols, 105
Think-aloud protocols, 107, 185
Time expansion, 131–134, 161, 209, 210, 214
Time period, 59, 108, 110, 148, 211
Time tag theory, 105
Trace strength, 66, 104, 105
Transition events, 108, 121, 123

W

Week schema, 20, 113, 114, 116, 118–123,
    186, 193, 195, 196, 199–201
Well-known other, 91
Workdays, 114, 116, 119, 120, 201

Y

Year schema, 121